**ONE SIGNAL**
**PUBLISHERS**

ATRIA

# The Genius of Judy

## How *Judy Blume* Rewrote Childhood for All of Us

# RACHELLE BERGSTEIN

ONE SIGNAL
PUBLISHERS

ATRIA

New York  London  Toronto  Sydney  New Delhi

ONE SIGNAL
PUBLISHERS

ATRIA

An Imprint of Simon & Schuster, LLC
1230 Avenue of the Americas
New York, NY 10020

First One Signal Publishers/Atria Books hardcover edition July 2024

**ONE SIGNAL PUBLISHERS / ATRIA** BOOKS and colophon are
trademarks of Simon & Schuster, LLC

Simon & Schuster: Celebrating 100 Years of Publishing in 2024

For information about special discounts for bulk purchases, please contact Simon &
Schuster Special Sales at 1-866-506-1949 or business@simonandschuster.com.

The Simon & Schuster Speakers Bureau can bring authors to your live event. For
more information or to book an event, contact the Simon & Schuster Speakers
Bureau at 1-866-248-3049 or visit our website at www.simonspeakers.com.

Interior design by Jill Putorti

Manufactured in the United States of America

1 3 5 7 9 10 8 6 4 2

Library of Congress Cataloging-in-Publication Data is available.

ISBN 978-1-6680-1090-7
ISBN 978-1-6680-1092-1 (ebook)

*For my son Curtis and his friends,*
*who make me excited about the future*

*But here she had*
*no children, no husband, and her mother was dead,*
*no one was far weaker or far*
*stronger than she, she carried her rage*
*unknown, hidden, unknowable yet,*
*she moved, slowly, under the arches,*
*literally singing.*

—SHARON OLDS, FROM
"VISITING MY MOTHER'S COLLEGE"

*The word police can fuck off.*

—MADONNA

# Timeline

1938—Judith Sussman was born in Elizabeth, New Jersey

1945—World War II ended

1956—Graduated from Battin High School

1959—Married John Blume

1961—Graduated from New York University; gave birth to Randy Blume

1963—Gave birth to Lawrence Blume; *The Feminine Mystique*
     by Betty Friedan

1966—The National Organization for Women (NOW) formed

1967—*Diary of a Mad Housewife* by Sue Kaufman

1968—Richard Nixon was elected

1969—*The One in the Middle Is the Green Kangaroo*

1970—*Are You There God? It's Me, Margaret*; *Sexual Politics*
     by Kate Millett; Women's Strike for Equality

1971—*Freckle Juice* and *Then Again, Maybe I Won't*

1972—*It's Not the End of the World* and *Tales of a Fourth Grade Nothing*

1973—*Deenie*; *Roe v. Wade* decision by the Supreme Court; *Fear of Flying* by Erica Jong

1974—*Blubber*; Nixon resigned due to the Watergate scandal

1975—Divorced John Blume; *Forever*; the Vietnam War ended

1976—Married Tom Kitchens in England

1977—*Starring Sally J. Freedman as Herself*; *It's OK If You Don't Love Me* by Norma Klein

1978—*Wifey*

1979—Divorced Tom Kitchens

1980—Ronald Reagan was elected; *Superfudge*; met George Cooper

1981—*Tiger Eyes*

1983—*Smart Women*

1987—Married George Cooper; *Just as Long as We're Together*

# Contents

# Preface

Judy Blume was my first.

She wasn't the first author I fell in love with, but when I was nine years old, she pulled me across another major milestone—she wrote a book that I wanted to hide from my parents. *Just as Long as We're Together*, about three middle school–aged best friends and their musical-chair friendship dynamics, started with a sentence so intoxicating it might as well have come with a chaser: *Stephanie is into hunks*. Was I into hunks? I wasn't sure. But I knew that I couldn't put the book down.

Stephanie's parents were getting a divorce. My parents were divorced, too! Her body, like mine, was turning into something alien. Black fuzz was sprouting in not-altogether-welcome places, and I was transfixed as Stephanie described her own evolving figure, replete with belly rolls, jiggling "glutes," and dark pubic hair.

My dad still read to me before bed at that age. But as soon as I got my hands on *Just as Long as We're Together*, I asked him to stop. Stephanie's world, filled with crushes, budding breasts, and pre-teen drama, wasn't one I wanted to share with him. And so that night, I shuffled to his bed-room in pajamas and slippers and announced that I was going to read myself to sleep. I recognized his sadness as I kissed him good night, and I felt it, too. But it was worth it. Blume offered me something nobody else ever had before: a mirror of truth and a portal to some not-so-distant future, all wrapped in a humble paperback.

*     *     *

Judy Blume is more famous than she's ever been since she started writing books for children in the late 1960s. She's a star who has exploded into a supernova, with multiple film and television projects (A documentary! A movie version of *Are You There God? It's Me, Margaret*! A Peacock series based on her 1998 novel *Summer Sisters*!). "The Judy Blume Renaissance is upon us," the *New York Times* declared in March 2023. "We Need Judy Blume Now More Than Ever," an April 2023 headline from the A.V. Club reads.

The latter referred to the post-Trump political climate, which has proven particularly favorable for book banners. To parental rights activists, a book like *Gender Queer*, a graphic novel by Maia Kobabe about adolescent gender dysmorphia, is "grooming," making it the most-banned title of 2022, according to the American Library Association. *All Boys Aren't Blue*, about author George M. Johnson's experience growing up Black and queer in Plainfield, New Jersey, is "indoctrination" and was banned eighty-six times, per the same list. Republican-led state legislators in Florida, Texas, and Iowa are feverishly removing books from school library shelves, leaving them half-empty. Not since the Reagan years have the attacks on books been so organized, and so vicious.

We need Judy Blume now because she understands this moment better than anyone. She is rightly being recognized for all the brave choices she's made in her long and celebrated career, from talking about periods in *Are You There, God?*, to having Deenie touch her "special place" in

*Deenie*, to showing an eighteen-year-old losing her virginity—without suffering any hideous consequences—in *Forever*. Tackling these controversial subjects earned her a dubious honor: she was the country's most-banned author in the 1980s, back when the Moral Majority was leading the charge against books the way the national right-wing group Moms for Liberty is driving efforts to remove books from school libraries today.

Blume is the grande dame of so-called dirty books. Her work, her voice, her face are all a comfort to the people who grew up with her, who watched her persevere against her attackers and go on to sell an astonishing ninety million copies of her novels to people around the world. Generations of readers are still rooting for her. Today, in her mid-eighties, she has graciously accepted her laurels and strolled into her role as a living legend.

I wanted to write this book to figure out why Judy Blume is still so beloved, when many of her contemporary young adult novelists, like Betty Miles and Norma Klein, have receded into history. I wanted to investigate why just the mention of Blume's name is enough to break the ice with a stranger and get a serious, otherwise put-together adult woman giggling. Try it: say the name "Judy Blume" to the nearest Gen X or millennial book lover and see what happens. Is it a smile? A fast flush of joy? I've seen this look so many times since I started researching Blume's life and work. A glimmer that floats across the eyes, almost like the person across from me is recalling a former flame.

What's the secret ingredient that makes Judy Blume's work so potent? The thing at the heart of her writing that makes it so sticky? Her name continues to show up in contemporary pop culture, in movies like *Easy A* (2010), *Ted* (2012), and *Deadpool* (2016). In interviews, Blume is consistent when she says that she wasn't sitting down at her typewriter trying to be a firebrand; she just wanted to tell honest stories. But in doing so, she created a cohesive, culture-altering vision of modern childhood. In writing about kids from the inside out, she hit on crucial universalities that transcended race, class, and even sexual orientation. Young readers saw themselves in Judy Blume's novels and felt she gave them permission to be truthful, too. More than truthful—to be *complicated*. In Blume's world, children are expansive enough to question their relationships with God one night and then bicker over trivialities with their best friends on the bus the next morning. Middle school crushes are valid, and important! Nice girls are allowed to challenge their parents. They're even allowed to criticize them.

This might not sound like a big deal now, but it was huge when Blume started writing in the late 1960s. Back then, children's literature clung to the wisdom that mother and father knew best. One of the reasons I loved *Just as Long as We're Together* so very much was that it validated my feelings. My parents divorced when I was five. Their split and subsequent remarriages had freaked me out and made me angry, but I held it all in. Unlike me, Stephanie expressed her displeasure with her mom and dad in all kinds of subtle and explicit ways. She was fundamentally a good kid—a doting older sister, a dedicated student—but she also wasn't afraid to tell her parents exactly how upset she was about their breakup. I couldn't imagine anything more delicious, or more deviant.

Judy Blume is special because she made young readers like me feel seen. That helps explain the nostalgia for her and her work, especially at a moment when the world—with a global pandemic, the existential threat of climate change, mounting combat overseas, and culture wars at home—feels so frightening. Blume's universe, filled with bicycles, bras, and boy books, is much simpler.

Certainly, that's part of the reason for the Blume-aissance. But it's not the whole story.

·    ·    ·

The answer, I've come to believe, is sex. Sex is the lifeblood that flows through her pages. Not selling sex for titillation's sake, the way her critics claimed, but sex as a fundamental part of being human. From Margaret

Simon's obsession with getting her period to Deenie Fenner's curiosity about masturbation, the children in Blume's stories all embrace puberty with open arms and take the ride into adulthood without shame. No matter how much they struggle, her adolescent characters are fundamentally empowered. Across Blume's books, kids approach sex as a crucial part of growing up, a key element in their cultural and biological destinies.

This was Blume's personal philosophy as well. She believed that kids deserved to have pressing and private questions about their bodies, and that they were entitled to the answers. Over the course of her life and career, she has recognized that women's interior lives and their sexual desires are deeply intertwined. Making that connection, and putting it into her books in the 1970s and 1980s, was radical at the time.

Hell, it's radical now.

Americans are still debating the value of sex education. Twelve-year-old girls are still getting catcalled on the street, while books that talk frankly about sex are getting dismissed as pornography. *Roe v. Wade* is no longer the law of the land and powerful men have announced that they're coming for birth control next. In Florida, Governor Ron DeSantis has greenlit a bill that prevents girls younger than sixth grade from even talking about menstruation in school. Kids in many states are prohibited from learning about the gender spectrum, or LGBTQ+ issues, or anything that falls beyond the traditional boy/girl binary.

This moment in history feels like a tipping point. When Judy Blume started writing in the late 1960s, the culture was at a tipping point, too. The sexual revolution presented an ocean of new ideas, but there were plenty of people trying to hold back the tide. Second Wave feminists—Betty Friedan, Gloria Steinem, Kate Millett—were fighting to change the world for women. The goal of women's liberation was to free wives and mothers from cages of domesticity and let them enter modern society.

Blume was a housewife and mother of two in her twenties when she first sat down to write. She wasn't a women's rights activist, but she was deeply affected by the ideas coming out of the movement. One of Second Wave feminism's aims was to demystify the female body once and for all, so that women could be more in control of their reproductive systems, their sexual experiences, and their lives. Tapping away at her IBM Selectric, Judy was absorbing feminist values and translating them, in real time, for her young readers.

This is the genius of Judy Blume. It's the single most important aspect of her legacy. Her work as a children's writer did something nobody else could manage: it helped ensure feminism's longevity. When Friedan published *The Feminist Mystique* in 1963, she argued that the activists who came before her—the First Wave suffragettes—had admirably won the vote but then hung up their sashes and failed to encode their values into American culture. "The fact is that to women born after 1920, feminism was dead history," Friedan wrote. Or, as Kate Millett put it in *Sexual Politics* (1970), "When the ballot was won, the feminist movement collapsed in what can only be described as exhaustion."

By the war years of the 1930s and 1940s, the country no longer had an active women's rights movement. The United States in the 1950s saw a return to patriarchal gender roles, leaving the Nineteenth Amendment in place but undoing much of the important social and cultural work of early feminism.

Second Wavers didn't want this to happen again. Friedan and Millett both agreed: a movement requires a multigenerational buy-in to maintain its momentum. And over in suburban New Jersey, a soft-spoken stay-at-home mom was listening. Writing cutting-edge books for kids, Judy Blume became the Second Wave's secret weapon.

This book is about how she did it. It takes elements from her life, her work (specifically, the controversial young adult novels she published between 1970 and 1980), and her battle against censorship to reveal how she brought up the next generation of women's rights activists. Her characters and stories were more than just entertainment. They were a roadmap of open communication, bodily autonomy, and even sexual fulfillment. They taught young readers that we were allowed to expect more from our lives than the women who came before us.

I am following that map from its starting point. Come with me.

*Rachelle Bergstein*
*Brooklyn, NY*
*October 25, 2023*

## Chapter One

# Housewife's Syndrome

*"I went in the closet and I cried."*

Before Judith Sussman had even graduated from college at NYU in 1961, she was married and pregnant. She had met a man—another New Jersey native, six years her senior—who could give her the life she thought she wanted: a suburban success story. When they first started dating, John Blume was a promising law student, preppy, clean-cut, with a round face and wry blue eyes. He had a job waiting for him at his father's law firm in Newark. Was Judy smitten? It was tough to say. Their backyard wedding, in August of 1959, had a feeling of inevitability.

It was inevitable, she later realized, because she had been pro-grammed to want certain things. Despite the fact that her high school yearbook listed her single most important ambition as "college," she was acutely aware that her degree in elementary education was actually a backup plan. Her mom, Essie Sussman, would have been mortified if she'd used it. In the shorthand of New Jersey's Jewish mothers, work was something a woman did when she couldn't find a husband to take care of her.

And of course Judy could find a husband—she was smart, bubbly, pretty. A good girl, if a bit of a flirt, with slim hips and a glinting, movie-star smile. When she had her first baby, a daughter she named Randy, in her early twenties, she had fulfilled her greater purpose according to contemporary standards. Her son, Lawrence, who they called Larry, followed soon after, in 1963.

By then, the Blumes had moved into a lovely new house in the affluent suburb of Scotch Plains, New Jersey. The four-bedroom home, which sat on nearly an acre of grassy land, had an airy front porch and a two-car garage. It was a twelve-minute drive from her mother. Judy framed her college diploma—already, school was starting to feel so far away—and hung it over the washing machine.

The family was thriving. As John Blume's wife, Judy frequented the local country club, taking tennis and golf lessons so she could go along with his hobbies, and enjoyed steak dinners at restaurants with crisp white tablecloths. She had to admit, she wanted for nothing. So what was that tug at the pit of her stomach? A hunger, gnawing and painful, like she was empty.

·    ·    ·

The sexual revolution was well underway, but it hadn't yet made it to Scotch Plains. The first *Playboy* magazine, with Marilyn Monroe in a black swimsuit beaming on the cover, had gone to press in 1953. Elvis rocked and rolled his hips on the *Ed Sullivan Show* just a few years later, in 1956. The birth control pill was approved for contraceptive use in 1960, and the Supreme Court's 1965 decision in *Griswold v. Connecticut* protected the rights of married couples to use it. Sex was in the air—or at least on the airwaves. "(I Can't Get No) Satisfaction" by the Rolling Stones topped the charts. Ponytailed schoolgirls watched the Beatles perform with desire shooting out of their eyes.

But in Scotch Plains, it was as if the 1950s had never ended. Even though it closed out its seven-year TV run in 1963, everyone was still playacting *Leave It to Beaver*. The men went to work every morning. The wives watched the kids, cooked dinner, and cleaned. If they were lucky enough to have free time, they gossiped and browsed clothing racks. "Those women weren't even shopping but simply going to stores, for lack of anything better to do," Blume later said of her fellow New Jersey moms.

Shopping didn't do it for Judy. It didn't do it for Betty Friedan either, who lived an hour away in Rockland County, New York. In 1963, mother of three Friedan published *The Feminine Mystique*, which described housewives' ennui as "the problem that has no name." Friedan argued that during World War II, when American women had flooded the workforce while the men went to war, they had been happier. Then, after D-Day, they had been corralled back into their homes. They subsisted on a substanceless media diet that told them they should entertain no ambitions beyond their "feminine" duties: Preparing gourmet meals. Scrubbing the floors until they sparkled. Cultivating their children's interests. Making it all seem lovely and effortless, so that it appeared, at five o'clock every day, as if they had been gift-wrapped just for their husbands.

Middle-class women were told they were lucky, that they led more pampered lives than any other species in the history of the world. "The American housewife—freed by science and the labor-saving appliances from the drudgery, the dangers of childbirth and the illnesses of her grandmother . . . was healthy, beautiful, educated, concerned only about her husband, her children and her home. She had found true feminine fulfillment," Friedan wrote of the cultural messages housewives received.

But then, Friedan asks: Why were so many women secretly dying inside?

They were miserable because they were bored, Friedan argued. More than bored—they were suffocating. And to top it all off, these women felt guilty about being unhappy. They yearned to understand why their comfortable, cosseted lives didn't nourish them. "I feel as if I don't exist," one interview subject confessed to Friedan.

Many suffered from unexplained illnesses. The "housewife's syndrome" or "housewife's blight," Friedan called it, describing a constellation of symptoms that appeared separately or all together: crippling exhaustion, anxiety, restlessness, teariness, lethargy, skin conditions.

Judy had pounding headaches and migraines that sent her to bed in the middle of the day. She had year-round sore throats, rashes, and other allergic reactions for no apparent reason.

"If you want to know about my illnesses, read *Wifey*," Blume said in the 1990 book *Presenting Judy Blume*. "It was another side of my life that I wanted to share."

In *Wifey*, Blume's first novel for adults, published in 1978, she references her weird afflictions in the character of Sandy Pressman: a stifled and sexually frustrated housewife who seeks fulfillment in a series of R-rated, extramarital affairs. Early on in the book, Sandy looks in the mirror to discover a crop of heart-shaped bumps erupting across her face. Despite taking a course of penicillin, she gets sicker. "Ten days later it returned, but much worse. A fever of 105, aches and pains in her joints, a strange rash suddenly covering her body; hivelike on her arms, measlelike on her stomach, blotches on her swollen face. She only wanted to sleep."

Judy (and Sandy) had the housewife's blight, all right. And who could blame her? While Gloria Steinem was publishing her explosive 1963 two-part series "A Bunny's Tale," about working as a cocktail waitress at the Playboy Club in New York City, Judy was making pot roast. While Friedan was promoting her book and gathering ground for women's liberation, Judy was tidying up the living room, driving the kids around, folding stack after stack of warm laundry. Randy and Larry grew from babies to toddlers to elementary schoolers, and Judy had more time on her hands—but she didn't know what to do with it. The truth was, she found tennis and golf boring. She couldn't stand the country club husbands, and their wives were somehow worse: catty and small-minded.

She needed a project. Something creative to pass the time.

As a girl, Judy had wanted to be a famous actress like Esther Williams or Margaret O'Brien, a child star turned ingénue. Growing up in the diverse city of Elizabeth, New Jersey, Judy—or "Judie" as she spelled it back then—was a cheerful, if somewhat high-strung kid. Her brother, David, who was four years older, made fun of her for being jumpy and liked to toss a sheet over his head like a ghost and sneak up on her. It was easy to get her to scream—she was always anticipating danger.

Her early childhood was defined by World War II. Born Jewish in February 1938, Judy couldn't remember a time without Hitler. Hitler, shouting sharply in German, was on the radio while the family ate dinner together at the dining room table. Hitler, with his Brylcreemed hair and bristly patch of a mustache, stomped through the newsreels that played when they went to the movies. Judy's father, a dentist named Rudolph Sussman, volunteered in town as an air-raid warden. Her mother, a housewife named Esther, or "Essie," knitted khaki sweaters for the boys overseas.

It was a frightening time, but Judy always had a place to stash her anxiety. Her dolls starred in elaborate dramas. She lived in a modest, two-story house on a residential street, and she spent hours bouncing a ball against the brick, making up stories. As she got older she took ballet lessons, acted in plays, sang in the school chorus, and joined the yearbook committee. She was always reading—her first favorite book was *Madeline* by Ludwig Bemelmans, which she took out over and over again from the local library branch. Then she graduated to Nancy Drew and eventually J. D. Salinger.

As an adult, Judy was missing a creative outlet. Washing dishes at night, she hummed along to the radio, thinking she might try her hand at songwriting. Quickly, the notion passed—John Lennon she was not. Then she turned her attention to arts and crafts. She bought yards and yards of colorful felt, fashioning it into splashy pendants to hang on children's walls. Much to Judy's delight, her local Bloomingdale's agreed to stock them and they sold for $9 apiece. She made over $350 (around $3,200 in today's dollars) before that enterprise got squashed by yet another malady, when her fingers started peeling because she developed an allergy to fabric glue.

Another idea came to her soon after. Reading bedtime stories to her kids, she wondered if she could be a children's book author and illustrator. She'd play around with words in her head—a little verse here, a mellifluous phrase there—and chuckle, imagining herself as the unlikely Dr. Seuss of suburban New Jersey. Her maiden name had been Sussman, she noted. Seuss, meet Suss. Was it a sign?

Probably not, but Judy started jotting down her ideas anyway. They came alive in colored pencil with simple, homespun drawings. Okay, she conceded, maybe she'd need to work with an artist. But when she wrote, she felt the zap of something familiar from her girlhood: something electric and joyful. A distant, yet sacred, creative force welled up inside her. She wrote one story, called "You Mom, You?" about a mother patiently explaining to her two young kids that she had once been just a silly child herself. The tots—enthralled by their mother's recollections, told in rhyme—are shocked by her playful history lesson.

Judy was proud of her short manuscripts and bound them with brass fasteners. She started researching where she might submit them: small children's book publishers and *Parents* magazine. One afternoon, she checked the mail and discovered a continuing education brochure from her alma mater, NYU. One class, offered on Monday nights, felt like it had been included just for her. It was called Writing for Children and Teenagers.

Judy signed up and started riding the bus from Scotch Plains into the city every week. Even the commute down to the West Village was fulfilling. There was something about taking herself into Manhattan that seemed both delightfully grown-up and reminiscent of her unencumbered college years. Seeing the steel frame of the George Washington Bridge rise up from the road, the silvery skyline shooting out in the distance, it was like she was traveling to another world, one shimmering with artistic potential.

In class, Judy was one of just seven students. The teacher was Lee Wyndham, a published children's book author, syndicated reviewer, and Russian émigré who wore flamboyant hats with feathers. Wyndham took a traditional view of children's literature—that all stories should have a good, clear-cut moral with no questions left unanswered in the end—but she also encouraged her pupils to play. Eager to find her own voice, Judy experimented with different perspectives, toggling between first and third person, and an array of narrative forms. She started carrying around a green-gray three-ring binder, which she used to take notes in class and scribble down any new ideas that came to her. On the inside cover Judy wrote down her address, as well as a phrase indicating the item's growing significance: *Reward if found.*

Between her lectures on everything from craft to writing strong cover letters to go with manuscript submissions, Wyndham consistently gave Judy warm, positive feedback. She was frank with the aspiring author, telling her that realistic writing, as opposed to fantasy, was her strength. Wyndham likely empathized with Judy; she also didn't start her professional career until after she had a family. When the class ended, Judy signed up to take it again. She had already started working on a full-length manuscript, about a young white girl whose sense of injustice is inflamed by her community's racist response to a Black family moving into town.

As Judy wrote, she was also sending out her stories. The first rejection stung. "I went in the closet—I didn't want the kids to see me," Blume told *CBS Sunday Morning* in 2015. "I went in the closet and I cried." Over time, however, her skin grew thicker. Eventually, by the late 1960s, she'd been rejected by every major publisher, from Harper & Row to Houghton Mifflin to Random House and Pantheon. But she had made progress, too. She sold a short story, called "The Flying Munchgins," to a children's magazine, about a little boy named Leonard who discovers a society of mysterious creatures—the Munchgins—living in the dirt. He traps them in a box and shows them off to his older brother and sister who, unimpressed, inform him that they're nothing special: just plain old ladybugs.

For another story, called "The Ooh Ooh Ahh Ahh Bird," Judy received $20—and a celebratory red rose from Wyndham.

"She was wonderfully supportive," Blume said of Wyndham at a 2015 book event hosted by the Arlington Public Library in Virginia. "She was wonderful to me, always," Blume recalled of her teacher, who died in 1978, even though she admitted Wyndham did not always approve of her tendency to leave the task of untangling moral complexities up to the reader.

Wyndham's support meant everything to her, especially because she felt she had so few others in her corner when it came to her writing. John wasn't bothered by her new passion, but he had trouble seeing it as anything more than a hobby. "He thought it was better than shopping," Blume said. He'd joke to their friends, "All I have to do is buy Judy some paper and pencils and she's happy!" At one point, John sent a few of her drafts to his friend who had worked in book publishing. That guy was discouraging to the point of rudeness. In so many words: *pack it up sweetheart and go back to baking.*

Judy didn't want to bake. She wanted to invent things—to dream. Then one day her dreams took root. In 1969, she received a phone call from an editor at Reilly & Lee, a Chicago-based publisher that had previously rejected her work. They said they wanted to publish her manuscript for *The One in the Middle Is the Green Kangaroo*, about second-grader Freddy Dissel, an aggrieved middle child who is sick of wearing his older brother Mike's hand-me-downs and being told to play nicely with his annoying baby sister, Ellen. When Judy hung up, she raced into the basement where Larry was having a playdate and started tossing the children's Silly Sand—the sloppy 1970s precursor to today's wet and pliant kinetic sand—into the air in celebration. "Larry's mother is crazy!" the friend later told her parents, according to a 1981 Scholastic mini-biography called *Judy Blume's Story*.

*Green Kangaroo*, in which Dissel goes from feeling like he will "always be a great big middle nothing" to getting the starring role in the school play (the titular green kangaroo), is not even close to Blume's best work. But it offers up hints of the humor and empathy that would eventually distinguish her as a writer. Judy was paid $350 (roughly $2,800 today) for the book, and when the mailman—who had grown accustomed to delivering rejections—came by with the check, the pair danced across the lawn together.

The publisher matched Judy with an artist, Lois Axeman, who provided the book's illustrations, though the pair never actually met. Judy dedicated her debut to John, Randy, and Larry.

When *Green Kangaroo* was published in the fall of 1969, her local newspaper, the Central New Jersey *Courier News*, did a small story on Judy. In an article titled "Mom Keeps Busy Writing Books for Little Children"—*Keeps busy! Honestly!*—the Scotch Plains resident and former Brownie troop leader shared that she was shopping another short manuscript, about a boy who swallows his brother's pet turtle, and already had a contract to publish another book, which she had completed in her writing class at NYU. The novel, called *Iggie's House*, featured a young protagonist named Winnie Barringer, who sought to befriend her new Black neighbors.

"The more I write, the more controversial I'm getting," Blume told the reporter mischievously, adding that she intended to dedicate her next book to Wyndham.

She revealed that *Iggie's House* would be published by Prentice Hall, based in nearby Englewood Cliffs, New Jersey. What Judy didn't say was that—when it came to putting her more cutting-edge ideas out into the world—she had found her perfect, fearless shepherd.

*Chapter Two*

---

# ʕKiddie ʕLit

*"It was the best $5,000 we ever spent."*

T here's one word people use to describe Richard "Dick" Jackson: "charming." As an editor for major houses like Macmillan and Doubleday, he knew how to work the room at a book party, flatter a sensitive writer's ego, and make even the stuffiest librarian smile. Jackson had practiced his people skills growing up among Detroit's upper crust as the son of a Hudson Motor Car bigwig, then moved east to attend Yale Drama. After graduating in 1957 he was drafted and did a two-year stint in the army. When he moved to New York and his acting career flopped, he enrolled in a master's program in publishing at NYU in 1962.

In 1968, Jackson co-founded his own company, called Bradbury Press, with his friend Robert "Bob" Verrone. The gregarious Verrone had been working at Prentice Hall at the time, and the pair opened up a small office within Prentice's sprawling North Jersey compound near the Hudson River.

"These two guys sort of considered themselves pirates, because they had gotten out of big publishing," remembered Peter Silsbee, a Bradbury

Press author who first met Jackson when he landed a job as his assistant in the early 1980s.

Jackson and Verrone set out to shake up the world of children's books. Back then, picture books were the name of the game: colorful, cozy reads that taught young readers life lessons. Verrone, who had what Silsbee called "an antic sense of humor," thought books for this age group could be more fun. Meanwhile, Jackson was lit up by an emerging area of the business: novels for readers ages eight to twelve, or the pre-teen set.

Middle grade didn't really exist as a publishing category until the 1970s. And of the novels for older children that got printed, the vast majority were fantasy stories. Think of E. B. White's *Charlotte's Web*, which came out in 1952 and put serious conversations about death into the mouths of talkative animals. Roald Dahl's books, such as *James and the Giant Peach* (1961) and *Charlie and the Chocolate Factory* (1964), were gorgeous, but absurdist. Then, in 1962, there was Madeleine L'Engle's *A Wrinkle in Time*, a brilliant intergalactic battle between good and evil.

The exception was Beverly Cleary's work, which featured ordinary children. Cleary dominated the children's market and Jackson wanted to publish more books like hers: "Books about real kids for real kids," Silsbee said of his onetime boss's mission. "He really hated anything remotely didactic . . . he wanted books that kids would pick and would just feel like they were a part of." Cleary had won over young audiences with her lively stories about middle-class white children, mostly living in the Pacific Northwest, where she had grown up. Young readers couldn't get enough of *Henry Huggins* (1950), *Ellen Tebbits* (1951), and *Beezus and Ramona* (1955), about nine-year-old Beatrice "Beezus" Quimby weathering the high jinks of her spirited younger sister. The pair starred in a wildly popular follow-up in 1968 called *Ramona the Pest*.

To find the next Cleary, Jackson and Verrone resorted to unconventional measures. They dug deep into their pockets and spent a precious $5,000 to take out an ad in *Writer's Digest*. It said they were seeking "realistic fiction" for eight- to twelve-year-olds. Soon, a manuscript arrived in the mail by way of an aspiring writer with no agent. Jackson picked it up, hoping to uncover treasure.

The book, called *Iggie's House*, was unpolished. The young characters were one-dimensional and the villain—an unapologetically bigoted local mom who rallies the town to reject and harass the new neighbors—was particularly overdrawn. Still, Jackson saw something in it. Among other things, he noticed that the author had a knack for capturing children's voices, with an impeccable ear for dialogue. Years later, Silsbee recalled him saying that the original manuscript for *Iggie's House* "wasn't very good . . . but there was something there."

So Jackson took a chance. He picked up the phone and called this untested writer. A woman answered, and her voice lifted when he introduced himself and explained why he was getting in touch. He could see she lived in New Jersey—would she be able to come by the office sometime soon?

Judy Blume could barely wait to get out her response.

"The day he called and said he'd like to meet me and talk about the manuscript was the most exciting day of my life," Blume later told *Publishers Weekly*. The morning of their appointment, she was so nervous her stomach lurched. She took a pill to try to settle it, which helped, but then the medicine dried out her mouth. Generally, her health had improved since she'd started writing, but a meeting with a real editor was stressful enough to throw her body back into crisis mode. Judy hopped into the car, hoping she wouldn't have to do too much talking.

When she arrived at Prentice Hall, Jackson—who was stylishly dressed and bore more than a slight resemblance to the freshly minted talk-show host Dick Cavett—greeted her warmly. Judy was taken aback by his good looks; he was "a stunningly beautiful man," she told the *New Yorker*. He led her to his cramped office, his desk piled high with stacks of manuscripts. Jackson confessed he wasn't sure about publishing *Iggie's House* yet, but he had some questions. The protagonist, for instance—who was Winnie, really? Beyond getting to know the new kids in town, what else did she want?

Judy wrote down everything he said. An hour and a half later, she had promised to revise the book for Jackson, in the hopes that Bradbury would give it a home.

• • •

Books in the swinging sixties were getting bolder. Just as there wasn't a defined middle grade category yet, there also wasn't a market around what we now know as young adult books, or reads just for older teenagers. There were books that *starred* teens, like *The Catcher in the Rye*, but Salinger's cantankerous 1951 manifesto was packaged as an adult novel. Then came *The Outsiders*.

Published in 1967, *The Outsiders* is widely considered to be the first young adult (YA) book. It was written by a teenager named Susan Hinton: her pen name was the gender-ambiguous S. E. Hinton, because her publisher thought no one would believe a girl wrote it. The novel focused on white-on-white grievance in Tulsa, Oklahoma. Its protagonist, fourteen-year-old Ponyboy Curtis, identifies with the "greasers": a group of underprivileged and all-but-unsupervised kids who overcompensate for their low social status with style and swagger. The greasers can't stand the "socs"—snotty rich kids who drive Mustangs and wear madras shirts—and the feeling is mutual. Late at night, the town becomes a war zone, fueled by class resentment. Among all the typical high school trip-ups, including drinking, depression, and teen pregnancy, the greasers have to worry about getting slaughtered by their rivals after the sun goes down.

*The Outsiders* pushed the envelope with its gritty subject matter, but still adhered to the industry's unwritten rule that books for young readers had to teach morals. For all its thundering violence, *The Outsiders* has an obvious, virtuous heartbeat. "Don't be so bugged about being a greaser," Johnny, the novel's much-abused sacrificial lamb, tells Ponyboy in a letter. "You still have a lot of time to make yourself be what you want. There's still a lot of good in the world."

For books that dropped the moral pretense, you have to look somewhere else, somewhere surprising: *Harriet the Spy*.

Today, Harriet is probably best known for the cute movie she inspired in 1996, starring future *Gossip Girl* pot-stirrer Michelle Trachtenberg, or more recently, the hip Apple+ cartoon voiced by Beanie Feldstein. But when Louise Fitzhugh published *Harriet the Spy* in 1964, she was testing boundaries of what was acceptable in books for kids. Harriet M. Welsch was a girl-detective, but she wasn't pretty and popular and polite like her predecessor, Nancy Drew. No, Harriet was opinionated and curious to the point of being unpleasant at times. She was bossy with her friends, and single-minded in her desire to unearth people's secrets. "*Harriet the Spy* was transgressing all over the place," said Roger Sutton, who was editor in chief of children's literature magazine and website the *Horn Book* from 1996 to 2021. "The adults [in the book] weren't always right. Sometimes you have to lie. She committed all kinds of felonious deeds that did not go punished."

Fitzhugh's next Harriet book took even bigger risks.

In 1965's *The Long Secret*, Harriet and her attractive but reserved friend Beth Ellen take their spy games to Southampton, where Harriet's Manhattan-based family is spending the summer. Harriet and Beth Ellen are on the cusp of adolescence; they daydream about what their lives will look like when they become women. The fingerprints of nascent Second Wave feminism tap across the pages (Fitzhugh herself was a queer feminist intellectual, drinking her way through Greenwich Village). Early in the book, Harriet asks Beth Ellen what she wants to be when she grows up. Shyly, Beth Ellen confesses that she doesn't "want to be anything at all . . . I want to marry a rich man. I want to have a little boy, and maybe, a little girl."

Harriet is disgusted by this answer. "You'll be a very boring person," she responds in her signature blunt style. "No one will come and see you. *I* certainly won't come and see you. *I'll* be working."

Later in *The Long Secret*, Beth Ellen is acting grumpy and Harriet screams at her on the phone: "WHAT'S WRONG WITH YOU?"

"I'm—menstruating!" Beth Ellen responds before unceremoniously hanging up.

That weekend, Harriet's friend from the city, Janie, visits Southampton. No-nonsense Janie wants to be a doctor, or a scientist, which is why she's comfortable talking about her body's inner workings to Harriet and Beth Ellen. Janie explains the whole monthly process to the two friends, with Harriet wondering why she hasn't gotten her period yet. "Now, you know the baby grows inside a woman, in her womb, in her uterus?" Janie asks them. "So, it's very simple. If you *have* a baby started in there, the baby lives on the lining; but if you *don't* have a baby, like *we* don't, then the body very sensibly disposes of the lining that it's made for the baby."

Janie's tutorial lasts a total of six pages and includes medical vocabulary previously unheard of in fiction for children, like fallopian tubes. Fitzhugh and her original publisher, Harper & Row, were bold to include the section, given that referencing female bodily functions in anything but gauzy, euphemistic terms was considered taboo (one popular Victorian-era nickname for the uterus was "mother room"). Indeed, the *New York Times* review of *The Long Secret* reverts to whispery language around the subject, even as it celebrates the book's candor. "*The Long Secret*, moreover, observes in so many words that being twelvish entails, for a girl, a few more changes than children's books have hitherto cared to recognize—heaven knows why," the reviewer writes.

•    •    •

*Heaven knows why.* That's what Judy thought, too. Why couldn't children's fiction tackle complicated or even controversial subjects?

Her revision of *Iggie's House* did enough to convince Jackson and Verrone to sign her. Silsbee said Jackson knew that the finished book still "wasn't up to what became her standard . . . but [he] just knew there was something there, and had to publish the book to get to know her."

*Iggie* was published in the spring of 1970, and the critics were underwhelmed. *Kirkus Reviews,* the industry's book reviewing mainstay, described a hapless yet well-intentioned Winnie—who among many gaffes, introduces her new friends, the Garbers, as being "from Africa," even though they've just moved from Detroit—as "the bumbling, besieged liberal at age eleven." Ultimately, the reviewer found Winnie's book-long crusade to garner support for Grove Street's integration to be "occasionally forced . . . loose though not slack—in fact evanescent except for the rueful truth."

Blume has since distanced herself from *Iggie's House.* In an afterword to a recent edition of the novel, she says that at the time she wrote it, she "was almost as naive as Winnie is in this book, wanting to make the world a better place but not knowing how." She explains that she had been moved by the race riots in Newark, which occurred in the summer of 1967, and the assassination of Martin Luther King Jr.

*Iggie's House* is flawed but it was progressive for its time in two ways: it deals with the real discriminatory practices of redlining and blockbusting, and it lets us watch as Winnie slowly calibrates her own moral compass, in a process that's sometimes painful. When her parents don't take an immediate stand against racism, she's deeply disappointed. And when the Garber kids don't really want to be Winnie's friend, despite her best intentions, she's angry and confused.

Jackson saw genuine possibility in the writer behind *Iggie's House.*

And by the time Bradbury inked the deal to publish it, Judy had already shared some details about a new project that was keeping her busy. "Judy was in my office one day and she said, 'I've written most of another book,'" Jackson, who died in 2019, said in *Presenting Judy Blume*. "'It's about a young girl who talks to God as if he's her friend.'"

When he read that manuscript, he knew he wasn't crazy. Many years later, he'd say of the money he and Verrone scraped together to buy the ad that brought in Blume: "It was the best $5,000 we ever spent."

## Chapter Three

# Pre-Teen Girls

*"Always in love"*

There's nothing remarkable about Margaret Simon. She is eleven years old, an only child who has just moved from New York City to the (fictional) suburb of Farbrook, New Jersey. She likes boys, wants to impress her friends, and is impatient to grow her hair longer. She finds adults and their preoccupations a bit funny, like when it's humid outside, she catches her mother sneakily trying to sniff her own armpits. She is neither shy nor especially outgoing. She's being raised in a dual-faith household, which in practice means a no-faith household, because the topic of religion is so fraught. As a result, it's up to her to figure out her own private understanding of God.

All of these details add up to a portrait of a regular adolescent girl. And *that's* what makes Margaret Simon special. She isn't remarkable—but she is real.

•  •  •

Letters to Jackson from 1969 reveal that while Judy was excited about publishing *Iggie's House*, the project that had captured her imagination was her as-yet-untitled novel-in-progress. Unlike *Iggie*, which took a child's view of a contemporary social issue, "Margaret Simon"—as Blume referred to the draft manuscript—was born from Judy's own memories. "In *Margaret*, I decided I'm going to write about what sixth grade was really like for me," she told the *Daily News* in 1976. "The personal parts about Margaret were true."

Judy turned eleven in the winter of 1949, four years after the war ended with a cataclysmic blast on the other side of the world and well into the Truman presidency, when everyone in America was just trying to go back to normal. Well, not exactly normal—the post-war economy was booming. The middle class had gotten a buff and a polish. Families of four or even five could thrive on one income, which meant kids were liberated from hovering psychic burdens like work and the draft and could concentrate on being children for a little bit longer than previous generations. That's how the adolescent, focused on school and social-izing, was born.

As a child, Judy was daddy's little girl. Her parents, Rudolph and Essie, both grew up in Elizabeth and met when they were finishing high school. They married young, him dark-haired and dapper, her slender, serious, and blond. They stayed in town, where they had lots of family living nearby. Essie, an introvert who loved books, was a guarded per-son, keeping her feelings under wraps. Rudolph, on the other hand, was dynamic—he was funny and charming. He owned his own dental prac-tice and was widely admired within the community. Judy thought of him as a natural philosopher who just happened to fix teeth for a living.

Her father was her go-to parent for comfort and affection, the one who indulged her in round after round of hide-and-seek, took her tem-perature when she was sick, and soothed her during thunderstorms (one boom was enough to send her leaping across the room). She rewarded him with a special nickname: Doey-Bird. Every night before bed, she gave him his "treatment," which was a series of kisses and hugs, always doled out in the same pattern. Blume described it in her 1977 autobiographical novel, *Starring Sally J. Freedman as Herself,* as "a sliding kiss, three quick hugs . . . finished with a butterfly kiss on his nose."

The Sussmans were Jewish, so Margaret's struggle with religion—in which she seeks out both Jewish and Christian experiences as part of a yearlong project to clarify her faith—wasn't Judy's. But when it came to Margaret's secret, intimate relationship with God, that was all her. From the first page of the book, Margaret whispers a prayer, as if conjuring an imaginary friend.

"Are you there God? It's me, Margaret," she begins, as she does with every quiet appeal to God throughout the novel. "We're moving today. I'm so scared God . . . Don't let New Jersey be too horrible. Thank you."

Judy spoke to God, too, mostly as a way of coping with her anxiety about her father's mortality. He was ostensibly healthy, but much of her childhood was shaped by illness and death. Not just the Holocaust, though whispers about the camps made her shudder. With many generations of family around, there were inevitably a lot of funerals, followed by intense, seven-day shivahs. She was terrified Rudolph was going to die young—at the age of forty-two, to be exact. He was the youngest of seven children and two of his older brothers, also dentists, had unexpectedly passed away at that age. *Please,* she prayed to whoever might be listening, *not Doey, too.* Sally has the same fear in *Sally J. Freedman*: "*Let Doey-Bird get through this bad year . . . this year of being forty-two . . . we need him God . . . we love him,*" Sally begs in her bed at night. "*You wouldn't let three brothers die at the same age, would you?* But somewhere in the back of her mind she remembered hearing that bad things always happen in threes."

Her fear of something happening to Doey was so overwhelming that Judy became compulsive. "I made bargains with God," Blume wrote in her 1986 collection of children's letters, *Letters to Judy: What Kids Wish They Could Tell You.* "I became ritualistic, inventing prayers that had to be repeated seven times a day, in order to keep my father safe and healthy."

She also felt like she needed to keep her worries to herself. Her brother, David, was the problem child, so she felt pressure to be perfect, fulfilling Rudolph and Essie's expectations for both of them. From a young age, David was brilliant but inscrutable. He was rebellious—once, he got sent home from kindergarten after kicking his teacher in the stomach. When Judy was going into third grade, David developed a kidney infection so persistent that Essie moved the three of them south to Miami for the year, hoping the sea air would cure him. It worked, but it also meant that Judy only saw her beloved father on holidays, when he could get away from the office and fly down.

More and more she learned to hide things from her family. Essie needed her to be easy, talented, popular, *happy*—and so Judy learned to give her just that.

·  ·  ·

It wasn't just Essie. American culture in the 1950s told adolescent girls that they should be pretty, popular, and happy, too. If America was a cake, that demographic was the icing, eye-catching and frothy. Teenagers, and particularly teenage girls, embodied frivolity and leisure. They were there to show the world just how far the United States had come.

In December 1944, *Life* magazine published a pictorial called "Teen-Age Girls: They Live in a Wonderful World of Their Own," featuring a handful of girls ages fifteen to seventeen, who were growing up in Webster Groves, Missouri. It described these coiffed, carefree creatures as "a lovely, gay, blissful society almost untouched by war." Their clothing choices (skirts and sweaters or loose-fitting blue jeans with button-downs), slang ("seein' ya" for goodbye and "uh-huh" for yes), and preferred pastimes (hanging out at record stores and hosting cheerful all-girl "hen parties") were presented with the kind of amused fascination usually reserved for toddlers and zoo animals.

"It is a world of many laws," *Life* explained. "They are capricious, changing or reversing themselves almost overnight. But while they are in effect, the laws are immutable and the punishment for violation is ostracism, swift and terrifying practice of ancient people."

In her new book, Judy recorded those laws. She didn't bring in an adult perspective to subtly swipe at them; rather, she took them as seriously as any other rite of passage.

Margaret starts to adjust to her new town when she meets her neighbor Nancy Wheeler, a chatty eleven-year-old with a turned-up nose and more than her share of bravado. Practically the first thing Nancy tells Margaret is that she can't show up to school wearing socks. "Loafers, but no socks," Nancy says solemnly. "Otherwise, you'll look like a baby." Margaret takes her at her word, despite her mother's protestations that she'll get blisters. "Well then, I'll just have to suffer," Margaret tells her, and she isn't wrong. The *Life* article outlines similar sartorial protocols, ephemeral but also somehow ironclad. "Months ago colored bobby socks folded at the top were decreed, not by anyone or any group but, as usual, by a sudden and universal acceptance of the new idea. Now, no teen-ager dares wear anything but pure white socks without a fold."

Having dutifully shown up to the first day of school sockless, Margaret scores an invite to Nancy's secret club, which she conducts with her two closest friends, Janie Loomis and Gretchen Potter. Together, the foursome form the Pre-Teen Sensations, or PTS's, a group where everyone answers to new, exotic names (Alexandra, Veronica, Kimberly, and Mavis), wears bras, and keeps Boy Books, in which they record their weekly list of crushes. These details came straight from Judy's own adolescence. In sixth grade, she also belonged to a club, called the Pre-Teen Kittens, with her best friends (an early draft of *Are You There God?* actually uses this name, with the members adopting feline identities like Tabby and Fluffy). The girls met up after school and, just like Margaret and her peers, unabashedly gossiped about boys and bodies.

Both groups—the fictional PTS's and the real PTK's—were obsessed with their slow-to-grow bustlines. "We must—we must—we must increase our bust!" the girls chant in *Are You There God?* immortalizing the same routine Judy used to do with her friends. She has demonstrated it in interviews and has talked about correcting the young actresses' form on the set of the 2023 *Are You There God? It's Me, Margaret* movie. Here's how it goes: you raise both arms to shoulder height and bend your elbows at right angles, then swing them back and forth rhythmically. "But it doesn't work," Blume joked in a 2013 interview with HuffPost Live, gesturing to her flat chest.

To Judy, it seemed weird that no one had ever thought to set down these kinds of details in a book for kids before. As far as she was concerned, bras and boy books were just a normal part of growing up. Not every kid had a horse, like Velvet Brown in 1935's *National Velvet*, but every girl had a body. She made Margaret boy crazy, the way she was in her junior high years.

Over the course of the novel, Margaret maintains a private crush on fourteen-year-old Moose Freed, who she meets through Nancy's older brother. Moose starts cutting the Simon family's lawn on Saturday mornings, after Margaret's father—a lifelong city dweller—nearly slices off his hand with the power mower. Margaret pines for Moose from the window while he works. "I pretended to be really busy reading a book, but the truth is—I was watching Moose . . . Moose would be number one in my Boy Book if only I was brave enough, but what would Nancy think? She hated him."

Instead, Margaret, as Mavis, picks the much less controversial Philip Leroy to top off her list of crushes. Philip is the safe choice—the cute guy in her class who everyone likes. But one afternoon before a school dance, Margaret admits to God that she, too, has been sucked into Philip's preteen gravitational pull: "It's not so much that I like him as a person, God, but as a boy he's very handsome. And I'd love to dance with him." Later that night, Margaret gets her wish, though the reality is considerably less transporting than she'd hoped. Philip is a clumsy dancer who steps on her toes and Nancy, standing right next to them in the school gym, almost starts crying because she's so jealous.

Margaret has her first kiss with Philip Leroy, at a party during a game of Two Minutes in the Closet. There, in the dark and between her nervous giggles, he gives her a quick peck on the lips. "A really fast kiss! Not the kind you see in the movies where the boy and girl cling together for a long time," Margaret says. Even still, she's pretty sure she liked it.

For Judy, channeling those awkward, early crushes came easily. As a kid, she was "always in love," she told the UK *Independent* in 1999 while promoting her adult novel *Summer Sisters*. By age fourteen, just a few years older than Margaret, she said she was regularly going to "make-out parties . . . you invited a group of boys and girls, and you turned out the lights, and you played."

Writing *Are You There God?*, Judy could convincingly borrow from those experiences in part because they still spoke to her, calling out from the depths of her memory. Compared to her committed, responsible twenties, her teenage years felt ecstatic and full of life. "When you're that age, everything is still there in front of you," Blume has said of her adolescence. "You have the opportunity to be almost anyone you want. I was not yet thirty when I started the book, but I felt my options were already gone."

Judy had discovered that working on a novel—from the early stage, of making up the characters, to the final phases, of polishing it with Jackson—offered her a welcome reassurance: life could still surprise her. As she chipped away at *Are You There God?*, she found herself diligently taking notes on a yellow pad as new ideas and themes surfaced, working out Margaret's unique relationship with God, for instance, and how the young character felt about her pubescent body. Margaret was quite a bit easier to evoke than Winnie. Maybe it's because in Judy's best moments

of writing, Margaret was emerging, all but fully formed, from somewhere deep inside her own consciousness.

And Jackson was shaping up to be the ideal literary midwife. By the
time Judy was ready to share her draft of the novel—which she plunked
out on her typewriter in a wildly creative six-week burst, in between
cooking, cleaning, and playing rounds of golf—she and Jackson had already established their routines. Judy would come by the Bradbury Press
office, where she'd ask him to open his windows to let in some air. Then
they'd sit down at his desk and talk for hours at a clip. They'd lay out the
printed manuscript between them and flip through the pages, one by
one. Jackson, who would have already discussed the draft with Verrone,
came armed with their combined thoughts and his pencil. As he and
Judy chatted, he'd scribble and erase. By the time they finished, Judy
would leave with her marked-up novel, the margins filled with Jackson's
handwritten notes.

With *Are You There God?*, one of Jackson's biggest concerns had to do
with Margaret's new best friend, Nancy.

In one of the book's most emotional moments, Nancy sends Margaret
a postcard from Washington, DC, with just three words: "I GOT IT!!!"
Margaret rightly understands this to mean Nancy's first period: a milestone that's taken a competitive turn for the PTS's. Margaret, feeling left
behind, is devastated. "I ripped the card into tiny shreds and ran to my
room," she says in the book. "There was something wrong with me. I just
knew it. I flopped onto my bed and cried." Here, Jackson didn't worry
about the subject matter. Instead, he wondered—is Nancy telling the
truth? Judy, who had been preoccupied with Margaret's internal experience, hadn't even considered it. But sure enough, when she thought it
over, she realized that yes, Nancy *was* lying.

In the final draft of the novel, Margaret finds out Nancy lied when
she spends the day in New York City with the Wheeler family. Nancy gets
her first period in the bathroom of a steak house after a trip to Radio

City, and—caught with her pants down, literally—begs Margaret not to expose her to the other girls.

While Judy, like any author, needed guidance when it came to building plot and character, her style—especially when writing in the first person—was always top-notch, as Jackson told *School Library Journal* in 2001. "It was the voice, the absence of adult regret, instruction or nostalgia," Jackson said, that always convinced him that Blume's books were a little bit magical. "She turns them over to the kids, to the characters," he continued.

And for Jackson, a children's book's greatest strength was always that rare whiff of authenticity baked into the pages. Jackson was dyslexic, which Silsbee said gave him a surprising advantage when it came to sniffing it out. "He told me, 'This is the reason I got into doing children's books, because I read at the same pace that children read.' So when he read a sentence, it was like this unfolding adventure . . . He said, 'That's why I think I'm a good children's book editor. Because I'm forced to slow down.'"

## Chapter Four

# Menstruation

*"Someday, it will happen to you."*

y the fall of 1970, when *Are You There God? It's Me, Margaret* was published, sex had busted out of the bedroom.

A *Time* magazine cover from July 11, 1969, with the cover line "The Sex Explosion," showed a nude man and woman about to embrace, shrouded only by a half-unzipped fig leaf. The models were members of the New York cast of the play *Oh! Calcutta!*, a surprise hit that had recently opened in an old burlesque theater where the actors performed almost entirely naked, portraying erotic acts from masturbation to group sex. The show, which got terrible reviews, was nonetheless packed night after night and commanded record ticket prices.

*Are You There God?* emerged into a rip-roaring, in-your-face culture. Girls still formed secret clubs, but they conducted them while songs like "American Woman" by the Guess Who—a guttural anti-Vietnam anthem—and "Lola" by the Kinks—about a guy boogying the night away with a drag queen or a trans woman—thrummed in the background.

*Hair* was on Broadway; the hippies barely wore clothes! The Summer of Love was in the rearview, as was Woodstock.

Sure, *Are You There God?*—which took its iconic name from a typist, who used the novel's first line as a placeholder—had its boundary-pushing moments, like when Margaret admitted to sneaking peeks at her dad's copies of *Playboy*, or when she stuffed her training bra with cotton balls and admired how she looked in the mirror. But 1970 was an entirely different world than the one Judy grew up in.

Or so she and Jackson thought.

The critics mostly liked Blume's slim coming-of-age novel. *Kirkus* gave *Are You There God?* a mixed review, calling it "fresh" and complimenting Blume's "easy way with words." However, the reviewer thought Margaret's obsession with her body was immature, and considered whether the book sent the right message, given that she doesn't gain perspective and grow out of it by the end. "The effect is to confirm common anxieties, rather than allaying them," *Kirkus* wrote, wondering if the story was perhaps intended as "satirical." As the reviewer noted with more than a shadow of judgment, the novel closed with Margaret getting her first period.

On the other hand, the *New York Times* described it as a "funny, warm and loving book, one that captures the essence of beginning adolescence." That same day, the *Times* included *Are You There God?* in a write-up of the year's outstanding children's books. Judy was overjoyed when she saw the paper. "That was the first time I felt 'I can really do this,'" she said in *Judy Blume's Story*. "These people are taking me seriously! It's not just pretend."

Her name was getting out there. She gained a frisson of notoriety in her town. She gifted three copies of *Are You There God?* to Randy and Larry's elementary school, but as she'd later tell it, the principal refused to put it in the library. He said that menstruation wasn't an appropriate topic for kids that age.

Then, there was the time the Blumes' phone rang and Judy picked up.

The person on the other end of the line—a woman—asked her if she was the one who wrote the novel.

"Yes," Judy said.

"Communist!" the voice shrieked, before quickly hanging up.

How bizarre. It was a strange thing to call someone who'd simply written a book about an American middle schooler and her friend group. Wasn't it?

.     .     .

These days, the Right uses a specific set of inflammatory words when it's accusing someone of exposing children to inappropriate material: "Indoctrination." "Pedophilia." "Grooming." "When I was 17 I discovered one of my younger siblings had been reading Judy Blume drivel at a friend's house," a Twitter user posted to their 18,000+ followers on April 16, 2023. "Their behavior became unacceptable. Judy Blume is a groomer." But in the Vietnam War era of the early 1970s, the shorthand for anything subversive was "communist." To a certain buttoned-up demographic, Communism was an encroaching political movement that had infected the minds of the American left wing. Loud and freewheeling rock music? Communist. Roll your eyes all you want, but it's true.

Widespread sex education? Definitely communist. Sex education in schools had been around for over half a century, but it was still an ideological battleground. It first cropped up in the 1910s when soldiers started coming home from the front lines of World War I. Many returned with unwanted reunion gifts for their wives, girlfriends, and sexual partners: gonorrhea and syphilis. The spread of venereal disease (as it was termed back then) was so swift and urgent that new, government-backed organizations popped up to deal with it. Billionaire oil-man John D. Rockefeller was a big supporter of sex ed in schools and he funneled money into the cause.

The thinking went that adults were already too far gone when it came to safe sex practices, but children and teens could be taught better habits. If the next generation received the right training, they'd be less vulnerable to disease and unwanted pregnancies. That said, institutional sex ed was controversial from the start. Over the years, detractors argued that devoting classroom time to sex and reproduction contributed to an overly permissive culture. They felt that schools had no right to butt into a conversation that had traditionally been entrusted to close adults at home.

The debate continued into the mid-century and through the sexual revolution, with pro–sex ed activists arguing it had a distinctly moral purpose. The landscape was changing, sex educators argued, and kids needed updated maps to navigate it. Teens who understood their bodies were bound to be more responsible with them. Appropriate sex education could escort young adults down the path toward married, monogamous sex.

Spearheading this conversation was SIECUS, the Sexuality Information and Education Council of the United States, established in 1964. Its founder was Dr. Mary Steichen Calderone, who grew up in the bohemian West Village as the daughter of the famed photographer Edward Steichen. She graduated from Vassar, went to medical school, and then became medical director at Planned Parenthood in 1953. But ten years later, she was ready to strike out on her own. In her work for the organization, she had started to suspect that Planned Parenthood was "looking at the problem [of unwanted pregnancy] from the wrong end of the telescope," said Jonathan Zimmerman, author of *Too Hot to Handle: A Global History of Sex Education*. "The problem wasn't the availability of contraceptives, although that remains a problem. The problem was Americans' ideas about sex itself."

Calderone started SIECUS with a few colleagues in her hometown of New York City after determining that young adults needed a clearer understanding of how sex worked and its place in society in general.

For Calderone, who was considered a firebrand in her day, sex wasn't something to be ashamed of—but it wasn't something to be glib about, either. She believed intercourse belonged in the marital bed, between a man and a woman. "Mary Calderone, despite what her enemies said, was no flame-throwing radical," Zimmerman said, citing the nickname her right-wing critics gave her: *Mary Stinkin' Calderone*. "She too thought that in the best case scenario, sex happened in what she called a long term, committed relationship . . . [She] didn't have a lot of time for gay sex. [She] was concerned about what she saw as the cheapening of sex that attached to the sexual revolution. But at the same time, she wanted a much more open and explicit discussion of the subject."

That involved advocating for frank sex education in public schools and in 1968 consulting on *How Babies Are Made*, a primer for children released by Time-Life Books. One of the first volumes of its kind, the no-fuss hardcover picture book—which has vintage, paper-cut color illustrations on every page—walks young readers through the cycle of reproduction, first using the example of flowers, then chickens, then dogs, and eventually, human beings. This approach followed the then-standard model of sex education, where the sperm and the egg were contextualized within the larger biological framework of plants in nature: literally, the birds and the bees. "The plants and animals stuff was a way to try to teach this stuff without making kids interested in it," Zimmerman said. "Because the goal is to prevent [sex]. It's not learn by doing, it's to prevent the doing."

*How Babies Are Made* works its way up to a man and a woman embracing in bed and describes intercourse in clear but clinical language. "The sperm, which come from the father's testicles, are sent into the mother through his penis. To do this, the father and mother lie down facing each other and the father places his penis in the mother's vagina." The obvious message is that it's all in service of perpetuating human life, by way of a process that's as natural as dusty yellow pollen fertilizing a blooming flower. However, there is a major difference, the book attests: "Unlike plants and animals, when human mothers and fathers create a new baby, they are sharing a very personal and special relationship."

But even this was too much for the critics of sex ed. The same year that *How Babies Are Made* was published, a former professor and religious zealot named Gordon V. Drake started churning out articles for Christian publications denouncing liberal sex ed as, yes, Communism. SIECUS, hand in hand with the National Education Association, were trying to "destroy the traditional moral fiber of America and replace it with a pervasive sickly humanism," Drake wrote in a forty-page screed called *Is the Schoolhouse the Proper Place to Teach Raw Sex?* He didn't approve of *How Babies Are Made* because it made no mention of marriage. Calling the people at SIECUS a bunch of "Johnny-come-lately pornographers," Drake attempted to tease out their various communist sympathies. He criticized their mission to get sex ed into more public school classrooms as evidence of a campaign to force religion and morality out of American life. "This, obviously drives a wedge between the family, church and school," he wrote. "If this is accomplished, and the new morality is affirmed, our children will become easy targets for Marxism and other amoral, nihilistic philosophies—as well as V.D.!"

•    •    •

Clearly, Judy disagreed. She eagerly picked up a copy of *How Babies Are Made* for Randy and Larry. She was determined to be honest with them about sex, partly because her own parents had made things so awkward. Her first introduction to menstruation came at the age of nine, when her family drove out to Long Island to visit her aunt, uncles, and cousins for the day. Her teenage cousin Grace wasn't feeling well and young Judy sensed it wasn't a run-of-the-mill cold keeping her down. As Blume recalls in her book *Letters to Judy*, she spent the whole car ride home asking about Grace, only to get stonewalled. "You'll find out when you're thirteen" was all her father would say.

But Judy was persistent and when she brought it up again at home, her father pulled her onto his lap and gave her the "talk"—which in this case was a vague, "confusing" story about eggs and the moon. "There was something about eggs dropping down, something about blood and something about the lunar cycle, leading me to believe that every time the moon was full, every female in the world over the age of thirteen was menstruating," Blume recalled.

Nobody gave her a special picture book to describe the inevitable physical changes that would come with puberty. Her mother wasn't much help, either. A year later, Judy watched Essie buy a menstrual pad in a public bathroom. When she asked what it was for, the mother-daughter pair had a clipped conversation that ended abruptly with Essie telling her, "Someday, it will happen to you."

Ten-year-old Judy nodded. "But I still didn't understand exactly what would happen or why."

When she finally did learn more about periods, she became desperate to get hers, especially after her friends started menstruating. In her mind it meant they were leaving her behind. "I wanted my period so badly," Blume said in *Judy Blume's Story*, "that I once put a pin in my finger to draw blood. I smeared it on a pad and wore the pad just to see what it would feel like."

She channeled that yearning when she was writing about Margaret. Unlike *The Long Secret*, *Are You There God?* doesn't spend time expounding on the physical mechanics of periods—there are no mentions of eggs or moons, let alone fallopian tubes. Instead, it treats menarche like a rite of passage so earth-shattering that schoolgirls are compelled to pray, cry, and lie about it. Margaret sees getting her period as an initiation into a new, grown-up world, marked by the trappings of female adulthood: bras, menstrual belts, and sanitary pads. In anticipation of the big event, she and her friend Janie slip into a drugstore to check out the personal care aisle. Perusing the selection, the girls settle on the brand they'd like to eventually use: Teenage Softies. They feel like rebels making the purchase, given that neither kid actually needs them yet. "Today I was feeling brave," Margaret narrates. "I thought, so what if God's mad at me? Who cares?"

When she gets home, Margaret tries on a pad in the privacy of her closet (early editions of the book have her using a menstrual belt, while subsequent printings are updated to reflect the advent of sticky tape, in a change originally suggested by Blume's British editor). "I wanted to find out how it would feel," she says, pulling her pants up. "Now I knew. I liked it."

No children's book had ever gone here before.

.    .    .

"You were never allowed to talk about [menstruation]," said Arlene LaVerde of the way things were during her childhood. LaVerde was born in 1967 and served as president of the New York Library Association from November 2023 to November 2024. "Now . . . the way we're able to talk about menstruation and periods, without fear—it starts with Judy Blume and what she started with that one book." LaVerde went on: "We wouldn't be where we are without her."

In Judy's day, girls ended up learning about Aunt Flo not from their parents, but from the people who wanted to sell them menstrual products. The overlap between physical maturity and consumerism—shopping for pads, picking out a brand—was as true for Margaret as it was for girls in the real world, writes Joan Jacobs Brumberg in her book *The Body Project: An Intimate History of American Girls*. With adults being ashamed to discuss periods with their daughters, it left a gap in the chain of communication that industry stepped in to fill. The first disposable sanitary napkins were manufactured by the medical and personal care corporation Kimberly-Clark, and sold under the name Kotex, which appeared on shelves in the early 1920s, after the company developed synthetic surgical cotton for use during World War I.

Quickly, according to Brumberg, Kotex became a status symbol among young, middle-class women, who could afford the monthly investment in a store-bought product that was immediately marketed as an upgrade in personal hygiene. Meanwhile, poorer girls, and particularly the daughters of immigrants, were stuck with the functional—but high-maintenance—washable cloth-rag pads used by their mothers and grandmothers. "Well into the 1930s and 1940s, there were some American girls who had to make do with homemade protection," Brumberg writes. But they weren't happy about it. "Daughters of immigrants understood, before their grandmothers and mothers did, that there was an American way to menstruate, and that it required participation in the larger consumer society."

By the time Judy Blume was writing about Margaret, that initiation often began in school, especially in more liberal enclaves like northern New Jersey. In 1946, Kotex and the Walt Disney company collaborated on an animated ten-minute film called *The Story of Menstruation*, an educational short that would eventually be viewed by approximately 100 million American girls. In it, a smoky-voiced actress with a fancy transatlantic accent walks viewers through the science of early puberty, starting with the pituitary gland. The cartoon, done in elegant, muted colors, is filled with wide-eyed girls who mostly resemble the title character in the studio's 1950 full-length take on the Cinderella tale.

The narrator—who pronounces the word "maturing" as ma-TOOR-ring—uses correct scientific terms, such as "uterus" and "ovaries," to explain the monthly cycle. In a sequence that describes the process that leads to menstrual shedding, a simulation of a woman's reproductive system appears on-screen, portrayed in bloodless shades of ivory, with an egg touring through a fallopian tube like a tiny pinball. "If the egg is impregnated, which happens when a woman is going to have a child, the egg will stay within the uterus," the voiceover actress recites in the film's only subtle nod to how babies are actually conceived. "Then the thickened lining will provide nourishment for the budding human being through the early days of its development. However, most eggs pass through the fallopian tubes without being fertilized."

*The Story of Menstruation* goes on to provide tips to girls for getting through their periods, including tracking them on a calendar, getting exercise, and eating right. At times, the tone borders on condescending: "Some girls have a little less pep, a feeling of pressure on the lower body, perhaps an occasional twinge or a touch of nerves." ("An occasional twinge"? Okay, try telling that to someone with mind-numbing cramps.) "But don't let it get you down. After all, no matter how you feel, you have to live with people. You have to live with yourself, too." As the film assures its young female audience, it's all part of growing up to be a healthy adult, within "nature's eternal plan for passing on the gift of life."

The film also mentions an accompanying pamphlet called "Very Personally Yours," which Disney and Kotex had produced as well to reiterate the cartoon's messages. In *Are You There God?*, Blume pokes fun at the kind of stuffy, in-school presentations that would have a junior high schooler like Margaret walking home at the end of the day with an illustrated period fact sheet tucked in her bookbag. One Friday afternoon, the sixth-grade girls gather in the auditorium to watch *What Every Girl Should Know*, which is being chaperoned by a representative from the fictional Private Lady company. "The narrator of the film pronounced it menstroo-ation," Margaret says. "The film told us about the ovaries and explained why girls menstroo-ate. But it didn't really tell us how it feels, except to say that it's not painful . . . it just said how wonderful nature was and how we would soon become women and all that."

Margaret is doubly unimpressed when she's handed a pamphlet after the movie, also called "What Every Girl Should Know." "It was like one big commercial. I made a mental note never to buy Private Lady things *when* and *if* I needed them," she says.

That irreverence and inborn skepticism are part of what make Margaret so relatable to young readers. It's also part of what makes her so needling to the kinds of parents who don't want their children exposed to sex ed. The problem is, sex is a part of human life and people figure out ways to learn about it, Zimmerman said. "Everyone gets sex ed, all seven billion people . . . They just get it from different places, and most of them don't get it from state-sponsored schools. They get it from Judy Blume novels. Or recently from porn on the Internet. Porn is sex ed. I think most of it is bad sex ed, but it's absolutely sex ed."

After publishing *Are You There God?*, Judy was officially in the sex ed business. Ironically, one of her next paying gigs was penning the very kind of period pamphlet that she sends up in her novel.

"Growing Up and Liking It" was commissioned by the Personal Products Company, a subsidiary of Johnson & Johnson based in Milltown, New Jersey. The booklet, published in 1970, was ten pages long and featured cheerful feminine doodles of flowers with smiley faces. In a series of short letters between pre-teens Patty, Donna, and Ginny, the girls discuss their changing bodies and menstruation. Patty is the knowledgeable one—she has an older sister and an open-book mother. Even though she hasn't gotten her period yet, she has already studied up on the subject. Ginny is preparing herself, too. She bought a "Starter Kit" from the Personal Products Company, which real kids could order for the price of $2.50.

At her request, Judy's name didn't appear anywhere on the pamphlet. She was well paid for her work, earning $5,000 for the chatty booklet (just over $38,000 in today's dollars), exactly the same amount that Bradbury spent on the ad that reeled her in. She was on her way toward financial freedom—no small task for a writer, or a woman for that matter, in the early 1970s.

## Chapter Five

# ℬad 𝒦ids

*"Sometimes I am a
mean and rotten person."*

**B**lume frequently uses the word "honest" to describe her work: an admirable word and—perhaps shrewdly—an uncontroversial one. But it sells her writing short.

Pioneer children's book editor Ursula Nordstrom, who published Louise Fitzhugh, E. B. White, Maurice Sendak, and other notables, has a famous quote that comes in handy here. Nordstrom described her mission as shepherding "good books for bad children," as opposed to all the "bad books for good children" she felt were crowding the shelves already. Nordstrom's quip makes a terrific soundbite, despite the fact that most early-childhood experts will tell you there are no truly *bad* children. But are there lots of kids who behave badly? Absolutely.

With *Are You There God?* and even more so in her next few books, Blume leaned into all the ways generally good kids could still be messy. Even contemplative Margaret has her moments of brattiness, like when she piles on the middle school outcast Laura Danker. Unlike the other girls in their class, Laura already has a curvy body, which leads to rumors that she uses it to entice boys. "I heard all about you and Moose Freed . . . about how you and Moose and Evan go behind the A&P," Margaret whispers to Laura when they get into a power struggle over a school project. "I don't know why *you* do it," she continues when Laura challenges her. "But I know why *they* do it . . . they do it so they can *feel* you or something and *you* let them!"

The exchange pushes Laura to tears, and Margaret regrets it immediately. But she never suffers any consequences—nor does she get a chance to make it up to Laura. She simply has to live with the shame of her own behavior. (On the other hand, the *Are You There God?* movie shows Margaret making up with Laura in the end and ditching Nancy—a false note in an otherwise faithful adaptation.)

Judy gave her characters the emotional legroom she felt she was denied when she was growing up. The older she got, the more she learned to hide her feelings. "My brother was so rebellious that my role in the family was to make everybody happy," Judy told *Bust* magazine in 1997. Photos of young Judy show her smiling so tightly you can feel the tension in her jaw. In the winter of 1951, when she was in eighth grade, three separate planes went down in Elizabeth on their way to and from Newark Airport. The crashes were a crisis for her hometown, and many people were killed. It must have been terribly frightening for everyone. Still, Judy tried to be the *happiest*.

"My mother used to say, 'We never have to punish Judy . . . if you look at her wrong, she cries,'" Blume wrote in *Letters to Judy*. "Well, yes . . . but I wish I had been able to risk showing my anger now and then. I wish I had felt secure enough to know that once I had gotten it all out I would still be loved."

· · ·

For her next book with Jackson, Judy created a character who holds in his feelings, too. *Then Again, Maybe I Won't* kept her firmly in the puberty zone. Like Margaret, Tony Miglione is weathering a big move alongside a flurry of physical and emotional changes. At the age of twelve, he's all set to start junior high in Jersey City when his father, Vic, a talented yet humble electrician, invents a new kind of electrical cartridge and lands a lucrative manufacturing contract with a heavy-hitting corporation in Queens. The job comes with plenty of money, which spells considerable economic mobility for Tony's multigenerational Italian American household. The family picks up and moves to a white house in Rosemont, Long Island, with a manicured lawn and a stately circular driveway.

Tony knows he's supposed to be excited about this impressive home, with its roomy closets and multiple bathrooms, and the fact that his parents can suddenly afford to hire household help, which means his aging grandmother doesn't have to cook anymore. But Tony is skeptical. Grandma seems depressed without anything to do, and his wealthy neighbor and schoolmate Joel is somehow more of a thug—shoplifting and making prank phone calls—than his far less privileged friends back in Jersey City. Tony is disappointed in his parents for throwing around their new money. They keep telling him he should be grateful to be on the receiving end of opportunities and material goods that his two older brothers didn't get, one of whom died young in Vietnam. "I wanted to say let me alone and stop trying to shove everything that Ralph and Vinnie didn't have down my throat!" Tony admits. "But I couldn't say that because that would have hurt their feelings and they weren't trying to be mean. But sometimes they're so full of bull it makes me sick."

This is not the way kids talk in Beverly Cleary's books. As if the move isn't stressful enough, Tony is also on the brink of a full-blown sexual awakening. Joel's older sister, Lisa, is sixteen and "the best looking girl I've seen in person anywhere," according to a lovestruck Tony. He's mesmerized—and a little bit ashamed—when he realizes he can see into her room at night from his window. He makes a habit of watching her undress. He knows it's wrong, but he does it anyway.

Recently, Tony has learned about wet dreams in gym class and he wonders if he'll ever have one. He's terrified he'll get an erection in school. "When I read Joel's paperbacks, I can feel myself get hard," Tony says, referring to the stash of adult books Joel keeps around, diligently cataloging the dirtiest passages. "But other times when I'm not thinking about anything it goes up too. I don't know what to do about that."

Judy worked hard to capture Tony's voice, prompting some rigorous tête-à-têtes with Jackson. In early drafts, Jackson found the storytelling less intimate than he'd come to expect from Blume. He felt she needed to convey Tony's feelings about the move to Long Island with more emotion, more care. Would Judy consider giving Tony a sentimental object that his mother, while packing up the house, wanted to leave behind in Jersey City? A week later, Judy came back with a scene where Tony asks to hold on to the junior high school pennant that hung over his bed.

"You'll get a new one . . . from Rosemont Junior High," says his mother, who is quick to toss out the remnants of her former life, in which she buried the older son who had originally owned the pennant.

"I want this one anyway," Tony replies. "It used to be . . . I almost said 'Vinnie's,' but I caught myself in time."

Jackson was pleased with the changes, and ultimately loved the manuscript. Judy dedicated the finished book to him: *For Dick*.

Unlike with *Are You There God?*, reviewers treated Tony's preoccupation with his changing body as utterly unremarkable. "Tony takes to carrying his raincoat everywhere, to use as a screen in case he has an erection in public—an event that does finally occur at the blackboard in math class, when a book provides the necessary cover," *Kirkus* said on October 18, 1971, calling scenes like this one "refreshingly light." A young male narrator, it seemed, could get away with referencing the physical trials of puberty in a book for children in a way a female character couldn't without raising questions.

Meanwhile, Judy was already getting involved with yet another novel for readers aged eight to twelve, called *It's Not the End of the World*. The conflicts were very different from those experienced by Tony Miglione but a similar, aching strain played throughout the pages—that of feeling like a stranger in your own home.

•   •   •

*It's Not the End of the World* is a book about divorce, told through a child's eyes. Like Henry James's classic novel for adults *What Maisie Knew*, published seventy-five years before in 1897, Blume's story lets readers watch a marriage fall apart by way of the observations and experiences of a sensitive daughter. Unlike in *What Maisie Knew*, the parents in Blume's tale are loving and almost entirely well-intentioned. But for sixth-grader Karen, their breakup still feels crushing—almost catastrophic. Eventually, she comes to accept that her mom and dad won't be getting back together, but not before she digs out the personalized cocktail napkins from their wedding, buys them an awkwardly timed anniversary card, and convinces herself that a handmade diorama about the Vikings is the perfect magical item that will help rekindle their love for each other.

Judy got the idea to write the novel after a wave of divorces hit her neighborhood, rattling her elementary school–aged children. In Scotch Plains and around the entire country, the seemingly solid suburban dream—erected by American culture in the boon years after World War II—started to splinter. The baby boom was over and another trend tiptoed across the country's green grassy lawns and began to chew away at the house frames: breakups. Between 1967 and 1979, the divorce rate doubled, affecting families of all racial and socioeconomic backgrounds.

"There are a number of different factors that go into really rapidly rising divorce rates in the sixties and seventies," said Suzanne Kahn, author of *Divorce, American Style: Fighting for Women's Economic Citizenship in the Neoliberal Era.* These included "everything from changing economic conditions, the feminist movement, more possibilities for women outside of the home . . . [and] rapidly changing divorce laws in the late sixties and early seventies that just make it easier to get divorced," Kahn said.

The divorce boom would soon yield some terrific art: *An Unmarried Woman. Kramer vs. Kramer.* Nora Ephron's *Heartburn.* But when *It's Not the End of the World* was published in April 1972, divorce wasn't the fertile creative ground that it is today, and especially not in books for children. Judy, then in her thirties, wrote the novel because she recognized that families were changing and kids were feeling unmoored. To learn more about how divorce affected children, she "did considerable reading and six months of crying," she told an interviewer.

Maybe she felt so emotional because she'd started to wonder if her own clan was headed in that same direction.

"I tried to reassure [Randy and Larry] but I really wasn't sure myself," she explained in *Letters to Judy.* "I wrote *It's Not the End of the World* at that time to try to answer some of my children's questions about divorce, to let other kids know they were not alone and, perhaps, because I was not happy in my own marriage."

When we meet the Newmans at the start of the novel, the New Jersey–based family of five's dinner time has devolved into chaos after Bill, the father, comes home late from work. Karen—a middle child sandwiched between fourteen-year-old Jeff and six-year-old Amy—watches as her parents get angrier and angrier with each other, until her mother, Ellie, tosses a sponge across the room. Karen guesses her dad will sleep on the couch that night, as he's been doing frequently. Still, she's blindsided when Ellie gathers up the children to tell them that she and Bill are separating. "I felt tears come to my eyes," Karen says, after her mom drops the news. "I told myself, 'don't start crying now Karen, you jerk.'"

But later, when she's alone, she gets emotional. "I would rather have them fight than be divorced. I'm scared . . . I'm so scared. I wish some-body would talk to me and tell me it's going to be all right. I miss Daddy already. I hate them both! I wish I was dead."

Over the course of the next few months, the Newmans struggle to adapt as Bill moves out and gets his own apartment and Ellie reconsid-ers her place in the world. Through it all, Karen tries to stay "depend-able" even though she's swollen with anger. "Sometimes I feel sorry for my mother and other times I hate her," she writes in her daybook, where she assigns every day a letter grade. It's been a long time since she's had an A.

She's also taken it upon herself to get her parents back together—and to stop Bill from going to Reno, where, due to New Jersey's strict divorce laws, he plans to live for six weeks to officially dissolve the marriage. When her painstakingly designed Viking diorama fails to successfully reunite them, Karen finally gives in to a full-blown tantrum. "I stamped on it with both feet until there was nothing left but a broken shoebox and a lot of blue sparkle all over my rug," she says.

For Judy, fine-tuning Karen's emotional range proved to be one of the trickiest parts of the editorial process. The eleven-year-old needed to be honest enough that young readers could see themselves in her, but not so bitter that she was off-putting. Early drafts of *It's Not the End of the World* show Blume striving to find that balance—with Dick Jackson's input, of course. Many of his notes had to do with making sure Karen had enough depth that she didn't come off as a whiner.

He wanted, for instance, to build in plenty of positive relationships on the page so that her rage toward her parents didn't seem like her default. Sure enough, in the published book, Karen has a supportive friendship with her lifelong neighbor Debbie Bartell and is intrigued when a new girl comes into her life—a wry, *New York Times*-obsessed child of divorce named Val, who shocks Karen by shaving her legs in front of her. Karen also looks up to her paternal grandfather, who she calls Garfa. Garfa lives in Las Vegas, and when he visits New Jersey in the wake of the separation, the pair conspire to stop the divorce in its tracks. She writes him private letters to update him on her progress, although her tone becomes increasingly resigned. "I have discovered something important about my mother and father," she says. "When they are apart they're not so bad, but together they are impossible!"

Judy also played around with the scope of the book, originally planning to track the Newmans through Bill's dating life and quick remarriage. Up through the third—and close to final—draft, he walked down the aisle with a woman named Sandy, who had a young daughter, Beth. Karen wasn't a fan of either of them. And eventually, Jackson suggested that Bill's second marriage plot was contributing to the problem of Karen's likability. Was it appealing, he wondered, to watch her begrudgingly accept her new stepfamily and continue to resent her father?

Judy agreed and lopped off the entire sequence. The finished novel ends with Karen making peace with the circumstances of the divorce and having a B+ day.

Blume worked to soften Karen's hard edges throughout the revisions but not at the expense of the character's righteous, and rightful, indignation. Karen is angry. At moments, she's mean and sarcastic. She doesn't bottle up her feelings like a nice girl. After she first finds out about the breakup, she gives Debbie a hard time just because she can. "I was making Debbie feel bad and I was glad," she says. "Sometimes I am a mean and rotten person." Later, in a fight with her mother, Karen takes a cutting snipe at her: "All you care about is yourself! You never think about me!"

Kids are allowed to blow off steam in Judy Blume's books, even if the fallout is ugly. And so Karen yells. Margaret taunts. Tony Miglione resents his parents and spies on his next-door neighbor while she changes. And it's not just the children in Blume's stories who act out—the moms and dads have their moments of gross humanity, too.

## Chapter Six

# The Fourth Dimension

*"In my heart, I was out there marching."*

Feminism seeped into the pages of Judy's new novel. In 1971, when she was writing *It's Not the End of the World,* the colossal momentum of the Second Wave was already reaching its peak. The year before, a college professor in her mid-thirties named Kate Millett had published her galvanizing treatise *Sexual Politics,* which argued that the modern world was organized around "a theory of patriarchy," where "sex is a status category with political implications" and women were a subjugated class, like Black people in America or Jews in Nazi Germany.

Her book is brilliant and ambitious, impossible to distill in just a few sentences. But Millett, like Friedan, believed that the economy benefited from the unpaid labor of wives and mothers. "Women who are employed have two jobs," she wrote, "since the burden of domestic service and child care is unrelieved either by day care or other social agencies, or by the cooperation of husbands."

And on August 26, 1970, feminists decided to do something about it. That day, which was the fiftieth anniversary of women's suffrage, Betty

Friedan led fifty thousand protesters down New York City's Fifth Avenue for the Women's Strike for Equality March, sponsored by the National Organization for Women, or NOW, founded in 1966. The action, paired with a countrywide call for wives and mothers to go on "strike" by putting down their brooms and dishrags for the day, was dedicated to three key issues: abortion rights, equal opportunities for women, and free child care. In major cities across the US, activists responded with complementary protests—amassing in Boston and Chicago, infiltrating men-only restaurants and social clubs in the South, demonstrating in Los Angeles, and swarming the capital.

Judy wasn't protesting—she was busy at home with her children. "I would have been marching if I hadn't lived in a suburban neighborhood with two kids," she told Samantha Bee in an interview in 2015. "In my heart, I was out there marching."

Before, Judy's political liberalism had been a secret. During the 1960 race between Richard Nixon and John F. Kennedy, she made campaign calls for Republican Nixon (her husband John's preferred candidate), but then got in the voting booth and mischievously pulled the lever for Jack. But now, the women's movement was everywhere: in the newspapers, magazines, and on television. Journalists Susan Brownmiller and Susan Kempton debated a smarmy but articulate Hugh Hefner on the *Dick Cavett Show*. A drawing of Kate Millett's face—hard-set, intense—stared back from the cover of *Time*. Housewife-turned-writer Judy was deeply affected by what she saw going on around her. And she found a way to symbolically get in on the action from behind her typewriter, while Randy and Larry played in the next room.

Judy vented her frustrations with being a wife and mother in the early 1970s by putting it all into the mouth of a proxy: Ellie Newman.

In the beginning of *It's Not the End of the World*, mother of three Ellie is raging after Bill gets home late from work and then starts complaining that dinner is cold. The fight escalates, and Karen notes that they've been arguing a lot recently, including one time the previous week when Ellie baked a cake for the family and ended up smashing it on the floor. She'd frosted it with mocha icing instead of the usual chocolate. When Bill snipped that he hated mocha icing but would scrape it off, Ellie got livid and hurled the whole dessert—plate and all—to the ground.

In the subsequent weeks and months, after Ellie and Bill announce their plans to split, Ellie starts opening up to Karen about why the marriage isn't working for her. At first, she offers simple reasons: "Daddy and I just don't enjoy being together," Ellie tells her impatient daughter. "We don't love each other anymore." Soon, however, Ellie shares her intention to go back to school to study English Literature. "I had you when I was just twenty," she says to her oldest child, Jeff, over a family dinner with the three kids. "I think I might like to get my degree. I never really had a chance to find out what I might be able to do."

The children—Jeff especially—are annoyed by this development, and even more so when Ellie changes her tune yet again and reveals that she's taking a part-time job as a receptionist at an insurance company. At that point their aunt Ruth, who is Ellie's overbearing older sister, questions Ellie's judgment.

"The children need you at home, Ellie," Ruth tells her.

"They're in school all day," Ellie assures her. "They won't even know I'm gone."

Woven throughout the pages is the sense that Ellie is aching for purpose, a vocation to transport her beyond the walls of her home. It's a quest that Judy—along with the feminists propelling the movement in general—knew particularly well.

Writing cured Judy of the housewife's blight. The constant buzz of ideas—which she jotted down in notebooks, on file cards, on tissues, and in the margins of old shopping lists—was better than any doctor's prescription. A deep wound had been treated and cauterized: "It was like the bacteria, the bad bacteria was coming out that was making me sick,"

Blume said at an event in 2015. "I never got sick again in the same way, that way. I couldn't wait to get up in the morning and get going."

The transformation made her wonder what her life would have been like if she'd figured this all out sooner. Thinking about it, she simultaneously resented and got sad for her mom. Essie never had anything beyond a husband and kids to keep her busy. "My mother had many, many talents and much to offer," Blume said in *Judy Blume's Story*. "Everyone would have been a lot happier, including my father, if she had worked outside the home."

Suddenly, Judy was questioning everything about their relationship. During adolescence, her childhood visions of becoming "the hero, the cowgirl, the detective" got replaced "with fantasies of growing up and getting married and having babies," she once said. She ascribed this switch to her mother's influence. Her whole life had been what *Essie* wanted for her, and the thought made her hot with anger. If she wasn't careful, she'd never stop being that anxious and agreeable schoolgirl.

Her mother's voice was such a part of her that she heard it ringing in her head like a relentlessly catchy jingle. *Your kids are what's important. Be a quiet and docile wife.* Had this ever been what she had wanted for herself?

She wasn't sure. There were other models of womanhood that had appealed to Judy, as far back as she could remember. Her married but childless aunt had been a school principal—a big accomplishment in her day. And then there was her father's longtime receptionist, Miss Fay. Miss Fay was a spinster who lived with her sister, a widow, and their parents. Not exactly the picture of success in the 1950s, but to Judy she was absolutely magnetic. "She had a Roadster with a rumble seat," she told *Bust*. "She smoked and could tell dirty jokes with the guys. She seemed exciting to me," Blume said, adding that it was Miss Fay who taught her how to use mascara before prom.

Judy was inspired by Miss Fay, enough so that she wrote a similar character into her 2015 novel for adults, *In the Unlikely Event*, which is set almost entirely in the 1950s. Daisy Dupree is the beautiful, eminently capable secretary to Dr. O, Elizabeth, New Jersey's most successful and beloved dentist (Judy has said Dr. O was based on her father). She's single and childless, and over the course of her career with Dr. O, she becomes a vital part of his ecosystem—booking his appointments but also babysitting his kids; cleaning up after him when he smashes a plaster-of-paris figurine in a private fit of rage; mentoring his newer employees; keeping his secrets.

Like Miss Fay, Daisy lives with her widowed sister. She had been married once and for only two weeks when a doctor diagnosed a congenital defect that meant she would never be able to have penetrative sex or bear children. Her husband had their marriage annulled. And Daisy, formidable, found freedom in his abandonment. "After that, she'd reinvented herself," we're told in *In the Unlikely Event*. "She'd learned to throw back a Scotch, to straddle a chair, smoke a pack of Camels a day and laugh at off-color jokes . . . a woman who made friends with men but who never let it get romantic. She was done with all that, with girlish dreams of houses with picket fences and little children calling her 'Mommy.'"

Near the end of the book, Dr. O picks up his dental practice and moves it across the country to a burgeoning boom town: Las Vegas. Daisy doesn't just follow him; she heads west first to set up the new office and hire and train the staff. She turns the heartbreak of being untethered into a decades-long adventure. Who wouldn't admire a person like that?

. . .

Second Wave feminists didn't look down on women who wanted husbands and kids. Betty Friedan herself had three children. No, the heart of the problem sat in women's isolation and lack of intellectual stimulation, brought on by traditional gender roles. Marriage and parenting, they argued, didn't necessarily mean that a wife also had to be an indentured servant. A vibrant home life didn't have to prevent a woman from becoming a vital contributor to her larger world.

Friedan saw this as the missing piece in so many women's lives. She called it the fourth dimension. In her 1976 book *It Changed My Life: Writings on the Women's Movement,* Friedan wrote that prior to the movement, women had been stuck "in the feminine mystique, which defines woman solely in terms of her three-dimensional sexual relationship to man: wife, mother, homemaker—passively dependent, her own role restricted to timeless, changeless love and service of husband and children."

The fourth dimension, on the other hand, opened up possibilities beyond those rigid boundaries. It could be entered only by unlocking a sense of purpose, whether through a fulfilling job, volunteer work, or continuing education. Admittedly, Friedan was appealing mostly to white, affluent women when she spoke this way, by making the assumption that outside employment was a choice. "Women who work because of a commitment [to their vocation] are more aware of themselves as individuals, take a greater joy in their own children, and know greater physical well-being than housewife-mothers or mothers 'forced' to work. The forced workers often have to quit a 'job' to find the fourth dimension," she writes, acknowledging those who take jobs for entirely financial reasons, but suggesting, perhaps naively, that an alternative path is available in most cases.

Friedan also blames the suburbs for housewives' malaise—but again, her solution turns up an economic blind spot. She endorses "a new kind of city living with close neighbors to organize cooperative nursery schools and swap babysitting with . . . maybe that suburban house will turn into a weekend retreat for the whole family instead of that onerous daily commute for the husband and a separate, isolated world for the wife and children."

As a middle-class mom, these are the issues that Ellie Newman is wrestling with in *It's Not the End of the World.* Whether she knows it or not, she wants the keys to the fourth dimension and she's rifling through her metaphorical purse to find them. Is she going to get her degree? Settle into long-term work? Sell the house and move the family to Florida? Or maybe she'll rent an apartment in New York City, where she always wanted to live before her responsibilities got in the way. The possibilities are, if not endless, pretty extensive for women like Ellie Newman. At the end of the book, she's still working out the details, but she knows she's ready for a change.

And one of those changes is getting away from Aunt Ruth. The novel is as much a coming-of-age for Ellie as it is for Karen. During a climactic fight scene, Bill shouts at her: "You never grew up! You're still Ruth's baby!" He's being cruel, but the book implies that he's also correct—Ellie hasn't been trained in making her own decisions. Her character arc is about learning to flex that muscle.

Finding the fourth dimension is the goal for Ellie; divorce is simply the exercise. And for Judy, clearly some of these issues were on her mind as she was writing. "At the time, my own marriage was in trouble, but I wasn't ready or able to admit it to myself, let alone anyone else," Blume explains in the afterword to the twenty-first-century edition of *It's Not the End of the World.* She hung on to the life she thought she had wanted for as long as she could. When the moment came to dedicate the book, she chose to honor her existing role as a devoted wife and jotted down, *For John.*

## Chapter Seven

# *Money*

*"It's scary to think about my mother with
no money to feed us or buy our clothes."*

Before Judy had a job, she and the children lived on John's income. John controlled the family's finances and doled out cash for her to pay for groceries and other household necessities. This made her, and all the other unemployed housewives out there like her, vulnerable. If a married woman had no money of her own, how could she leave? Or worse—what would she do if her husband left *her*?

The women's movement wasn't just about personal fulfillment. It was about women renegotiating the terms of their very survival.

The realities of divorce woke up a lot of otherwise privileged white women in the late 1960s, said Suzanne Kahn. The divorce rates had gone up for women of color as well, but it was generally white women who were blindsided by the struggle that came next. "The reason that divorce became the politicizing moment for many white women was because they had been so included in the culturally dominant narrative, and also in public policy. Black women were already suffering from many different forms of exclusion, both political, legal and cultural," Kahn said.

From a political perspective, white women had sauntered through their milestones and, at the same time, divested themselves of power. They had gone to work after college, but then quit their jobs the moment their pregnant bellies started to pop. After that, a wife's income, health insurance, and retirement benefits flowed through her male partner. As did her purchasing power: If a married woman wanted a credit card, her application needed to be cosigned by her spouse. An unmarried woman was usually compelled to produce some kind of male guarantor, like her father or her brother, if she had any chance of taking out a card in her own name. It wasn't until the Equal Credit Opportunity Act of 1974 that lenders legally had to approve female credit card applicants if their finances were viable.

Until then, and for a long while after, a good marriage was sometimes the only thing standing between a woman and the poverty line. When a divorce blew through, it was terrifying. "They were really sort of economically displaced," Kahn said of these mostly middle-class women after their breakups. Like Judy, they had made all the "right" choices up until that point, and the fear and disappointment of being financially gutted mobilized them. "They start to organize and a lot of them find a home at some of the biggest feminist organizations of the twentieth century, like the National Organization for Women," Kahn said. "They really start advocating for shifts in the social insurance system that gives them access to all these economic resources they've lost."

The movement welcomed them with open arms. "If there is any one thing that makes a feminist it is to grow up believing somehow that love and marriage will take care of you the rest of your life—and then to wake up at forty or fifty or even at thirty and find out it isn't so," Friedan wrote in *It Changed My Life*. She found that women whose marriages had crumbled needed the teachings of Second Wave feminism to help them make sense of what had happened. "They were suffering not only loneliness and guilt and hostility—the psychological scars of that inequality that had been responsible for destroying so many of the marriages in the first place—but real economic deprivation."

In other words, women were ending their marriages—only sometimes by choice—and then watching helplessly as their quality of life plummeted. Even more heartbreaking, they couldn't provide for their kids in the same way the entire family had come to expect. And so the movement was clear: in the future, married women should not leave their jobs. In order to make that feasible, the government had to step up and offer families the kinds of services that would allow mothers to flourish in the workplace. "Women should be educated to do the work society rewards, and should be paid for that work," Friedan writes. "And since women are the people who do have children, there should be maternity leaves—and paternity leaves—and child-care centers, and full income tax deductions for child care and home maintenance."

And advocates wanted other things, too. If the structure of the American family required a woman to stay home, acting in a support role to her male, breadwinning partner, then "homemaker" should be considered her job—and thus, she was entitled to benefits. Friedan wanted these wives, after a divorce, to get severance pay, as well as Social Security payments reflecting the time they'd put in. She also thought husbands should be on the hook to cover their ex's post-split educational needs, to give them a shot in an increasingly competitive marketplace. Finally, Friedan supported the idea of mandatory marriage and divorce insurance, which would guarantee child support and other monthly payments in case a union splintered.

Unlike some more radical feminists—"Until all women are lesbians, there will be no true political revolution!" declared *Village Voice* writer Jill Johnston in a 1971 debate moderated by Norman Mailer, commemorated in the 1979 documentary *Town Bloody Hall*—Friedan, a divorcée herself, still believed in the institution of heterosexual marriage. She also bristled at the accusation that feminism was to blame for the cascade of nationwide breakups. To her, the rising divorce rate was a clear-cut reflection of gender inequality, and it would stabilize as soon as the problem of women's systemic oppression was solved. After that, legal partnerships would look different, and better, for everyone. "Our movement to liberate women and men from these polarized, unequal sex roles might save marriage," she wrote. "And marriage is probably worth saving. The intimacy, the commitment—the long-term commitment of marriage—is something we still need."

The feminists hoped that their work would one day make life better for their daughters and granddaughters. They wanted young girls to grow up expecting more than they did from their marriages, and from their lives. And in many ways, Blume's books chanted from that same pulpit. From the very first line of *It's Not the End of the World*, Karen tells us that she hasn't bought into the fairy tale. "I don't think I'll ever get married," she says. "Why should I? All it does is make you miserable."

Are we meant to believe her? Maybe. But what's clear is that she's rejecting doing things her parents' way.

Blume understood that divorce introduced kids to serious worries. Throughout the novel, Karen struggles with the idea of her mom and dad dating new people. She's very anxious about money, even though she knows nothing of the family's finances. "My mother has no money that I know of," Karen thinks to herself after a friend suggests that Ellie must have "plenty" of it if she's getting divorced. "It's scary to think about my mother with no money to feed us or buy our clothes or anything." Later on in the book, the kids complain about going to Howard Johnson's for dinner with Ellie. Amy, the youngest, whines that "Daddy always takes us out for steak."

"Daddy can afford to," Ellie tells her—a sharp and surprising reaction that Karen immediately clocks.

As she penned *It's Not the End of the World*, Judy was a visitor in the province of divorce, but she hadn't yet set up residency. Her work was satisfying but also useful—quickly, she was building up her nest egg. The check for "Growing Up and Liking It" was a windfall. When *It's Not the End of the World* came out, she already had five books behind her. *It's Not the End of the World* wasn't a smash—the *New York Times* dismissed it as "self-help reading, a guide for those troubled by divorce, that will have little interest for those that aren't"—but she had other irons in the fire.

While she was writing her middle grade and young adult novels, Judy was also publishing books for younger children. These cheerful, humorous stories bricked her path to financial freedom. *Freckle Juice*, about a second grader who wants freckles so badly he falls for another classmate's gross-out recipe, published in 1971. Her first mega-hit came the following year, in 1972, with *Tales of a Fourth Grade Nothing*. Unlike the Newmans, the Hatchers were a delightfully tight-knit family. They could handle anything together, including a full-fledged natural disaster in toddler form: the inimitable, hysterical Fudge.

*Tales of a Fourth Grade Nothing* had started as a short story back in the Lee Wyndham days, about a wild little boy who accidentally swallows his older brother Peter's pet turtle. Another piece—about a mother who is so worried about her son's meager appetite that she indulgently lets him eat on the floor, like a dog—was an obvious predecessor, too.

Jackson, who was mostly interested in novels for older readers, turned down the early draft of *Tales of a Fourth Grade Nothing*. It was a decision he'd eventually come to regret, as he told *School Library Journal* in 2001. At the time, it was a picture book and he didn't see its stunning potential (*Tales*, beloved, eventually yielded three sequels about the Hatcher family and one spin-off, about the inner life of Peter's neighbor and nemesis, the swaggering Sheila Tubman). Judy's agent sent it to another editor, named Ann Durell, who worked at the children's book publisher E. P. Dutton. Durell read it and invited Judy to lunch, suggesting the story might make more sense as a longer novel. Judy got straight to work and Durell made an offer on the revision soon after.

Blume has since revealed that the inspiration for Fudge was her own son, Larry, who occasionally ate on the floor, calling himself Frisky the Cat. He never actually choked down a turtle—that idea came from a newspaper article Judy saw in the late 1960s—but he did suck his fingers like Fudge and left an embarrassingly big mess behind at more than a few restaurants. But if Blume was anything like Ann Hatcher as a mother, she could handle it. Ann is patient to a fault with her youngest son, barely cracking when he's so rowdy around her husband's biggest advertising clients that they flee the apartment, taking their account with them. Warren Hatcher, the dad, is a bit of a hothead, but Ann, a stay-at-home mom, remains steady throughout the book, at least up until the denouement when Fudge eats the turtle. "Oh no! My angel! My precious little baby!" she shouts when she realizes what he's done.

In the next book, *Superfudge*, Warren takes a leave from his job to write a book, and Ann considers what her life might look like after her kids are grown up. One evening, she tells Peter she'd like to go back to school and get a degree in Art History. The Hatchers have just had a third baby, nicknamed Tootsie, and Peter can't understand why his mother would even be thinking about another major change.

"Someday she'll grow up and go to school and I'll want to have a career," Ann tells him. Peter is nonplussed.

But by the time *Superfudge* was published in 1980, Judy's own life had changed dramatically. *Tales* was a great success and some of her earlier novels, including *Are You There God?*, had found a slew of new readers after coming out in paperback. The freedom—financial, creative—emboldened her. In between *Tales* and *Superfudge*, Judy Blume became a star.

## Chapter Eight

# Mothers

*"One thing I'm sure of is I don't want to*
*spend my life cleaning some house like Ma."*

Judy's illnesses didn't start with her marriage. She had always been a delicate kid. In seventh grade, she had a massive outbreak of eczema, worsened by an allergy to the ointment a doctor prescribed to soothe it. "This 'flare-up,' as the doctors called it, caused a disfiguring rash that covered my whole body," Blume wrote in *Letters to Judy*. "My face swelled and my eyes shut . . . I felt very sorry for myself."

She got sick with mono her first semester in college and had to come home from Boston University to recuperate in New Jersey. She spent a month weak and glassy-eyed in bed, staring at the walls, and by the time she felt better, she was so embarrassed that she decided to transfer to NYU. "I never want to see Boston again," she informed Rudolph and Essie. She needed a fresh start, somewhere she wouldn't be the sickly girl who vanished after orientation.

Her body had been uncooperative throughout much of her teens and twenties. Although there hadn't been long-lasting repercussions of her various ailments, she could easily imagine what that might feel like for a junior high student.

*Deenie* is the story of a thirteen-year-old aspiring model who gets diagnosed with scoliosis and has to wear a bulky back brace. But scratch the surface and you'll see that Blume's 1973 novel is also a story about mothers and daughters.

•   •   •

Ellie Newman's journey is about slow but steady self-actualization. Thelma Fenner's story is a cautionary tale. In movement terms, Thelma, Deenie's mom, is melting in the crucible of the feminine mystique, but she doesn't know it. She's bored, unfulfilled, childlike. And all it takes is one family crisis, centered on the battleground of her adolescent daughter Deenie's changing body, to blow the lid off and expose her.

The book opens with tension between Thelma and Deenie. The pair, who live in Elizabeth, New Jersey, with Deenie's father, Frank, and older sister, Helen, are headed into Manhattan to see a modeling agent. Deenie is beautiful, and Thelma wants her to capitalize on it. "The thing that really scares me is I'm not sure I want to be a model," Deenie admits to the reader, while curled up on a bus on the New Jersey Turnpike. She'd rather join the school cheerleading squad than get a job, even a potentially glamorous one that will help her "make a lot of money and maybe get discovered for the movies, too," according to her mother.

Yet Deenie is painfully aware of her role in the family. "Deenie's the beauty, Helen's the brain," Thelma tells anyone who's willing to listen, including their bus driver. By categorizing her daughters this way, Thelma invests in them differently. With Helen, she's rigorous about her homework, making sure nothing distracts her from her academic promise. Meanwhile, Deenie's grades are tossed off as irrelevant. "Nobody expects much from my schoolwork so I get by with hardly ever cracking a book as long as I don't bring home any D's or F's," Deenie says.

Instead, Thelma rides Deenie about more superficial things. Deenie, for instance, is not allowed to wear sneakers, because "they make your feet spread so your regular shoes don't fit anymore." Deenie's also aware that her eating habits are policed in a way that her sister's are not. "She's really fussy about what I eat," she says of Thelma. "She leaves Helen alone but watches me like a hawk. She thinks if she's in charge of my diet I'll never get pimples or oily hair. I hope she's right."

At the start of the book, Deenie is well aware of the discrepancies between how she and her sister are treated, but it's clear she doesn't quite know what to do about it. She isn't sure if she wants to be a model—but like any self-conscious adolescent girl with a middle school crush and an overbearing mom, she doesn't want acne and greasy hair, either. Her looks, she tells us before her highly anticipated cheerleading try-out, don't occupy her thoughts all that often, although she's conscious of being pretty and the advantages that come with it. "Most times I don't even think about the way I look but on special occasions, like today, being good-looking really comes in handy," she says.

Yet the audition doesn't go the way Deenie had hoped. She doesn't make the squad, and the next day, her gym teacher asks her to swing by so she can take a closer look at Deenie's posture. Soon, she's off to see a specialist about her uneven hips and rounded shoulders. The would-be model gets diagnosed with idiopathic scoliosis, a condition that arises most often in pre-teen girls, where their spines start to grow in a curved shape. The doctor says she'll need to have an operation or get fitted for a cumbersome back brace. With that, Deenie leaves the fold of her mother's expectations and enters the world of disability.

Blume has said that she got the idea for *Deenie* after a real-life encounter in 1970. One night, she met a woman at a party whose fourteen-year-old daughter was recently diagnosed with scoliosis, and she had to wear a back brace to correct it. "This woman was falling apart," Blume says in *Presenting Judy Blume*. Judy then met the daughter and was impressed by her poise and resilience, casting a completely different light than her stressed-out mom. "She was very open about her problem and shared some of her feelings and experiences with me," Blume later wrote about her.

She researched scoliosis and visited a hospital where she observed kids getting fitted for their Milwaukee braces: the restrictive, full-torso support garment that Deenie has to wear. Judy recalled her struggle with eczema and decided to write that into her new book, too. She created a character named Barbara Curtis, the new girl in Deenie's class who becomes a mirror for Deenie's eventual self-acceptance. Barbara, like the real-life Judy, has a rash all over her body, which at first Deenie finds "disgusting." Secretly, Deenie nicknames her the Creeping Crud, and prays she won't get partnered with her in gym class.

But after Deenie starts wearing the brace to school, she looks at Barbara Curtis differently. Barbara is kind to her during her awkward adjustment period with the medical device, helping Deenie tie her shoes when she can't figure out how to bend down and reach them. "I felt like the world's biggest jerk," Deenie admits to the reader at that moment. Later, she introduces Barbara to her friends. "She's a nice kid," Deenie says. "I think I must have been really weird to not like her just because of her creeping crud."

For Deenie, opening her mind to the experiences of disabled people within her community allows her to make peace with her new reality, which is that she'll have to wear the Milwaukee brace for four long years. No matter how she tries to camouflage it, the device—which she needs to keep on almost twenty-four hours a day in order to reroute the growth of her spine—pokes up past the base of her neck and shows through her clothes. Her appearance, which has defined her at home for much of her life, is being compromised. But Deenie is surprisingly spunky. After years of avoiding eye contact with "Old Lady Murray," the hunchbacked woman who sells magazines on the street corner, Deenie tries talking to her. Old

Lady Murray isn't terribly interested in conversation and it doesn't go well. But Deenie is facing up to the fact that she and the "crazy" town peddler now have something in common: kyphosis, or a rounded upper back.

Deenie's diagnosis also encourages her to reconsider Gena Courtney, a neighbor and schoolmate who was hit by a delivery truck when she was in first grade. The accident cost Gena her eyesight in one eye and she has to wear braces on both legs. Early in the novel, Deenie admits that she's never known how to treat Gena since then. "I always feel funny when I pass her house—like I should stop and say hello—but then I think I better not, because I wouldn't know how to act or anything," she says. By the end of book, Deenie sees her through fresh eyes, too. "I wonder if she thinks of herself as a handicapped person or just a regular girl, like me," Deenie thinks.

After getting used to her back brace, Deenie's ability to still see herself as a regular girl has to do with her baseline temperament—her admirable pluck—and the kindness of her friends at school, who, after getting their questions out of the way, treat her exactly the same. Even Buddy Brader, the boy she's been flirting with, is still interested in Deenie. Just before their second kiss, at a party in her friend's basement, Buddy asks if she can remove the brace. Deenie, despite having packed a change of clothes for just that reason, holds her ground in the moment. "I have to wear it all the time," she tells him.

"Oh well," Buddy says, all but unaffected.

These flashes of acceptance buoy Deenie, who begins to trust that scoliosis won't ruin her life. Unfortunately, the same can't be said for Thelma.

.  .  .

Thelma is devastated by Deenie's diagnosis. If part of a parent's job is modeling strength for one's children, she fails at this almost immediately. To be fair, neither Deenie's mother nor her father reacts well to the news that she has scoliosis that requires aggressive intervention. "You're not telling us Deenie's going to be deformed, are you?" Frank asks the doctor who identifies Deenie's condition. Meanwhile, Thelma panics. "Ma started whispering, 'Oh my God,' over and over again," Deenie says.

On the drive home from the doctor's office, the adult Fenners bicker about which side of the family Deenie inherited her scoliosis from. They're not at all attuned to their daughter, who herself is emotionally free-falling in the backseat of the car. "I expected Daddy to explain everything on the way home . . . Instead, he and Ma argued about whose fault it was that I have something wrong with my spine until we pulled into our driveway. It was almost as if they'd forgotten I was there."

But in the weeks that follow, Frank adjusts to the family's new normal while Thelma continues to spin. In her eyes, Deenie's brace clutters up her tidy organization of their family. How can Deenie be the beauty if she's confined to an ugly piece of medical equipment for the next four years—a period of time she views as critical to Deenie's burgeoning modeling career? That's why Thelma treats the brace like a misfortune that's happening to all of them. "I had to fight to keep from crying," Deenie says when she first sees it. Meanwhile, Thelma holds nothing back. "Just when I thought I was going to be okay Ma started. 'Oh my God,' she cried. 'What did we ever do to deserve this?'" She blames Deenie for slouching, despite the fact that the professionals are clear with the family that idiopathic scoliosis is an inherited disease.

The problem, Blume seems to be telling us, isn't just that Thelma's insensitive—she's immature. The feminine mystique has left her ill-equipped and puerile. She can't even drive: a symbol of her dependency. Frank has to act as her chauffeur, or she hitches rides with Aunt Rae, her best friend whose kids are grown up and "has nothing better to do" than to cart Thelma around. Aunt Rae—who is not actually related to the Fenners—is almost as invested in Deenie's modeling as Thelma is. At one point in the book, Deenie comes home and finds Thelma and Aunt Rae doing each other's hair like schoolgirls.

By the age of thirteen, Deenie is positive about one thing: she wants more. "She spends hours and hours cleaning the place," Deenie says of Thelma's role as a homemaker. "One thing I'm sure of is I don't want to spend my life cleaning some house like Ma." Deenie confesses that sometimes she's jealous of Helen's brain because it means that she'll grow up to have the kind of demanding job that keeps her too busy for things like washing the floors until you could eat off them, like her mother does. Modeling isn't a sure thing, nor does it seem like the kind of skill that guarantees lifelong independence, Deenie muses. Toward the end of the novel, she thinks to herself that she might like to become an orthopedist.

The crisis ends up freeing Deenie, loosening her from the grips of a controlling mother. And while Thelma doesn't quite see it that way, she's also forced to admit that she's been living out her own dreams through her girls. Helen and Deenie are hard on her near the close of the book, when it comes out that bookish Helen has been skipping her study dates to go hang out with her secret boyfriend. Helen, it turns out, doesn't like being labeled, either. "I used to tell myself it didn't matter if I wasn't pretty like Deenie because I have a special brain and Deenie's just ordinary," Helen sobs. "But that didn't help, Ma . . . because it's not true!"

Thelma doesn't apologize. She gets defensive. But her defense is revealing of the ways her own regrets have guided her parenting. Her last line in the book serves to let her daughters know exactly why she's been so meddlesome. "I wanted better for you," she tells them as Helen and Deenie cry together. "Better than what I had for myself. That's what I always planned for my girls . . . is that so wrong?"

"I think of the story as one about parental expectations," Blume writes in the afterword to the twenty-first-century paperback edition of *Deenie*. "What happens when a parent pigeonholes their children?" Judy took this question of pigeonholing seriously; Helen and Deenie are birds learning to flee the nest, figuring out who they'll be when they land. Pigeons even figure into Deenie's personal journey. The first day she wears the brace to school, the vice principal calls Deenie into her office to tell her that due to her diagnosis, she's now eligible to ride "the special bus," which is free. Instantly, Deenie rejects this idea—riding the bus with kids like Gena Courtney would reaffirm that she's different—and she glances out the window, trying to hide her tears. On the ledge, she sees a pigeon and thinks, "Ma says pigeons are dirty birds with lots of germs and I should stay away from them." The vice principal gives her a form and tells her to bring it home for her parents to sign.

Deenie conveniently loses the form and two weeks later, the vice principal checks in about it. By then, Deenie's bad attitude about wearing the brace has lifted. She's not pleased about it, but she's willing to withstand it as a temporary burden. "I looked out the window and no pigeons were on the ledge," Deenie says, nodding to her ability to rise above her mother's fears and biases.

The pigeons are brief visitors in the manuscript, but Judy was quite proud of them, according to Dick Jackson. Their work together on the book focused on Deenie's growth away from Thelma, as expressed through her relationship with her two best friends. An early draft of the novel established that Deenie was adopted, which served to distance her from Thelma as Deenie's biological destiny started to unfurl. But Jackson wasn't convinced this was the right way to do it. Instead, he and Judy talked it through and decided that Janet and Midge—Deenie's closest schoolmates—could help to more robustly reflect Deenie's maturation. Blume then built moments into the novel, including the trio shopping for a nightgown and going to the movies together, that illuminated all the stops on Deenie's path.

As always, Blume and Jackson were in lockstep when it came to their editorial vision for the project. And interestingly, one aspect of *Deenie*— by far the book's most controversial plotline—they barely touched at all.

## Chapter Nine

# *Masturbation*

*"I rubbed and rubbed
until I got that good feeling."*

**L**ike many adolescents, Deenie has a secret.

Or maybe "secret" isn't the right word. Deenie has a private ritual, something she does when she can't sleep. She doesn't know why, but it makes her feel better. Touching her "special place" helps stave off her worries. Or, as she puts it, "I have this special place and when I rub it I get a very nice feeling."

Let's be clear—until *Deenie*, girls didn't masturbate in children's literature. Inventive, now classic characters like Pippi Longstocking and Ramona Quimby were zany and unpredictable, but they certainly never told us where their hands wandered when they were alone. Even now, the mention of self-pleasure in a young adult book is enough to get it yanked from school libraries. Sherman Alexie's terrific, award-winning 2007 novel *The Absolutely True Diary of a Part-Time Indian* brings up masturbation within the first thirty pages: "If there were a Professional Masturbators League, I'd get drafted number one and make millions of dollars," the fourteen-year-old narrator Arnold Spirit Jr. jokes.

*The Absolutely True Diary of a Part-Time Indian* has been banned over and over again, across the country, for years. And that's male masturbation; examples of adolescent female masturbation in books for teenagers are still fewer and far between. Melissa Febos writes about discovering self-pleasure as a pre-teen in 2021's *Girlhood*—an essay collection for adults—and even now, her words feel radical. "The first time I slid on my back to the bottom of the tub, propped my heels on the wall aside the faucet and let that hot water pummel me, I understood that to crack my own hull was a glory," she remembers. "Alone I was both ship and sea, and I felt no shame, only the cascade of pleasure."

Over the course of Blume's novel, there are three separate instances where Deenie refers to touching herself. In case there's any question about what Blume means, she makes it crystal clear in a scene in the middle of the book, when Deenie attends a sex ed class at school. The gym teacher, responding to an anonymous question that Deenie wrote down and dropped in a box on her desk, tells the kids—and the readers—outright.

"Does anyone know the word for stimulating our genitals?" the teacher, named Mrs. Rappoport, asks the class. When a student timidly offers up the answer "masturbation," Mrs. Rappoport is enthusiastic, encouraging the group to all say it aloud in unison. "Now that you've said it," she goes on, "let me try to explain. First of all, it's normal and harmless to masturbate."

Deenie is relieved. After that, she's happy to touch her special place as a way to de-stress. When she gets a nasty rash from wearing her brace with nothing under it, she takes a bath and tries to make peace with the fact that she'll have to start wearing an undershirt to school, which she's been resisting because it seems babyish. "The hot water was very relaxing and soon I began to enjoy it," Deenie says. "I reached down and touched my special place with the washcloth. I rubbed and rubbed until I got that good feeling."

*Deenie* wasn't the first of Blume's books to use the word "masturbation," but it was the first one to portray it. *Then Again, Maybe I Won't* does everything but—Tony Miglione talks about reading dirty novels, spying on his attractive neighbor as she gets changed, having wet dreams, and getting erections, but he doesn't actually put his hands down his pants. The word comes up in a book, *Basic Facts About Sex*, that his father gives him after awkwardly bumbling through the sex talk. "There's a whole section on wet dreams and another on masturbation," Tony says after leafing through it. "Maybe they do know me after all!"

With *Deenie*, Blume was pushing the envelope and Jackson allowed it. And why not? It was 1973.

·   ·   ·

Stevie Wonder had radio listeners second-guessing their "Superstition." There was "Smoke on the Water"—hair-raising, electric—and Marvin Gaye got people singing along to his smooth and sultry bedroom hit "Let's Get It On" from behind the steering wheels of their cars. *"There's nothing wrong with me loving you. / Baby, no, no,"* Gaye crooned—and you believed him. Nixon was still president but nobody trusted Tricky Dick anymore. The wheels of the Watergate scandal were already turning, poised to roll him straight out of the Oval Office.

Popular reading material was getting more explicit. *The Joy of Sex: A Gourmet Guide to Lovemaking* was written by an English physician named Alex Comfort, and it was a how-to manual for being more adventurous in bed. Comfort's inspiration was *The Joy of Cooking*, the home cook's go-to that had made elevated recipes more accessible. With his book, Comfort wanted to show how regular couples could also expand their erotic palates. The guide to everything from oral sex to light bondage even included line drawings of different sexual positions, which Comfort and his second wife, Jane Henderson, who had been his longtime mistress during his first marriage, had posed for. Clearly, there was an appetite for this kind of material—after it published in 1972, *The Joy of Sex* topped the *New York Times* bestseller list, and remained on it for much of the early 1970s.

Feminists were also doing their part to empower people with knowledge about their sexuality. In 1969, a group of women in their twenties and thirties, who called themselves the Boston Women's Health Collective, set out to make teaching moments out of topics that had previously been considered unspeakable. They had met at a series of informal consciousness raising groups on the MIT campus, where attendees had gotten to talking about their frustrations with their male doctors. These physicians, they complained, were condescending and couldn't be bothered to answer questions about their bodies. Finally, they had a safe space to open up about their concerns: What really happened to their insides during pregnancy? Why were they so miserable each month before getting their periods? And was there a trick to enjoying—like, *really* enjoying—sex?

The group, which was eventually whittled down to twelve women, made a list of topics and started researching them. They wrote up their findings in a booklet, published by the New England Free Press. The first print run of *Our Bodies, Ourselves* was 1,000 copies, and it sold out quickly. Another printing followed. After they sold over 200,000 books, major publishers started calling. In 1973, Simon & Schuster published an expanded version of *Our Bodies, Ourselves*, which covered everything from menstruation to abortion to postpartum depression. The illustrated tome, which included detailed drawings of the female anatomy and encouraged women to examine their vulvas and feel inside their own vaginas, was a phenomenon.

Even the informational books written for children were getting less stuffy. *Where Did I Come From?*, published in 1973, was the Age of Aquarius update on *How Babies Are Made*, featuring colorful, cartoon-like illustrations. Unlike the 1968 Time-Life staple, *Where Did I Come*

*From?* scraps all references to the birds and bees and skips right to the important part: naked humans. The book features pictures of two doughy, average-looking adults in the buff, and walks young readers through their relevant anatomical differences. Living up to its promise "to tell the truth," it spends five full pages explaining the process of sexual intercourse, making reference to erections ("the man's penis becomes stiff and hard"), ejaculation, and orgasms.

The latter was especially daring, a break from popular wisdom that health education for kids should gloss over the part where sex feels good. This book, while sticking with the idea that heterosexual intercourse is necessarily procreative, broke new ground by acknowledging that sex isn't just "special" and romantic—it's pleasurable. "When the man and woman have been wriggling so hard you think they're both going to pop, they nearly do just that," author Peter Mayle explains. "All the rubbing up and down that's been going on ends in a tremendous, big shiver for both of them," which the book then goes on to compare to "a really big sneeze."

*Where Did I Come From?* is often silly, as when it describes sperm as "romantic" and illustrates the point with a drawing of a googly-eyed, tadpole-like creature draped over a heart, sniffing a rose and decked out in black tie. "There's some joy and fun in that book," said Cory Silverberg, author of a series of gender- and family-inclusive sex ed books, including *Sex Is a Funny Word.* "A lot of the sex ed books feel like textbooks for kids, and *Where Did I Come From?* didn't, because it was goofy."

The playfulness of *Where Did I Come From?* made it innovative. It also signaled a new approach to sex ed that was primed to infuriate conservatives.

*Deenie* was published in September 1973, and as with Blume's previous titles, reviews were mixed. The *New York Times* praised its "touching authenticity" as well as its candor: "It is also comfortably frank about the preoccupations of young teen-agers with sex, and deals in a tactful and reassuring way with such once undiscussable subjects as masturbation." *Kirkus*, however, wasn't keen on *Deenie*. Dismissing the novel as "bibliotherapeutic," the trade magazine slammed Blume for the amount of space she devoted to the details of Deenie's medical journey. Then, it got worse. "Instead of giving Deenie any personality or independent existence beyond her malady, the author throws in the subtopic of masturbation . . . which only makes the story's hygienic slant more pronounced," *Kirkus* said.

Judy dealt with bad reviews by scribbling bad words all over them with a red pencil. She believed, really believed, in what she was doing. "I had never heard the word masturbation when I was growing up," she wrote in *Letters to Judy*. "Yet at twelve I knew I had a special place and that I could get that good feeling by touching it. I talked about it with some of my friends . . . I never found anything relating to my early sexuality in books, so there was some comfort in finding out from my friends that I was not alone."

She held this line throughout her career. "I wrote the truth, what I knew to be the truth," Blume reiterated in 2015. "I knew that I would have been very satisfied if I could have a book that said it was okay to masturbate."

.     .     .

Just like in *Then Again, Maybe I Won't*, Deenie's burgeoning sexuality signals a natural drift away from her mother. Like Tony Miglione, she's becoming more autonomous, scrutinizing her parents and honing her own values. A point of view that first appears in *Are You There God?* gets sharpened with *Deenie*, where female sexuality becomes shorthand for female subjectivity. It's strongly implied in Blume's later works—and particularly those intended for adults—that they're one and the same.

At age thirteen, Deenie is more sophisticated than eleven-year-old Margaret. She's cavalier about periods—at the start of the book, she says she's gotten hers exactly once, which doesn't quite make her an expert, but she's not a total newbie, either. She's adept at tracking down information. Deenie explains that she sent out for a booklet about menstruation and read it, so she knows it could be a while before her cycle is regular. When she starts to have questions about boys, she casually asks Helen to loan her her "sex book."

Deenie and her friends are old enough that their giddy schoolgirl crushes are being noticed and even reciprocated, with all the attendant exploration that entails. Over the course of the novel, she goes from sweatily holding hands with her classmate Buddy Brader at the movies to kissing him in the locker room during the seventh-grade mixer. While Janet and Barbara are out having fun on the dance floor, Deenie stiffens as Buddy starts touching her over her shirt. "I know he was trying to feel me," she says. "I also knew that Buddy wasn't feeling anything but my brace, which only made everything worse."

Even though she likes him, her nerves get the better of her at that point and she darts out of the locker room. But the next time she sees Buddy outside of school, at a party in Janet's basement, things go smoother. After telling him that she can't take off her brace, Deenie lets herself relax into the moment—mostly. "This time when he kissed me, I concentrated on kissing him back. I hoped I was doing it right," she says.

But when it comes to masturbation, Deenie is more or less in the dark. She leaves the question about it in her teacher's dropbox because she wants to know if what she's been doing is "normal." After Mrs. Rappoport reads Deenie's anonymous query out loud, it becomes clear that most of Deenie's peers are underinformed about it, too. "I wasn't the one who wrote the question but I've heard that boys who touch themselves too much can go blind or get very bad pimples or their bodies can even grow deformed," one classmate offers. That last possibility sends waves of fear—and embarrassment—through Deenie. "Maybe that's why my spine started growing crooked!" she thinks, while her face gets hot. "Please, God . . . don't let it be true, I prayed."

Mrs. Rappoport is quick to correct this line of speculation. First, she tackles the suggestion that it's only boys who explore their own bodies. "It's very common for girls as well as boys, beginning with adolescence," she says. "Nobody went crazy from masturbating, but a lot of young people make themselves sick from worrying about it."

Deenie—who, under different circumstances, might have spent the next four years choking down portions of shame and self-disgust—instantly feels relieved. She's grateful to have had the class discussion and looks forward to the next one. Unfortunately, plenty of real American kids weren't quite so lucky.

●    ○    ●

Judy spoke directly to her readers in her books, and sometimes that meant writing an adult character who represented an ideal: a mouthpiece for how Blume believed things should be. Mrs. Rappoport is the model sex ed teacher, tackling Deenie's question without awkwardness or judgment. Yet in classrooms all across the country, put-upon teachers were stumbling through their school's health or "family life"—the de rigueur title for sex ed in the 1970s—curriculums. The contents of these classes varied from place to place. Depending on where an educator worked, he or she might be open and informative or tight-lipped and moralizing. They might also be scared of getting fired for saying the wrong thing.

Family life education, or FLE, was an approach to sex ed that came out of the 1950s. It tucked all the uncomfortable body stuff into the pocket of a larger, gender normative curriculum about courtship and marriage: chaste dating tips, engagement rituals, even balancing family budgets. Intercourse was a part of that. "Family life education was the first time that American educators actually acknowledged that adults had sex and described it," Jonathan Zimmerman said. "But they did so with the goal obviously of keeping it within what today we'd call straight marriage." Any other kinds of sex were treated as depraved and even dangerous. Students were told that premarital sex could result in sickness and unwanted pregnancy, but they weren't always informed about contraception.

In FLE, contraception was considered a lightning rod topic, along with abortion, homosexuality, and masturbation. "Those were called the 'Big Four,'" Zimmerman said, and by the 1960s and early 1970s, they were taught only in districts where parents and school boards were more or less united in their liberal perspectives, such as in New York, New Jersey, and areas of California. Why? Because the Big Four unhook sex from procreation. Masturbation, according to Zimmerman, is so controversial because "it's explicitly about pleasure. And only that, it's not about anything else, it's not procreative."

Historically, kids had been taught that fondling themselves led to all manner of issues, some of which get recited in *Deenie*. Since the Victorian era, children were told that "self-abuse" was shameful and caused problems ranging from dim-wittedness to full-blown insanity. At its heart, the prohibition against masturbation grew from the emphasis on self-control in late-nineteenth-century American culture, Jeffrey Moran writes in *Teaching Sex: The Shaping of the Adolescent in the 20th Century*. "Once a young man touched himself in that way, he threatened the entire structure of Victorian character. Self-discipline, social responsibility, character—masturbation symbolically toppled all the pillars."

The idea that a girl might do such a thing was even more outrageous. Early moralists accepted that boys had undeniable sexual urges, and part of the task of becoming a man involved wrestling down the beast. Girls, on the other hand, were assumed to be naturally chaste, and it was a woman's job to support her man in his ongoing struggle toward virtue. If a young man slipped—whether by touching himself or seeking out sexual intercourse—it was disappointing, but understandable. Young ladies, meanwhile, were given no such freedoms. Within the framework of Victorian morality, "girls who fell prey to self-abuse were clearly aberrant," Moran writes. Women who gave in to premarital sex deserved everything—whether it was community-wide shunning, disfiguring disease, or unwanted pregnancy—that happened afterward.

These attitudes evolved during the sexual revolution, but they still remained foundational to the American understanding of sex. In a 1965 article about the birth control pill for the *New York Times*, Cornell political science professor Andrew Hacker unpacked the expectation that easy access to contraception would encourage immorality. "For a long time there has been a certain ritual, not without moral undertones, connected with birth control as practiced by unmarried people," he wrote. "The young man is 'prepared' on a date; the girl is not. If there is a seduction, he takes the initiative; she is 'surprised' . . . Vital to this ritual is the supposition that the girl sets off on the date believing that it will be platonic; if it ends up otherwise she cannot be accused of having planned ahead for the sexual culmination."

In other words, the ritual became more about defending a young woman's honor than her chastity. Mid-1960s readers had begun to accept that people had premarital sex, but the charade helped maintain a bulwark of the Victorian perspective: that boys still wanted it more than girls. The idea that scores of unmarried women were, of their own initiatives, taking daily medication to prevent pregnancy was a blow to the very structure of cultural mores around sex. The growing popularity of the Pill, much like female masturbation, toppled the premise that women were only interested in sexual intimacy in the context of making babies.

By the early 1970s, some sex ed teachers in public schools, like Blume's fictional Mrs. Rappoport, really did acknowledge the Big Four, and they did so with SIECUS's full approval. But they were taking a risk, Zimmerman said. "If [the teacher] does that at PS3 down in the Village, she'll be teacher of the year, and if she does that in wherever bumfuck

Indiana she'll be canned. One can well imagine on the Upper West Side, this being completely fine, right? But there are lots and lots of places where it wouldn't be, up until today."

And even in areas where topics like masturbation and contraception were allowed, the familiar yarns of conservatism were often knitted through the conversations. The SIECUS curriculum, while comprehensive, still depicted girls as potential victims when it came to their male peers' wild, raging sex drives. The message to young women was the same as it was back in the Victorian era: male sexuality is a storm. *Be strong enough to hold it off until marriage, and then submit to it, passively, ever after.*

Professor and researcher Michelle Fine was "shocked" when she went back to high school in New York City in the mid-1980s to investigate why the dropout rates among low-income students were so high, and found that something essential was missing from family life instruction: the existence of female sexuality. Even in the anything-goes Big Apple, she saw that teenage girls were being taught about sex—"'Say No,' put a brake on his sexuality, don't encourage"—in a way that stopped them from developing a healthy sense of agency and entitlement in their inevitable sexual encounters.

"This was about, 'you're a victim, bad things will happen,'" Fine said. There was "no analysis of hetero male sexuality . . . they didn't have to say 'boys will be boys' although that was in the air."

While male sexuality was being "normalized," female sexuality was being erased. Fine, who published her findings in the *Harvard Educational Review* in 1988, argued that "the missing discourse of desire" contributed to the school's high rates of teen pregnancy, which ultimately caused young mothers to drop out. She says that cutting a girl off from her own natural desire for pleasure can potentially mute her voice—and her ability to articulate her sexual needs—in harmful, enduring ways. "I just think people can't say no if they can't say yes," Fine said. "Being able to assert a clear sense of desire, yearning, hope, aspiration, enables one to then articulate conditions under which [something is okay]—or a clear no."

This remains true for so many girls and women, who grow up in a world where "unacknowledged social ambivalence about female sexuality"—per Fine—has contributed to decades-long mixed messages about whether women should be hyper-sexed male fantasies, passive sex objects, or utterly sexless. But *Deenie* blazed an alternative trail.

"I still go into classrooms where I'll say the word 'masturbation' and kids will say, 'I thought that's something only boys do,'" said Rachel Lotus, an independent sex educator based in Brooklyn. "And I'm talking about kids who are on the precipice of puberty, who have maybe heard the word or heard the phrase 'jerking off' but they still believe that that is limited to people with penises only. So it's a huge priority for me to name it, to normalize it, to talk about it being everybody's right. Whether you do or you don't is up to you, but it's something that everybody can do and enjoy."

Lotus, who was forty-two at the time we spoke, recalled reading *Deenie* as a kid and feeling an enormous weight off her shoulders. "[The book] completely changed my understanding of everything and was a huge relief. I mean, huge. 'Oh! There's a word for this, other people do it?' This isn't weird or scary or shameful, it doesn't need to be stigmatized."

She believes sex educators like her owe Judy an enormous debt. "I don't think you'll talk to any sex educator who doesn't think that Judy Blume is the most badass, radical, incredibly brave author . . . *Deenie* is still, however many years later, still so radical for having that scene."

# ᴠVirginity

*"Nice girls didn't go all the way."*

ᴿandy Blume was almost exactly the same age as Judy's pre-teen characters; she was twelve when *Deenie* was published. From early on, she had been one of her mother's most trusted readers. She gave Judy book ideas, pointed out errors, and corrected her dialogue if it missed the mark, especially when the junior high slang came off as inauthentic.

They'd started that routine with *Then Again, Maybe I Won't*. An elementary school–aged Randy had insisted on reading an early draft and Judy let her, even though she worried that the subject matter might be too advanced. But much to Judy's amusement, the puberty stuff went right over Randy's head. She thought Tony carried the raincoat to cover his face if he got embarrassed and interpreted his nocturnal emissions as him peeing.

As Randy approached her teenage years, she started reading novels that were circulating among kids her age, including 1967's *Mr. and Mrs. Bo Jo Jones* and 1969's *My Darling, My Hamburger*. In both books, starlit high school romances give way to teen pregnancies—with disastrous consequences. One young woman marries the baby's father, miscarries, and then her future dissolves into a heavy haze of responsibility and grief. Another girl has an illegal abortion and nearly hemorrhages to death, missing her graduation.

The alternative to these stories were Maureen Daly's 1942 classic *Seventeenth Summer* and Beverly Cleary's *Fifteen* from 1956, which veered too far in the other direction, filled with *aww shucks* soda fountain dates and *gee whiz* sentimentality. Randy suspected that there was more to teenage relationships than what she read in these page-turners-cum-morality-tales. In passing, she told her mother that she wanted a book where a young couple has sex—but nobody dies and their lives aren't ruined. She also told Judy that she hated the way the male and female characters were being stereotyped. "In these books, the boys had absolutely no feelings, and the girl 'did it' not because she was excited sexually, but because she was mad at her parents," Blume said in *Presenting Judy Blume*. "And she was always punished for it."

Judy agreed that the classic teen romance was ripe for an update and got to work. She dug into the emotional nuances that would lead a pair of lovestruck high schoolers to have sex. *Forever*, about seventeen-year-olds Michael Wagner and Katherine Danziger, emerged from there. "I set out to teach very few things in my books," Blume explained. "But I did set out in *Forever* to show that boys can love just as hard, feel just as much pain."

·　　·　　·

*Are You There God?*, *Deenie*, and *Forever* form a triptych, with eleven-year-old Margaret, thirteen-year-old Deenie, and seventeen-year-old Katherine creating a progressive portrait of the new American girl. All three are smart, spunky, and in touch with their bodies. They're all white, middle class, and from the suburbs—Judy wrote what she knew—but together, they embody an ideal for Blume that transcended race or class. The trio offers a vision of how the up-and-coming generation could digest the feminist and sexual revolutions. They're good girls with a twist; they're all in touch with sexuality, but they have futures.

By the time she wrote *Forever*, Judy was no longer pulling directly from her own experiences. She had come of age in the 1950s, when premarital sex represented a barrier that "nice girls" just didn't cross. "When I was growing up, we had very firm rules about how far to go," Blume wrote in *Letters to Judy*. "Nice girls didn't go all the way. We were supposed to be virgins until we were safely married." Although she knew girls who slipped up, Judy played within the lines, more or less. As she told a reporter for the *Independent* in 1999, "[I] was a virgin until I got married, or at least until I got engaged. But not even early in my engagement. Very late in my engagement," she said.

However, she was no stranger to sexual exploration. She was the envy of her friends because her parents trusted her to have her boyfriends over to their house in Elizabeth, where she'd make out with them in the sunroom. This gave her "years of kissing experience," as she told a reporter in 1976. Blume later elaborated in the *Independent*, explaining that her mother and father allowed this because they were nervous about the dangers of "parking," in which unsupervised high schoolers fooled around in dark cars. There were rumors of distracted kids getting attacked by bloodthirsty strangers. Just once, Judy decided to try it anyway. "I wanted to know what it would feel like to make out in a car," she said. "No sooner had we pulled off the road than a cop was there at the window with a flashlight."

The policeman warned them that necking in the shadows was a recipe for getting assaulted. "He said, 'Don't do this—this is dangerous!'" Blume recalled. "And I said, 'I know! I've never done it!'"

She found other ways to sneak around the "nice girl" fence. "My friends and I played sexual games, sexual games between girlfriends, ending in orgasm," she said in the same article. "I played with one friend—she and I took turns being the boy." (Blume's main characters in *Wifey* and 1998's

*Summer Sisters* have a similar history of same-sex exploration; like Judy, both protagonists grow up to sleep with and eventually marry men.)

By the time Judy was a mother herself, the world had changed, as had her own perspective. Her marriage to John "lacked intimacy," she told the *Independent* years after their divorce, and she found herself wondering what she had missed out on by settling down at an all but virginal age of twenty-one.

She didn't want Randy to have the same regrets. She knew that abstinence before the altar wasn't realistic anymore, nor was it necessarily a recipe for an erotically fulfilling partnership. And so, Judy started imagining the new teenage girl: one who was nice—but also free.

•   •   •

*Forever* is a traditional teenage love story with a twist, and that twist has a name: Ralph. Ralph is what the male character calls his penis. Boy and girl meet; boy and girl get swept off their feet—and then, *oh hello*, Ralph has joined the party. *Forever* was the first book of its kind to show a young couple's sexual journey.

The writing is explicit, for sure; there are descriptions of nudity, orgasms, and semen. But Judy was careful to avoid pitfalls that would make *Forever* easily dismissible as smut. For one thing, the emotional relationship between the pair is just as nuanced as their physical connection. Equally important, Blume is intentional in the way she presents the two main characters. They aren't rebels or burnouts or outsiders, sneaking around in the streets after dark.

They're sweet, wholesome kids.

Michael and Katherine are seniors in high school: she's from Westfield, New Jersey, and he's from the neighboring town of Summit. They meet at a mutual friend's fondue party—the tamest possible teenage get-together—where they flirt and banter. The next day, they go on a drive and talk about their interests. They're both athletes, with Michael a skier and Katherine an avid tennis player. The colleges on their wish lists are competitive: Penn State, University of Vermont, Middlebury. Michael's favorite food is literally spinach! Katherine tells Michael that she volunteers at the local hospital once a week as a candy striper.

Katherine in particular is family oriented. Her dad is her most frequent tennis partner; the first thing she does after her date with Michael is go home and tell her mom about him. Her younger sister, Jamie, is a precociously talented artist and cook, but Katherine doesn't let her own insecurities get in the way of their sisterly bond. Other details, offered early in the novel, telegraph Katherine's level-headedness. She has a "92 average" in school, and she's thin. "We are exactly the same size—five-feet-six and 109 pounds," she says of her and her mother. It's one of the few times Blume provides a physical description as specific as a character's weight. You get the sense that she's using Katherine's svelte body as a shorthand for self-control, which wouldn't fly now but was par for the course in the diet-obsessed 1970s.

When it comes to sex, Katherine is equally disciplined. She's still a virgin and broke up with her last boyfriend, she tells us, because he pressured her in bed. "He threatened that if I wouldn't sleep with him he'd find somebody else who would," she says. "I told him if that was all he cared about he should go right ahead."

Like Judy, Katherine has been warned by her parents about the dangers of parking. After her second date with Michael, she invites him back to her house, where they make out in the den. Michael wants to go farther, but Katherine holds him off, dutifully performing her role as the good girl. "Let's save something for tomorrow," she says when he tries to reach up under her sweater.

In the chapters that follow, the pair engage in the familiar, gendered pas de deux, with Michael angling for more action and Katherine keeping him at bay. What makes her—and *Forever*—so interesting is that she's actually enticed by the idea of sex. As their relationship unfolds, it becomes less about if for her, than *when*.

"In the old days girls were divided into two groups—those who did and those who didn't," Katherine muses. "Nice girls didn't, naturally. They were the ones boys wanted to marry." She continues to say that just because the rules have changed, it doesn't mean that her entire generation takes sex lightly. "It's true that we are more open than our parents but that just means we accept sex and talk about it. It doesn't mean we are all jumping into bed together."

Katherine isn't jumping into bed with anyone—but in her town, teenage hanky-panky is hardly rare. Her best friend, Erica, lives on a hill, where "she's always finding used rubbers in the street." Erica herself is sassy, extroverted, and less sentimental about sex than Katherine is. "I've been thinking," Erica tells her one day, "that it might not be a bad idea to get laid before college." When Katherine balks because Erica doesn't have a boyfriend, Erica is unfazed. "We look at sex differently," she says. "I see it as a physical thing and you see it as a way of expressing love."

In the months that follow, Erica gets involved with Michael's friend Artie: a promising high school actor who thinks he might be gay. Erica is more than happy to help him figure himself out, though he's mostly interested in her as a formidable board game opponent. She gets frustrated with him but there's also a sense that in the world of the book, she and Artie are doing right by each other. By giving Artie the space to understand his sexuality—a plotline that turns tragic when he tries to take his own life—Erica slows down enough to realize that she cares more about sex than she thought she did. "I've been doing a lot of thinking and have decided I don't want to fuck just for the hell of it," she writes in a letter to Katherine near the end of the novel. "I want it to be special."

It's clear that Erica has come around to the right way of thinking about teenage sex. *Forever* makes a case for the wrong way, too. The novel opens with a shocker of a phrase: "Sybil Davison has a genius IQ and has been laid by at least six different guys." Sybil is Erica's cousin, who hosts the New Year's Eve fondue party where Michael and Katherine first meet. We learn that Sybil is fat and Erica thinks she sleeps around to make up for her low self-esteem.

For the most part, Sybil exists as an off-screen character. She shows up in Artie's school play looking "fatter than ever" and then disappears from the action, until Erica tells Katherine that Sybil is pregnant. Nobody knows who the father is and she's too far along to get an abortion, which means she'll have to carry the baby to term. Sybil has decided to go the adoption route and is looking forward to having the baby "for the experience."

The birth goes well, and Erica and Katherine visit Sybil in the hospital. Sybil seems nonchalant—she describes labor and delivery as "no big deal"—but a few things she says imply otherwise. She's disappointed that she won't be able to attend her high school graduation. She talks about the girl baby's full head of hair in a way that suggests feelings well beyond indifference, and admits that she hopes the adoptive parents will name her Jennifer.

Sybil's life isn't ruined by the slipup—she tells her friends that she plans to go to Smith College in the fall, with a brand-new IUD. But later, Erica informs Katherine that Sybil won't talk about the baby, and that the "whole experience was more than she bargained for."

In *Presenting Judy Blume*, Blume explains that with Sybil's character, she wanted to show "that a girl like Sybil might have a genius IQ but she has no common sense." Put another way, Sybil is tripped up by her hunger. She's brilliant but *oh*, her appetites.

Katherine, on the other hand, thinks things through. She has a good head on her shoulders thanks in part to her female role models: her mother and her grandmother. Her mom, named Diana, is the foremost children's librarian at the nearby public library. When Katherine starts talking to her about sex, Diana doesn't shut her down. "Were you a virgin when you got married?" Katherine asks one morning in the car on the way to school. Her mother answers her honestly, admitting she was a virgin until Katherine's father, Roger, proposed and that if she were to do it all over again, she probably wouldn't have gotten married so young, at age twenty.

Then, she delivers the most concrete piece of advice about sex that the book has to offer. "You have to be sure you can handle the situation before you jump into it," Diana tells her daughter. "Sex is a commitment . . . once you're there you can't go back to holding hands."

Diana goes on to say that whatever decision Katherine makes, she just hopes she'll behave responsibly. Later, she saves a column from the *New York Times* and brings it up to Katherine's bedroom. The article—which is real—is called "What About the Right to Say 'No'?" and was an op-ed written by a Yale professor and doctor, Richard V. Lee, published on September 16, 1973. It argued that the sexual revolution put too much pressure on adolescents to have sex before they were ready and created shame around virginity, rather than sexual experience, for girls as well as boys. In an unexpected cultural twist, teen and twentysomething virgins were being treated by both their peers and adults like uptight losers. "The new ideology is that sex is good and good sex means orgasm and any body can," Lee wrote. "The result has been to turn the pleasures of sex into a duty. Along with all this goes the 'knowledge' that if you don't have intercourse, you'll go crazy—and that virginity is a hang-up."

Lee provided four questions that teenagers could ask themselves to help assess if they were truly prepared for intercourse, including "Is sexual intercourse necessary for the relationship?" and "Have you thought about how this relationship might end?" Reading along in *Forever*, Katherine gets prickly around the latter. In her mind, her feelings for Michael are permanent—thus the "forever" of it all.

Still, she's open when Diana brings up the article at breakfast the next morning. They have a quick, pleasant conversation in which Katherine—who has already lost her virginity, unbeknownst to her mother—doesn't feel judged. In Diana, Blume gives readers an example for positive parent-child rapport over a sensitive subject. "Not that I don't identify with Katherine, but I could see myself as Katherine's mother," Blume once said. "And I like her."

She also clearly likes Katherine's grandmother. Hallie Gross is a lawyer who once had an unsuccessful run for US Congress. At almost seventy, she's still working, while also dealing with her longtime husband's deteriorating health and volunteering for Planned Parenthood and NOW. Ever since he had a stroke, Katherine's grandfather has trouble walking and talking, but you'd never know it from the patient and loving way Hallie treats him. She's an active feminist who also adores her family; one time, we learn, she drove to her apartment in New York City and back just to grab the exotic spices needed to try out a new recipe.

Like Diana, Hallie isn't afraid to talk about sex. After first meeting Michael, she tells Katherine that "he's a nice boy," but she should "be careful." When Katherine asks her why, Hallie is matter-of-fact. She wants her granddaughter to be mindful of catching a venereal disease or getting pregnant. Katherine, more than a little surprised, tells Hallie that they aren't even sleeping together.

"Yet," Hallie replies.

Hallie makes it her business to educate her granddaughter about sex, too. One afternoon, Katherine arrives home to a package from Hallie and tears into it, thinking it might be an early birthday present. Instead, she finds a quick note and a stack of pamphlets from Planned Parenthood. Katherine is annoyed by Hallie's presumption and calls her up at work to tell her so. But Hallie doesn't back down. "Sometimes it's hard for parents to accept the facts," she says in her own defense, implying that at her age, she's evolved enough to face the realities of her granddaughter's awakening sexuality. As Hallie writes in her note that came with the pamphlets: "I don't judge, I just advise."

And Katherine eventually takes Hallie's advice to heart. She has strong mentors in Diana and Hallie, and Katherine, ever sensible, becomes a diligent student.

.   .   .

Throughout history, a girl's virginity has been everybody's business. For Victorian parents, an explicit part of the contract of marrying off one's daughter included the assurance that she was "pure," meaning that she'd never had sex. Doctors were employed to check the state of a would-be bride's hymen; Kate Millett described this practice trenchantly as "a sign of property received intact." A young woman who strayed brought shame upon her family, and "ruined" herself.

By the Jazz Age this had started to change, with flappers cutting their hair and embracing their sexual freedom, like men. But flappers weren't "nice" girls. They gave up their claim to niceness in exchange for the thrill of shadowy corners in speakeasies, illicit liquor fueling the fire in their bellies. Up through the mid-century, there were two kinds of girls: those who went "all the way" and those who didn't, as Katherine recounts. The ones who didn't had an easier time getting hitched. As Diana tells her daughter: "There were double standards then . . . boys were supposed to get plenty of experience before marriage," while good girls were still expected to keep their legs closed.

Then, in the 1960s, the importance of female virginity started to wane. This dovetailed, interestingly, with a development in women's health: the widespread acceptance of tampons. The first commercially available tampons appeared on the market in 1936, under the brand name Tampax, which were invented by a male doctor named Earle Cleveland Haas. Three years later in 1939, Tampax was featured at the World's Fair in Flushing, Queens, in the Hall of Pharmacy. The exhibit boasted the world's largest medicine chest, demonstrations of pharmaceutical chemistry, and an area devoted to "the drug store of tomorrow." Married women—in other words, those who were "appropriately" sexually active—embraced the product easily, appreciating the efficacy and discretion of tampons as opposed to bulky sanitary pads.

But the idea of tampon use among teens remained much more controversial. Would Tampax interfere with virginity? Would adolescent girls be more inclined to masturbate if they got comfortable inserting something into their bodies? Physicians were invited to weigh in. Referencing a 1945 paper in the *Journal of the American Medical Association*, Joan Jacobs Brumberg writes that a doctor named Robert Latou Dickinson used a sketch to show "that a tampon took up no more room than a standard nozzle for douching and it was smaller than the average penis. As for the old Victorian bugaboo that anything in the vagina had to be 'stimulating,' Dickinson said that if there was any erotic stimulus it was both 'momentary' and 'negligible.'"

Tampon use among teenagers slowly became more socially acceptable. By the time Blume was writing *Forever*, the vast majority of high school seniors would have at least tried them. Girls teaching each other how to insert them became a typical right of passage, Brumberg explains. During Katherine's first pelvic exam, when the gynecologist holds a mirror between her legs to help her get acquainted with her genitals, Katherine notes that it reminds her "of the time that Erica taught me how to use tampons. I had to hold a mirror between my legs then, too, to find the right hole."

Tampons helped to temper the cultural importance of the hymen. Even with the assurance that a girl could physically remain a virgin while using internal menstrual products, the taboo of penetration started to lose its teeth. This, along with changing social mores and the rise of heavy petting in cars, all meant that by the 1970s, a girl's virginity had a lot less to do with her eligibility for marriage. To use the parlance of the time: there were still sluts and prudes, but you didn't need to stay a cherry to land a husband anymore. Katherine and her family come together around the topic not because she's in danger of ruining herself, but because they care about the safety and sanctity of her first sexual experience. They want to make sure she treats the milestone with the appropriate reverence, that she acknowledges it as special.

. . .

Reading *Forever* through today's lens, Michael comes off as pushy, or worse. In a TikTok from 2022, a Gen Z–appearing user rants: "Michael is like a predator. This man pressures her so many times into sexual intercourse that I feel like she eventually just gave in . . . Michael was just so nasty." He's not as bad as Katherine's former boyfriend—the one who gives her an ultimatum—but he's still written as a "typical" horny teenage guy trying to drive their sexual exploration to the finish line as quickly as possible.

After they've been seeing each other for a little bit over a month, they split off from a double date with Erica and Artie and start making out in Katherine's den. When Michael tries to unbutton Katherine's jeans, she stops him. She doesn't want to go so far with their friends playing Monopoly in the next room. Michael says he understands but then asks for a minute to himself. "This is really rough," he tells her.

The next time they're together, Jamie's the only other person in the house. Katherine asks for privacy to change her clothes but Michael follows her into her bedroom. Michael—who has only had sex twice, with a girl he met on the beach in Maine—makes a show of testing out the mattress, noting that "soft mattresses are good for making love." Katherine humors him, but then asks him to leave because she wants to take off her bra. Instead, he tells her he'll just help her with the hook but then reaches around to cop a feel. "Please Michael . . . don't," Katherine says. Michael pushes back, but then they're interrupted by Jamie calling from downstairs.

Katherine draws a firmer line after another date. They're fooling around in the den again and this time, Michael reaches down her pants. "I'm not ready, Michael," she says after he tells her how much he wants her. When he points out that she seems turned on, she clarifies that she's not "mentally ready . . . a person has to think . . . A person has to be sure." Michael concedes that they can satisfy each other without intercourse and Katherine agrees—just not right then. "If I didn't know better, I'd think you were a tease," Michael says, before dismissing her assurance that she isn't as "Promises . . . promises."

Katherine tells Michael that taking it slow "isn't easy for [her] either," and she means it. From her internal monologue, it's clear that she's genuinely engaging with the question of whether or not to have sex. After Michael accuses her of being a tease, she lies in bed that night contemplating what it would feel like to lose her virginity. "Sometimes I want to so much," she admits. "But other times, I'm afraid."

This is how Blume carefully modulates the nice girl. As an author, she acknowledges Katherine's very real sexual urges, but imbues her with the self-confidence, and self-control, that allow her to hold off Michael long enough to make peace with her own desires. She's waiting for love, for one thing. The first time Michael tells her he loves her, on a ski trip to Vermont with his sister and brother-in-law, Katherine isn't sure she wants to say it back. "I was thinking, *I love you Michael*. But can you really love someone you've seen just nineteen times in your life?"

By the end of the ski weekend—and after Katherine has officially met, and touched, Ralph—she's ready to reciprocate. She tells Michael that she loves him, too, and when she arrives back home to her parents, they ask if she and Michael are going steady. Katherine gets annoyed as her mom and dad start reminiscing about their own high school steadies and the love tokens they'd treasured at the time. Diana shares that she once wore a classmate's class ring around her neck on a chain; Roger talks about how he gave a fellow tenth grader his ID bracelet.

For Katherine, these comparisons to her own relationship are invalidating, but she stays quiet. "I didn't tell them that with Michael and me it's different," she says. "That it's not just some fifties fad, like going steady. That with us it is love—real, true honest-to-god love."

She doesn't see the similarity when Michael gives her a silver necklace for an eighteenth birthday present. He's had the round pendant engraved with both of their names and the word "forever."

"In my whole life nothing will ever mean more to me," Katherine says with tears in her eyes.

By the time she's sporting Michael's gift around town, Katherine is no longer a virgin. One afternoon, Michael surprises her with the key to his sister's empty apartment in nearby Springfield, New Jersey. Katherine says she isn't sure she wants to go and Michael assures her they don't have to "do anything"; they can "just talk." Katherine knows better but it's all part of the dance—Michael is giving her plausible deniability. By the rules of the day, no matter what happens next, Katherine's moral position is upheld by the pretense that it wasn't her idea.

The first time Katherine sees the apartment, she and Michael follow the same old script: just talking leads to just kissing, which ends in them satisfying each other with their hands. But the next day, something has changed. Katherine feels ready. They're at the apartment again, and Katherine says that "when we were naked, in each other's arms, I wanted to do everything—I wanted to feel him inside of me." She's conscientious of course; she asks Michael if they can move from his sister's bed to the floor, because she's worried about stains. She also insists that he wear a condom, even though she's just finished her period. "I'm thinking about getting pregnant," Katherine tells Michael when he assures her that he doesn't have a sexually transmitted disease. "Every woman had a different cycle."

That night, they have intercourse twice. Both times, Michael comes immediately. Katherine is disappointed, but she doesn't let it show. On her way home from the apartment, she's buzzing with her new reality—she's no longer a virgin. "Still, I can't help feeling let down," she muses, because it wasn't so pleasurable for her. "Everybody makes such a big thing out of actually doing it. But Michael is probably right—this takes practice."

And practice is exactly what Katherine resolves to do. This is where Blume steers *Forever* off the preexisting road map, where the novel goes from merely explicit and bold to something revolutionary.

*Chapter Eleven*

# Pleasure

*"Can we do it again?"*

A round the same time that *Forever* was published in the fall of 1975, the *New York Times* printed a brief op-ed called "Recreational—and Procreational—Sex." The writer was Dr. John Money, a New Zealand–born sexologist (that's right, *sexologist*) who founded the Gender Identity Clinic at Johns Hopkins University in 1966. In his essay, Money argued that a "new ethic" was required for sex, in response to a massive paradigm shift surrounding intercourse and its purposes.

"Our old ethic is, like Venice, sinking imperceptibly into the sea," he wrote colorfully. "We have succeeded neither in shoring up the old customs and morality of sexual relationships nor in restructuring them to meet the new tide of history."

The new tide was one in which the rules around sex were in flux. There have always been two approaches to intercourse—recreational and procreational—and traditionally, the latter was righteous while the former was sinful. The ethics of sex were built around this long-accepted binary: pleasure was bad; making babies was good. But now, Money said, the whole framework needed restructuring. The upcoming generations were no longer buying into it, thanks in part to changes in life expectancy. "Men and women both, therefore, may plan years of recreational sex together during which they are either too young or too old to embark on parenthood," he wrote.

The increased availability of contraception made a major difference, too. Money argued that teenagers in particular needed guidance about how to navigate this new world—but they weren't getting it. "The established generation of adults has pretty much abdicated its responsibility toward youth," he charged, adding that "parents look backward rather than forward." In the meantime, young adults had already started devising updated rituals for sex and courtship. Money described a "new code of betrothal" that was slowly developing, "a relationship of recreational sex that is not promiscuous but that also is not a permanent commitment to procreation."

In other words, teens were embracing a kind of serial monogamy in which they tested out potential mates—and sex partners—before finding one who they wanted to marry. While conservatives viewed this as a symptom of widespread moral breakdown, Money saw it as a distinctly positive development with the potential to lower the divorce rate, which had more than doubled between 1963 and 1975.

Money's perspective was winning the culture wars. The public acceptance of recreational sex was happening on a national level, in the hallowed halls of the capital. Two recent Supreme Court decisions had revealed that as far as the American government was concerned, citizens were no longer required to limit their sexual experiences to the willful pursuit of pregnancy. When it came to straight couples at least, these decisions implied that people's bedrooms were inherently private spaces. And that privacy yielded another entitlement—the right to experience pleasure.

•   •   •

For a real girl around Katherine's age, the consequences of premarital
sex were quite a bit less severe than they would have been for her grandmother or even her mother. Over the course of a century, virginity had
gone from a physical status to a mostly symbolic one. Equally as important, pregnancy was no longer a foregone conclusion of heterosexual
intercourse. The medical field had effectively severed the rope between
the two—and in recent years, the government had tied off the knots.

The biggest development on this front was *Roe v. Wade*, the landmark 1973 Supreme Court ruling that allowed women in all fifty states
the right to an abortion within the first three months of pregnancy. *Roe*
was one of the feminist movement's flashiest victories, representing
years of grassroots activism and advocacy to shore up public support
for the procedure. The decision was controversial, but not among the
justices. The court ruled 7-2 that from a constitutional standpoint, a
woman's right to an abortion was justified by her well-established legal
right to privacy.

Another landmark case, decided less than a year earlier, had a major
impact, too. *Eisenstadt v. Baird* declared that unmarried people should
have access to contraception. Until this ruling in 1972, the Pill—which
came on the market in 1960—was only available to married women.
*Eisenstadt v. Baird* changed sex for the Michaels and Katherines of the
world. For the first time, a young woman could be completely in control
of her fertility.

After Katherine makes the choice to have sex and receives guidance from Diana and Hallie, she calls Planned Parenthood in the city to
schedule an appointment. She's nervous, and when the medical receptionist on the other end of the line asks her age, she answers, "Does it
matter?" The Planned Parenthood rep assures her that she doesn't need
parental permission to come in, but they have "special sessions" for teenagers. Katherine is just shy of eighteen, which qualifies her for a group
chat with a doctor and social worker.

Blume devotes an entire chapter to Katherine's Planned Parenthood visit, as if she's making a point of showing readers how nonthreatening an appointment like this can be. After the group session, Katherine meets with a social worker for private counseling, during which she answers questions about her sex life and her menstrual cycle. Then it's on to the exam, where the male gynecologist patiently walks her through the steps, showing her the speculum and letting her see her own cervix. She's nervous but still confident enough to advocate for herself. When the social worker suggests that a diaphragm might be the best birth control method for her, Katherine firmly states her preference: "I'd rather take the Pill."

The office respects her wishes and gives her a two-month supply of birth control pills, plus a prescription. She hasn't yet told Michael about the Planned Parenthood visit and she can't wait to surprise him with the news. For a girl like Katherine, there's nothing wrong with indicating that she intends to have sex with him again. The dance is over—as is the phase in which Michael is clearly taking the lead. Unbeknownst to him, Katherine is setting the stage for a whole new act.

What's amazing about *Forever*, Rachel Lotus said, is that it foregrounds Katherine's enthusiastic consent. "Katherine absolutely wants it and is in touch with her own desire and feels ready," Lotus said. "They both are going into this situation knowing that that's what they want . . . and how refreshing. To have her take ownership of her own experience in that way."

The next week, Michael invites Katherine to his house. Up until this point, she's spent a lot of time around Michael's older sister, but she hasn't met his parents or even been to the family home. Michael describes his mom and dad as "a little stuffier" than Katherine's, but "basically they're good guys." Still, she's hesitant to come over, even though Michael assures her that his parents will be out until midnight. "We don't have to do anything . . . we can just go there and talk," Michael tells her. This time though, the charade has been dropped and Katherine isn't even pretending to fall for it. "I think I've heard that before!" she jokes.

Once she's through the door, Katherine is fascinated by what she sees. The furniture downstairs is "big, heavy and dark." She has fun inspecting Michael's bedroom, where he displays his team pennants and trophies. She even goes through his medicine cabinet, laughing that he "use[s] more junk" than she does and has "at least six different kinds of after-shave." They banter back and forth about it until Katherine raises the stakes.

"Do you ever put it on your balls?" she asks.

Michael says no, and then wonders if she would like to do it for him. Katherine accepts the challenge, then boldly inspects Ralph in the light of the bathroom. They have sex right there, though Katherine remains unsatisfied. But an hour later, they try again, this time in Michael's bed. For the first time, he's able to last a little longer, giving Katherine a chance to get into it. "I grabbed his backside with both hands, trying to push him deeper and deeper into me," Katherine says. "I spread my legs as far as I could—and I raised my hips off the bed—and I moved with him, again and again and again—and at last, I came."

Katherine isn't ashamed. Far from it—she's celebratory. "I actually came," she tells Michael afterward. "I've never felt so close to you before." Then, "Can we do it again?" Michael says he needs to rest. They go out for hamburgers and Michael brings her home, where they sit in the den for a while. "I thought how nice it would be if we could go upstairs, to bed, together," Katherine says. "I was hoping we'd make love again but Michael said he was kind of exhausted."

By this point, Katherine's sexuality has been fully awakened. In the logic of the novel she's done everything right, and her reward is getting to enjoy her intimate experiences. The next time they have sex, after Michael's high school graduation, she doesn't just let herself go—she actively pursues pleasure.

Back in the den, Michael notes that she's being "aggressive" as she kisses him all over his body. She straddles him and asks if it's okay to do it "this way," with her on top. "Any way you want," Michael answers. Katherine describes finding the rhythm between their bodies and savoring every moment. "I couldn't control myself anymore," she says. "I came before he did. But I kept moving until he groaned and as he finished I came again, not caring about anything—anything but how good it felt."

Michael isn't threatened by Katherine's newfound sexual confidence. The next generation of boys, Blume seems to be saying, should be able to meet empowered good girls where they are. While they're holding each other, Katherine gets lost in her post-coital musing. "I thought, there are so many ways to love a person," she says. "This is how it should be—forever."

·    ·    ·

Although she never explicitly tells them so, Katherine's parents are aware that she's having sex with Michael. They also know that the young couple are actively plotting out how to stay connected through college, with the intention of being together for the rest of their lives. That's what makes Diana and Roger's next steps so unique from a historical perspective. For the parents of yesteryear, the only way to salvage a sexually active young woman's future would be to persuade her gentleman caller to marry her. But the Danzigers don't want their daughter to marry Michael, despite the fact that he's traditionally suitable—smart, employable, and from a similar socioeconomic background—and also that they like him. Even with all that in mind, Diana and Roger set out to help Katherine understand that she should end the relationship.

To them, Katherine's prospects are actually more promising if she gives herself time before settling down. This wouldn't have been true at any other time in American history, but thanks to the sexual revolution and the women's movement, an intelligent, levelheaded girl like Katherine had real options outside of just landing a decent man and getting pregnant. Much to Katherine's disappointment, her parents arrange for her to take a job teaching tennis at Jamie's sleepaway camp for the summer. "We both think you could use a change of scenery," Diana says vaguely when Katherine accuses them of trying to keep her away from Michael. "Camp is just seven weeks," Roger says firmly as her protest escalates.

Ultimately, they make it clear that Katherine doesn't have a choice—she's going to New Hampshire. She's scared to tell Michael, but then finds out that his parents have decided to send him out of town, too. They've helped him get a job in North Carolina, with his uncle who owns a lumber yard. The pair vow to stay together, despite any geographical challenges. "So they'll find out that separating us won't change anything," Michael tells Katherine. "Then maybe they'll leave us alone."

At the end of June, they both leave to start their new jobs, vowing to write each other every day. Their letters are mushy: "I miss you," "Ralph misses you," "Love forever," etc. But slowly, Katherine finds her footing at camp. She starts spending time with Theo, the tanned, mustached, twenty-one-year-old head tennis counselor. One day, he asks her about her necklace. "What's *forever* supposed to mean?" he says, flipping it over. When Katherine tells him, then asks him what he thinks, he's honest: "I think forever's a long time for a kid like you."

Katherine takes issue with being called a kid, especially by a guy who's not much older than she is. Over the next few weeks, their banter evolves into flirtation, and she's startled when she wakes up from a vivid sex dream about him. Immediately, she writes Michael a four-page letter as penance. But soon, her letters to him start slowing down. When her grandfather dies, she turns to Theo for comfort.

Michael shows up at the camp to surprise her one afternoon, and Katherine immediately knows it's over. They go to his motel room and start making out, but she can't pretend that she's into it.

"There's another guy, isn't there?" Michael says.

"In a way, I guess . . ." Katherine says—and Michael freaks out.

Remember: *Boys can feel just as much pain*, Blume said. Michael takes the breakup hard. He shuts himself in the bathroom and flushes the toilet over and over so Katherine can't hear him crying. Then he drops her back off at camp, telling her it's fine, actually he "screwed [his] way around North Carolina." The statement has the ring of a lie, and Katherine calls him out. But it doesn't matter. When she gets out of the car, Michael pulls away so fast that his tires "left marks on the road."

It was important to Blume to show the depth of Michael's suffering. Equally important: the fact that it's Katherine, not Michael, whose intense feelings fade. The morality tale version would show Katherine being used; once she's had sex, she's no longer a conquest. But *Forever* doesn't take that stance. It's Michael, not Katherine, who is left behind.

They see each other once more back in New Jersey, in an awkward run-in. They exchange quick pleasantries and Katherine thinks to herself that she has no regrets. "I'll never regret one single thing we did together because what we had was very special," she says. "Maybe if we were ten years older it would have worked out differently." When she gets back home, her mother tells her that she missed a call from Theo.

Katherine isn't miserable—she hasn't been punished. She still has her whole life to look forward to. And for a surprising number of parents, that wasn't acceptable.

## Chapter Twelve

# ℘Paperbacks

*"We'd all whisper and
certain pages would fall open."*

Even with *Are You There God?* and *Deenie* behind her, *Forever* wasn't what readers expected of Judy Blume. Dick Jackson and Bob Verrone—who had moved Bradbury Press from northern New Jersey to the Westchester, New York, town of Scarsdale—knew as much. To protect themselves they created an entirely new division and released the novel as Blume's "first book for adults."

"Labeling it an adult book . . . was our way of saying that it didn't belong on children's shelves," Jackson said years later, "and that we were not recommending this for every fourth grader."

Judy herself disagreed with that decision. She told *School Library Journal* that seeing the book described that way right on the hardcover flap came as a "shock." By then, Judy had clout and employees at Bradbury were told to do whatever it took to keep her happy. "Dick told me, 'Judy Blume is our big author, Judy Blume is the person who keeps this business going, basically,'" Peter Silsbee remembered. "She kept the lights on." But in this case, Jackson did what he thought was best to keep himself and his star writer out of hot water.

Blume had become wildly successful, thanks in part to a paperback deal with Dell. "The way Dick told the story was, they published her first books, all in hardcover, but then when they went to paperback . . . that's when they really got into the hands of kids," Silsbee said. A paperback at the time cost around $1.75, which was quite a bit less than the hardcovers. "They were on racks in the drug store. And that was it, it was all word of mouth. Like one kid would read it and pass it to their friend, pass it to *their* friend, and pretty soon you had this huge fan base."

That huge fan base was ravenous for books by Blume. In August 1976, the *New York Times* reported that Dell had printed over 1.75 million copies of her titles, calling her "a kind of heroine to the kids who read and re-read her books." She was a complicated figure for parents, who supported their kids in reading but weren't always in love with Blume's subject matter. The paper of record's review of *Forever*, which had run the previous winter, called the novel "a convincing date-by-date account of first love." It made no mention of the various sex scenes, but rumors of the book's contents traveled swiftly from kid to kid, mother to mother.

"Rest assured the kids manage to wangle copies of 'Forever,'" the *Times* wrote.

The trade magazines panned the novel. *School Library Journal* hated it, saying, "Obviously it's not a quality book, but that fact won't bother the many girls who will read it." *Kirkus* was also dismissive. "Cath [sic] and Michael fall in love when both are high school seniors, and Blume leads up to It date by date and almost inch by inch (hand over sweater, hand under skirt)," the reviewer writes. "As usual with this immensely popular author, *Forever* has a lot of easy, empathic verity and very little heft."

*Forever* had at least one powerful ally in its corner. Mary Calderone at SIECUS—with whom Judy would eventually develop a warm relationship—thought the book was excellent. In May 1977, SIECUS put out its monthly report with a front-page story devoted to the topic of sex in children's literature. Writer Pamela D. Pollack, who worked as a book reviewer for *School Library Journal*, rounded up a series of recent titles that dared to tackle the carnal experiences of teens. Pollack did not include *Forever* in her story, and offered a fairly bleak assessment of the way these books portrayed premarital sex. "Not too long ago, if sexual matters were mentioned at all in children's fiction, a single standard of abstinence-or-else was applied unilaterally to the unmarried and underage," she wrote. Now, she said, writers acknowledged the existence of teen sex but often did so by presenting the "extreme repercussions" that Randy Blume had mentioned to her mother: unwanted pregnancy, plummeting self-esteem, rape. Even the gentler versions presented "boys at the mercy of their hormones and girls as being at the mercy of boys." Pollack expressed the need for a novel that guided young adult readers toward a healthier, more humane view of sexuality: "What is necessary is some notion that sex should be a satisfying experience shared by people who care about each other," she wrote.

And as far as Calderone was concerned, she had found it. Later in the same issue, SIECUS's president reviewed *Forever*, calling it "very well-written" and "in good taste." She also suggested that it was parents, not adolescents, who needed this book the most, agreeing with John Money that authority figures were failing their kids in a rapidly evolving culture. "I believe this is a book that parents (mothers and fathers both, please note) should be reading, not in order that they may fix an accusatory gaze upon their teenage daughters, but so that they might perhaps be helped to face at last how much the world in which *their* children, their own darlings, are growing up is different from the world that they remember at the same age," she advised.

*     *     *

Whether or not parents were buying *Forever*, kids were getting their hands on it. The biggest story surrounding Blume's novel had to do with the way young readers were smuggling it around their social circles like contraband. One tween would snag a copy, inhale it, and then surreptitiously pass it along to a curious classmate.

Bronx-based middle and high school librarian Julia Loving recalled checking out *Forever* from the New York Public Library, where her mother and father had given her written permission to borrow books from the adult section. Now in her fifties, Loving was a devoted fan of Blume and loved *Deenie* in particular. "Being Black, I always assumed that Deenie was white, but I didn't really think of any difference between her and me being Black and her being white as characters," she said. "I just knew we were girls and we liked boys."

Loving remembered reading *Forever* and then sharing it with a close middle school girlfriend, who was a grade below her. "Her parents found out," Loving said. "And because it was a mature book, basically [her father] came up to my parents' house and spoke about me lending the book and this and that, because it was very saucy at that time."

New York City elementary school librarian Lauren Harrison had a similar experience. "There was a copy of *Forever* that was passed around in fifth grade," recalled Harrison, who was forty-six at the time that we spoke. Like Loving, her parents allowed her to read whatever she wanted; her mother is a librarian, too. But Harrison was aware that the book was tricky stuff for other kids her age. "I didn't have to hide it," but her friends did, she said. "I remember just sort of, we'd all whisper and certain pages would fall open," she added, referring to her crew crowding around the novel and perusing its most descriptive sex scenes.

This phenomenon was so widespread that in 1978, the novelist Joyce Maynard—who was also Judy's friend—did a twenty-column story about it for the *New York Times*. Maynard went to the "pretty, mostly white, upper-middle-class community" of Bath, Ohio, where *Forever* was making the rounds among the girls—and making waves among their mothers.

Maynard sat down with a group of kids and moms to hear about their experiences of the book. She learned that Heather Benson, then thirteen, had borrowed a friend's copy on a choir trip, then brought it home, where her mom, Pat Benson, discovered it. Pat knew Blume's name but hadn't heard anything about her latest publication and was shocked by what she saw. She stopped short of forbidding Heather from reading it but put it away in a drawer while her daughter thought over their chat. Heather ended up steering clear of the novel—or at least that copy of it. "I know she didn't [read it]," Pat, who was fifty at the time, told the *Times*, "because she knew which drawer I put it in and I arranged a strand of hair on the pages and it's still there—which is the kind of trick you've got to know to keep on top of what's going on."

Another mother, Jan Worrall, described buying a copy of the novel at her daughter's request and then, after bringing it home and paging through it, returning it to the bookstore. In her interview, she told Maynard that she would have preferred for her daughter Jocelyn, then age eleven, to read "pornography . . . at least then she'd know that was wrong, instead of having this book about a nice, normal girl who has sex and then it ends and the book's over." She felt Blume had dropped the ball when it came to using her platform to mold kids. "Judy Blume had this beautiful opportunity to teach kids a lesson, if she'd just given an example of suffering or punishment. But the girl doesn't get pregnant or have a nervous breakdown," Worrall said.

Some of the other moms were less incensed, but still wary of Blume's latest. One noted that although she didn't like the book, she hoped that if her daughter Christiane were to have premarital sex, she would take a cue from Katherine and use birth control. Another mother, named Ellie Griffith, took a different stance. "She has the right to publish what she wants," Griffith said about Blume. "But when she comes out with a book like 'Forever' she should use a pen name."

Despite their mothers' objections, the girls all seemed well acquainted with the book's contents, so much so that "mention of [certain] page numbers alone is enough to set off shrieks," Maynard wrote. (This was the analog precursor to BookTok, where among more literary-minded chatter, young influencers point their followers toward reads with particularly spicy sex scenes.) And even though the girls were fluent in *Forever*'s juiciest passages, not one of them was actually having sex or planning to do so anytime soon. Most of the girls were thirteen years old, and to them, the boys at school were still "weird" and "gross."

"How could you look them in the eye afterward?" Christiane said about doing the deed.

Maynard interviewed Blume for the article, and the author defended *Forever* the same way she would stand up for all her most controversial titles in the years to come. She said that children are not immune to life's harshest realities, and silence from adults doesn't help. "I hate the idea that you should always protect children," she said. "Sexuality and death—those are the two big secrets we try to keep from children, partly because the adult world isn't comfortable with them either. But it certainly hasn't kept kids from being frightened of those things." She also maintained that despite the notoriety of certain passages, sex was not why kids were voraciously reading *Forever*, or any of her novels. "I can't entirely explain why they do, myself," Blume said. "I know I'm no great literary figure. But it has something to do with my feeling about kids."

More likely it was a mixture of both. This was long before the internet and iPhones dropped the virtual Kama Sutra into everybody's pockets. Judy was offering up information kids couldn't find anywhere else and she was doing it in an accessible, entertaining way. Schools weren't telling adolescent girls that they'd have to practice at sex in order for it to be pleasurable. Parents, for the most part, weren't volunteering information about birth control, or about being "mentally ready," or what it might feel like to have intercourse and then fall disappointingly out of love. Without access to this kind of nuanced education—beyond the birds and the bees—children turned to Blume.

Cory Silverberg, who is nonbinary and was fifty-three at the time we spoke, said that reading *Forever* as a pre-teen in Canada in the early 1980s opened the door to self-exploration about their gender identity. "I read that book so many times," Silverberg said. "The thing is, I identified with the girl and I in no way understood that." It wasn't until many years later that they found language to describe their gender, but *Forever* offered insight that was missing from sex ed at the time. "I basically turned off sex education because 'this doesn't apply to me.' Because you're either going to do it this way [as a boy] or this way [as a girl], so I was looking for possibility. I wanted to grow up to be [Katherine]."

*Forever* was pivotal for Jonathan Zimmerman, too.

"I was fourteen and I remember reading [*Forever*] and it taught me more about sex than anything I'd ever read," he said. "My parents had *The Joy of Sex*, these sort of hirsute figures doing strange and hairy things, but that was not the same. 'Cause it wasn't kids."

The fact that Blume animated Michael and Katherine with genuine desires and feelings is what made the book both magic and extremely contentious, Zimmerman explained. "I think it was explosive and it remained so because, I know this can sound pedestrian, but it framed kids as autonomous sexual beings. And it took their sexual lives seriously." As simple as it sounds, no one had ever thought to do that before.

With *Forever*, Blume cemented her reputation among children as a writer who would tell them the truth. And, Judy realized, it was about time she started telling the truth in other ways as well.

## Chapter Thirteen

# Rebellion

*"He had married this little girl,*
*and he was happy that way."*

Judy wasn't happy in her marriage. At low moments, she wondered if it had been doomed from the start. Five weeks before her and John's wedding, her beloved father, her Doey-Bird, had died suddenly of a heart attack at the age of fifty-four. She was holding his hand when he lost consciousness. Judy was still crumbling under her grief when she walked down the aisle.

Sixteen years later, and just three years after the Blumes bought a bigger house with a swimming pool, Judy asked John for a divorce in the spring of 1975. He agreed, but then they decided to live together until June so that Randy, then fourteen, and Larry, then twelve, could finish out the school year before moving. After that, the kids headed off to sleepaway camp and Judy packed up their lives and moved to a townhouse an hour away, in Princeton.

She was thirty-seven years old and alone, she realized, for the first time in her life.

The kids hadn't taken the separation well. Before Judy and John told them, Judy had consulted a family counselor who warned her that the children would have questions—and she needed to come prepared with answers. Unlike other kinds of unhappy couples, the Blumes weren't demonstrative in their moments of friction. They weren't big yellers or fighters. As far as young Randy and Larry were concerned, their polite, upstanding parents were perfectly content. "It was a nice marriage," Blume later said, "but inside I was dying."

To explain herself, Judy wrote letters to the kids before they left for the summer, which they read alone in their rooms and then came together to sob. When home feels safe, divorce can be catastrophic to the children. Judy knew that all too well, having put herself in Karen's shoes to write *It's Not the End of the World*. Despite the book's sunny title and its optimistic ending, Judy recognized the pain that it took to get there.

Still, she felt she had no other choice. A few years before she initiated the split, Judy felt herself, at the age of thirty-five, undergoing a massive change—one that she'd eventually describe as an adolescent rebellion, just delayed by twenty years. Essie, who she spoke to twice a day, became representative of Judy's subtle, lifelong indoctrination into a role—the self-annihilating housewife—that no longer suited her. That perspective transformed John in her eyes from a good-enough spouse and a solid provider to a figurehead of her mother's middle-class values. Judy was sick of it all: the PTA meetings, the dinners at the club, the aqua-lined pool in the backyard. Suddenly, she felt an overwhelming urge "to taste and experience life," she said in *Presenting Judy Blume*. "I wasn't terrible. I was responsible. I was working. I loved the kids. But I was rebelling . . . My divorce was all part of that rebellion."

Judy recognized a level of childishness in herself, which she came by honestly, having gone straight from her parents' house to her husband's. She felt immature in ways she didn't like, and realized that John treated her in kind, like something delicate and unformed. Before the divorce, Judy had understood—with a level of dread—that she wanted desperately to take shape. She wished to be a person with edges and depth and firm, well-defined corners, just like one of her characters.

•     •     •

John blamed *Fear of Flying*. Erica Jong's unrestrained roman à clef, about marriage and a successful female writer's messy interior life, came out in 1973, before the Blumes separated. Isadora White Wing is a twice-wed Jewish poet from New York who, five years into her second marriage to psychoanalyst Bennett Wing, finds herself desperate for adventure and sexual novelty. She still loves Bennett but can't deny the sense of yearning that has cast a shadow over her daily life with him. "What *was* marriage anyway?" Wing wonders early in the novel. "Even if you loved your husband, there came that inevitable year when fucking him turned as bland as Velveeta cheese: filling, fattening even, but no thrill to the taste buds, no bittersweet edge, no danger."

"*Fear of Flying* was a very, very important book to me," Blume told *Bust* magazine in 1997. "I was becoming aware. My husband blamed it for my unhappiness—which is simplistic, to say the least." Over the course of Jong's novel, Wing comes to understand that her quest for passion—and the infamous "zipless fuck"—is part of a larger identity crisis about being an artist, a wife, and potentially a mother (she's grappling with the decision of whether or not to have kids). "Was I going to be just a housewife who wrote in her spare time?" Wing asks herself at a crossroads between her husband and another man. "Was I going to keep passing up the adventures that were offered to me? Or was I going to make my fantasies and my life merge if only for once?"

Wing chooses the latter, running off with Adrian Goodlove, another analyst who is the crude and domineering funhouse image of her rigid and respectful husband. The book's title refers to Wing's very real phobia—she's terrified of air travel—but also the nagging suspicion that she's always holding herself back. When she leaves with Adrian for a road trip across Europe, she feels, at least at first, like she's finally taken flight. But as time wears on, Adrian's shortcomings start to surface. He's mostly impotent, for one thing. He's also full of crap. When he leaves her without warning to go back to his wife and children, Wing finds herself alone in a hotel room in Paris, wide awake through a bout of insomnia and raking herself over the coals. What had she done to her life? "Leaving Bennett was my first really independent action," she resolves as the night wears on. It was the first thing she'd ever done that directly defied her parental and cultural programming.

By morning she understands that she's always been afraid of growing up. "I was afraid of being a woman," she says. "Afraid of all of the nonsense that went with it. Like being told that if I had babies, I'd never be an artist, like my mother's bitterness, like my grandmother's boring concentration on eating and excreting, like being asked by some dough-faced boy if I planned to be a secretary. A secretary!" In the end, she goes back to Bennett. After all, he's kind, smart, and good in bed, and it isn't his fault that the world makes it nearly impossible for women to be on their own. Isadora can only hope that he'll live up to his surname and help her soar.

*Fear of Flying* spoke to Judy, as did another feminist novel published in 1967, called *Diary of a Mad Housewife*. That book, by Upper East Sider and Vassar graduate Sue Kaufman, follows New York City mother of two Bettina Balser in the throes of a nervous breakdown. Balser, thirty-six, is a Smith College–educated former artist who can quote Baudelaire and Proust, but whose life now revolves around shopping, decorating, cooking, and throwing parties. It's all at the behest of her husband, Jonathan, a former activist turned nouveau riche social climber who demands that his wife head up their home life to his exacting standards. With no outlet to express her anger, Balser—who shakes uncontrollably when Jonathan issues his unreasonable orders—takes to drinking, smoking too much, and writing in a secret journal. She also starts having an affair with a piggish playwright named George Prager. He isn't very nice, but the pair share an explosive sexual connection.

Prager is dominant in bed, and Balser finds that she likes it. For a while, that uncomfortable truth scares her. But then she begins to understand that what she's acting out with her lover is just another angle on her relationship with Jonathan. "Why should I be disturbed by the sado-masochistic aspects of that relationship, when I have another one going?" Balser writes in her diary. "Why not face the truth: it's an enormous relief to have that sort of thing out in the open and act it out, instead of having to deal with it in a disguised form, all veiled and gussied up with domestic overlay as it is with Jonathan and me."

Although Balser can't stand who her husband has become, she understands she's trapped—after all, he controls the money. At one point, her period is late and she believes Prager has gotten her pregnant. Her options, or lack thereof, flash before her. "Without a cent of my own, without a checking account, the only other way [beyond asking Prager for cash] I could have paid for an abortion would have been to try and get the money secretly from my father, and even I shied away from all the filthy implications of that," she realizes. Luckily, her period shows up and she doesn't have to debase herself. But even that relief doesn't solve the problem of the larger social constructs that frame her marriage, in which she has to be the "submissive woman," the "obedient wife" to the "forceful dominant male" breadwinner.

Blume nods to *Diary of a Mad Housewife* in *Wifey*, when Sandy's sophisticated best friend, Lisbeth—who lives on the Upper West Side and who is experimenting with an open marriage—slips her a copy. Sandy wonders if she should be offended: "Did Lisbeth think she was a mad housewife too? Was that why she'd given her the book?" The novel doesn't come up again until Sandy's husband, Norman, mentions it during a fight, when Sandy is trying to express why their relationship leaves her unsatisfied.

"Have you been reading that book again?" Norman snipes.

"What book?"

"The one Lisbeth gave you."

"This has nothing to do with Lisbeth or books," Sandy says.

Like Bettina Balser, Sandy feels she has to choke her own voice down in order to stomach her marriage. Like Isadora White Wing, Sandy worries that she'll never know true sexual liberation firsthand. Did Judy relate to these predicaments, too? And if so, what did she do about it?

●　●　●

Blume is forthright about one part of her "rebellion," which overlapped with Isadora Wing's—her marriage to John left her feeling inept. "He had married this little girl, and he was happy that way," Blume told a reporter for the *Chicago Tribune* in 1985. Divorcing him meant she would have to grow up, which wasn't easy, either. John was cold toward her; the kids were angry. Judy found that the period after her divorce left her more confused and depressed than ever.

"Just getting through the day was a real struggle for me," she writes of that time in *Letters to Judy*. "I woke up crying every morning and I went to bed crying every night. I wasn't sure I could cope. I had very little left over for my kids."

She worried a lot, fearing that she'd ruined all their lives. The only thing she didn't have to stress about was money. Thanks to her career, she wasn't financially ensnared like Bettina Balser. She wouldn't have to work as a cocktail waitress—"That's what divorced women on TV always turn out to be—cocktail waitresses," Karen muses in *It's Not the End of the World*—or transform herself into the sad woman Sandy's sister, Myra, describes in *Wifey*.

Myra is having a turbulent moment with her wealthy gynecologist husband, Gordon. She doesn't trust him anymore, but she can't imagine leaving, either. "If I divorced him, I'd have to give up the house and move to an apartment in Fort Lee, with all the other divorcées," she whines. She'd have to "eat at Howard Johnson's instead of Périgord Park, get a job in a department store." For Myra, who has embraced the upscale suburban lifestyle in ways Sandy cannot bring herself to do, it's a nonstarter. She'll have to look past his suspected dalliances (it's only one, with Sandy incidentally) and stand by him.

Judy didn't have to brave financial ruin to leave John, and so the exes settled into their new routines as co-parents. She had the kids during the school week, in Princeton, and on the weekend they went to John's, where he would take them out to fancy dinners and plays in the city. "He entertained them lavishly," Judy later explained, "not to compete with me, but because he didn't know what else to do. He wanted to show them that he cared."

This went on for a bit, until John realized that he couldn't sustain paying for expensive outings every time he had his children with him. The big-ticket jaunts abruptly stopped, which disappointed them. It took a while, Blume has said, for the family to find its rhythm within their joint custody arrangement. And then, another change upended their shaky balance.

## Chapter Fourteen

# ❧Mistakes

*"From the beginning, we fought."*

𝒥udy had gotten involved with someone, a man named Tom Kitchens. He appeared to be John Blume's total opposite—a native Texan, a Christian, an academic, with deep brown eyes, a goatee-style beard, and a headful of curls. They'd met before the divorce was finalized, when Judy took the kids on a cross-country flight to accept an award for *Tales of a Fourth Grade Nothing*. Kitchens sat across from Judy and they struck up a conversation.

He came off as youthful and carefree. "My son and daughter thought he was a kid," Blume told *People* magazine in 1978. "He thought I was their big sister, and I thought he was a ski bum." Instead, Tom told her, he was a physicist at the National Science Foundation who traveled the country bestowing government grants on innovative labs, like "a 12-month-a-year Santa Claus," he said with a twinkle. At forty, he was a bit older than Judy and was five years out of a marriage that had yielded three daughters. At the end of the trip, they exchanged contact information. After his next flight, Tom sent her a postcard saying that he'd sat in the same seat, and the ride had been a lot less fun.

As Judy moved out of the family's house in New Jersey, she and Tom became pen pals. He was based at the time in Washington, DC, and she sent him one of her books to read. After she officially became single, she invited him up to attend a party. Tom was compelling to Judy, in part because he lived a life that seemed so different from the one she had known. He'd traveled widely. This was not a guy who needed to tee off every Sunday morning—he was curious and outdoorsy, with a sense of adventure. Suburban life had felt like a trap to Judy. Suddenly, Tom Kitchens appeared, offering what looked like a handsome escape hatch.

When Tom was assigned to a short-term position in London, he invited Judy and the kids to come with him. This—*this* was the kind of person Judy aspired to be. A woman whose radius extended well beyond her small town's outer limits. A globe-trotter. A sophisticate who could give her children the experience of six months in Europe.

She said yes—she, Randy, and Larry would go with him. In the winter of early 1976, they left the townhouse in Princeton for their new, temporary home in North West London. She and Tom got married that spring, less than a year after her divorce from John. It was fast, but for the first time, Judy was letting herself go wherever the universe took her. Was it crazy that she had started seeing someone so quickly?

In retrospect, maybe a little bit. She certainly didn't have to commit herself so wholeheartedly, so *officially*, to the very first man she dated, she later realized. "I could have had affairs, but instead I got married because that's what I thought you did," she explained after the fact. "So I married the first man who said, 'Hello, how are you?'"

•   •   •

They'd moved in together without really knowing each other, and Judy had an inkling that things weren't working out even before she and Tom tied the knot. For instance—he'd been impressed by her career at first, but quickly grew resentful of all the time, between writing and book promotion, it took for her to maintain it. Instead of falling head over heels for the new guy in their mother's life, Randy and Larry were ambivalent toward Tom.

"I would say, 'Isn't he wonderful?'" Blume wrote in *Letters to Judy*. "And my kids would just look at me as if I were crazy. They didn't dislike him. But they didn't think he was so great either."

Larry was having a particularly hard time, acting out because he was angry about the divorce but refusing to admit it. Yet Judy felt she had no choice but to marry Tom. She had already uprooted her children by moving them to London, and making the relationship official seemed like the only way to ground that livewire decision. The idea of going back to Princeton—without Tom—was mortifying. The day they went to sign their marriage license in Hampstead, Judy had an allergy attack. "It was very hard for me to get married again," she told *People* about reciting her vows with red eyes, runny nose, and a puffy face. "I walked around the block three times: I was scared of the connotation of being somebody's wife again."

She liked London, but after Tom's tenure there ended he took a job as a researcher at the Los Alamos Scientific Laboratory (LASL), where in the 1940s Robert Oppenheimer headed up work on the first atomic bomb. Oppenheimer had handpicked Los Alamos, New Mexico, for its off-the-beaten-path location, and after World War II, the facility—which was eventually renamed the Los Alamos National Laboratory—remained devoted to weapons development, among other national security projects. For Judy, Los Alamos felt considerably more foreign than London. The insular community revolved almost entirely around the lab. Looking at the mountainous canyon landscape, she might as well have been on the moon.

The family struggled in Los Alamos. Judy wasn't thrilled with the schools, and Randy hated it there almost immediately. She grew increasingly hostile, transforming from a shy, artistic, responsible adolescent into a full-blown angry teenager. One day, she didn't come home when she said she was going to. As the hours passed, Judy grew more and more anxious, until she did something she swore she never would do as a parent and reached for Randy's diary. "In spite of my vow to respect her privacy, I finally opened it and read the last few entries," Blume writes in *Letters to Judy*. "It was clear she was feeling alienated, frightened and confused and that we needed help."

Judy couldn't really blame her; she didn't like Los Alamos, either. The area was teeming with ambitious husbands but it was almost impossible to find any equally fulfilled wives. "It is a town with very frustrated, resentful, talented women who have very few outlets and few job opportunities," Blume said later.

In her 1981 novel *Tiger Eyes*, which mostly takes place in Los Alamos, Blume depicts it as an odd little world filled with narrow-minded white people who carry guns for no reason and look down their noses on minorities. Davey Wexler, the book's fifteen-year-old protagonist, clashes with her aunt and uncle who live there and have taken her and her family in. Uncle Walter is a pedantic, neurotic type who works for LASL and imposes rules on Davey that she resents. "You're the one who's making the bombs," she yells at him after he warns her that learning to drive is too dangerous. "You're the one who is figuring out how to blow up the whole world. But you won't let me take Driver's Ed."

Judy was lonely there, and not just because she had trouble making friends. Her marriage to Tom was falling apart. They'd hardly known each other when they moved in together, and despite the initial attraction, they had very little in common. She'd gotten married to save face, to protect her kids from any harmful gossip—a divorcée living with a man out of wedlock was enough to spin the rumor mill in the 1970s—and of course, to satisfy her mother. But in the process, she'd once again managed to sacrifice her own happiness. Tom, whose kids were older, didn't approve of her parenting and competed with Randy and Larry for her attention. Judy had two abortions during that time, to avoid the prospect of the pair of them raising a baby together. Their home wasn't peaceful. "From the beginning, we fought," Blume said. "We fought, I think, because we didn't take the time to get to know each other. Each of us had invented the person of our dreams and then we were disappointed when we turned out not to be."

So Judy leaned into her professional life: *The Career*, as she called it. In many ways, it was the only thing keeping her sane. In 1977, she published *Starring Sally J. Freedman as Herself*, a highly autobiographical novel about an imaginative Jewish girl growing up in the post–World War II era. It's 1947 and Sally lives with her family in Elizabeth, New Jersey: her kindly dentist father, her reserved mother, and her brilliant yet troubled older brother, Douglas, whose stubborn case of nephritis prompts a temporary move down to Miami Beach, Florida, for the winter. Her dad—Doey-Bird—stays up north to work, so her mom taps Ma Fanny, Sally's grandmother, to go with them. Sally puts on a brave face for her parents, but she's a fundamentally anxious kid whose thoughts are always roiling about the war. She wonders if Hitler is still alive and is posing as her mustached neighbor, Mr. Zavodsky. She writes Zavodsky letters that she never sends: "I think I know who you are. I think you are a person people hate. I think you are a person who is wicked and evil."

Sally is also making sense of another kind of injustice—her very first experience of the Jim Crow South. To save money, the family takes the train from New Jersey down to Florida, and Sally is secretly relieved because she's afraid to fly. On the train they're seated across from a Black woman, who introduces herself as Mrs. Williamson, and her three young children, including an eight-month-old baby named Loreen. One morning, Sally wakes up and they're gone, which is strange because they're also going all the way to Miami Beach. She asks her mother where they went. "They had to change cars," her mom explains.

"We're in a different part of the country now Sally . . . and colored people don't ride with white people here."

Sally is appalled, even more so because her mother doesn't seem all that upset about it. A few months later, she's hanging out in town with her new friend Andrea when the girls stop for water. As Sally is drinking from the fountain, a stranger comes and grabs at her, mid-sip. The woman gestures frantically to the label on the fountain: *Colored*. "What would your mothers say if they knew what you'd been doing?" she scolds them, handing Sally a tissue to wipe her mouth. "God only knows what you might pick up drinking from this fountain . . . you better thank your lucky stars I came along when I did."

Andrea is another Northern transplant and the two girls are stunned. Walking home, they talk through the experience. "Did you know they had two fountains?" Sally asks. Andrea says she didn't. They go on to discuss how in Florida, people with dark skin need to ride in the back of the bus.

"My mother says you have to follow the rules," Andrea says.

"So does mine," Sally confirms, before telling her that back in New Jersey, she and the family's housekeeper, Precious Redwine, were fine using all the same cups and dishes.

You can feel the gears turning in Sally's head: Is segregation all that different from what happened to the Jews in Europe? Unfortunately for Judy, most reviewers weren't moved by Sally's story. "While Ms. Blume's book is teeming with social value, its literary qualities are less conspicuous," the *New York Times* wrote. "Her characters are so recognizable that they don't matter." Reviewer Julia Whedon treated Blume's popularity with subtly snobbish curiosity: "It's evident that her appeal goes beyond sexual frankness," Whedon wrote. "She must be conveying a certain emotional reality that children recognize as true."

This—the idea that Judy had endeared herself to young fans by indulging their immature tastes, instead of feeding them what they needed—had been following Blume for a while. Mostly, it didn't bother her; she didn't see herself as a member of the literati, either. But she also felt protective of Sally. After all, it was the closest she'd come in fiction to sharing the facts of her own childhood (like so much of the book, the incident on the train really happened to her). And so when reviewer Jean Mercier panned the novel in *Publishers Weekly*, Judy was devastated. The write-up felt extreme and mean-spirited. "Blume's approach will be resented as frivolous by many readers, since Sally's own relatives are victims of the Nazi death camps, not the stuff of humor," Mercier wrote. "Neither are some of the other details in the book. In fact, parts are sickening."

*Sally* was sickening?! It was all too much for Judy. The divorce, the awful new marriage, Los Alamos, her unhappy kids—and now a respected children's book reviewer claimed that treasured memories from Judy's own past were so repulsive that she almost lost her lunch. She couldn't take any more. Overcome by emotion, Judy picked up her bulky IBM Selectric and walked outside to the edge of her yard. Breath heavy, she hovered the typewriter over the arroyo. What would it feel like to hurl it down? To watch the keys pop out in a cathartic crush of metal?

"I held it out to drop it and then I thought, 'Are you crazy?'" Blume told an audience at the Arlington Public Library event in 2015. The review was awful but the notion of quitting writing was much worse.

"You're gonna let one person stop you from doing what you love to do?" She turned around and walked back inside the house.

## Chapter Fifteen

# Monogamy

*"Oh Mother, dammit! Why did you bring*
*me up to think that this was what I wanted?"*

Instead of tossing her career into the abyss, Judy wrote a letter to Jean Mercier. She had her habit of writing curse words over reviews she didn't like, but this was the first time she'd confronted another professional about a bad write-up. In April 1977, she penned a respectful note to Mercier, telling her she was entitled to her opinion of *Starring Sally* but couldn't understand why she'd called the book "sickening." What was it about the creative pre-teen's inner life that turned her stomach?

Mercier wrote back right away. Apologetically, she confessed that she was a great fan of Blume's, which made her experience of *Starring Sally J. Freedman as Herself* all the more disappointing. She said she had read the book twice, hoping for a different impression the second time around. But alas—she thought Blume could do better, as she had many times already. As for the "sickening" comment, Mercier explained that she was referring to one scene in particular. Toward the end of the book, the Freedmans order Chinese food in Miami and find a cockroach in their chop suey.

Perhaps Judy was feeling vulnerable because she had already started work on a new novel; one that would expose her to criticism in an entirely different way. For one thing, it was her first project that was genuinely intended for adults. It also was unapologetically frank about sex and marriage, just like some of the highly controversial books that inspired her, by Erica Jong and Sue Kaufman. But in comparison to many of Blume's books for children, this one wasn't coming as easily. She had rented a small office in Los Alamos over a donut shop, and she had spent three months tinkering with the opening pages in order to get the main character's voice pitch-perfect. In the meantime, she scarfed down way too many glazed donuts. Judy gave up the office and went back to writing from home.

She kept going with the manuscript, likely knowing that this new book would drive some people crazy. It starts off with a bang—a housewife oversleeps and wakes up to find a naked man in a motorcycle helmet pleasuring himself on her front lawn. She calls the police, who treat her like a bored mom who made up the whole thing for attention. After that, her life becomes even more outrageous. Something about that motorcycle-riding exhibitionist—who later returns for a repeat performance—sets off a chain of events in which his audience-of-one suddenly recognizes that she's stagnating. She leaves the house and stirs things up. She's sick of being a wifey, and tired of being good.

*       *       *

*Wifey* is Judy Blume's *Fear of Flying*. Like Isadora, Sandy also hates planes, but she braves a flight early in the novel when the Pressmans head down to Sandy's sister's lavish new vacation property in Montego Bay. Her best friend, Lisbeth, gives Sandy advice about how to get over her phobia. Lisbeth "explained it as Sandy's need to control her own destiny," Blume writes. "If you were the pilot," she said, "you wouldn't be afraid. What you really ought to do is take flying lessons."

The novel expresses the deep frustrations of a housewife who is hand-cuffed to a humdrum husband. In *Wifey*, Sandy and Norman Pressman have two kids and a boring sex life. They get it on once a week, on Satur-day nights, in their maid-tidied home in Plainfield, New Jersey. As lovers go, Norman is as predictable as they come: he climbs on top of Sandy, thrusts for "three to five minutes," washes up afterward, and falls asleep. Foreplay isn't really his thing. Sandy, who describes herself as "an ado-lescent at 32," finds herself desperate to try something, or someone, new. Before she strays, she resolves to single-handedly spice things up in the bedroom. She buys a "pictorial sexual encyclopedia" and studies up be-fore breaking out some new moves on Norman and getting on top of him. But Norman is resistant:

> *"What are you doing?"*
> *"Let's try it this way."*
> *"No, not with you on top."*
> *"It's a very common position, Norm . . ."*
> *"For dykes, for women's libbers who want to take over."*

Sandy gives up and they have quick, missionary sex, just how Norman likes it. She's left unsatisfied and a short time later, she's having her first tipsy extramarital experience with her brother-in-law, who also happens to be her gynecologist. It's pleasurable but ultimately disastrous, as is her next affair, with her best friend's impotent husband (Sandy doesn't feel quite as guilty about this one, as Lisbeth has an open marriage). She fan-tasizes about, and eventually reconnects with, her high school boyfriend Shep—the one she didn't marry because he failed to impress her mother. In bed, Shep is just as exciting as she remembers, but he won't leave his wife for her.

The language in the book really goes there. The good sex scenes read like sweaty romance novel fare, with Shep and his "silky mushroom" proving almost irresistible to Sandy. "I used to know that [sex scenes] were good if I turned myself on while I was writing them," Blume said at the *New Yorker* festival in October 2023.

And then there are the bad sexual encounters. When Lisbeth's husband loses his erection, he ends up weeping in her arms. Early on in the book, she gripes that Norman prefers lovemaking to be as bland and antiseptic as possible. "That's why I douche with vinegar . . . cunt vinaigrette . . . to make it more appetizing . . . you know, like browned chicken," she jokes.

Sandy's freewheeling summer comes to a screeching halt when she gets gonorrhea, without any idea who she caught it from. She has to tell Norman and then weather the consequences.

*Wifey* is a book about marriage and sexual fantasies, but it's also a story about breaking free from the stranglehold of childhood programming. Throughout the book, Sandy's inner monologue is mixed in with imagined commentary from her overbearing mom, Mona. Mona's voice represents the part of Sandy that married Norman instead of Shep. "I won't forbid you from seeing him, Sandy, but I want you to know how unhappy Daddy and I are about this," Mona scolded her about dating Shep when she was younger. "He's not the right kind of boy for you. He has no background. His mother scrubs floors. Did you know that?" She urges Sandy to reconsider "that nice boy who took you to the ball"—aka Norman Pressman. Sandy listens and thus, the frustrated housewife blames her mother for her unhappiness.

Mona is a widowed traditionalist. She's well-intentioned, but without even thinking about it, she's spent a lifetime indoctrinating her daughters into the old ways. Myra, the elder of her two girls, has grown up to embrace her wisdom. But Sandy—Sandy is at war with herself. Nearly every negative question she has regarding Norman and her lifestyle is countered by a broken-record answer from her inner Mona.

Marriage 101, by Mona: "Make his interests your interests. Make his friends, your friends. When he's in the mood, you're in the mood. Dress to please him. Cook to please him. What else matters? A happy husband is the answer to a happy life." As Sandy's dissatisfaction grows, her mother's voice in her head gets louder. "Was she wrong to want more out of life?" Sandy wonders about herself. "She wasn't sure. If he beat her, she could complain. If he drank, she could complain. If he ran around, she could complain. But Sandy had no *real* reason to complain . . . *Nobody loves a kvetch* [whiner], Mona had said. *Remember that, Sandy . . . especially not a man who's worked hard all day.*"

In rejecting Norman, Sandy has no choice but to reject her mother, too. "Is this what my life is all about?" she thinks to herself one afternoon. "Driving the kids to and from school and decorating our final house? Oh Mother, dammit! Why did you bring me up to think that *this* was what I wanted?"

Sandy's mother-in-law, Enid, is even worse. While Mona clearly loves her kids, Enid expresses nothing but resentment toward her two daughters-in-law. Norman's brother is married to a woman named Arlene, who Enid casually describes behind her back as Miss Piss. When Sandy goes against Enid's wishes and names her own daughter Jennifer, instead of Enid's choice of Sarah, Sandy gets her own nickname: Miss High and Mighty. "To me she'll always be Sarah, no matter what Miss High and Mighty calls her," Enid says of her new grandchild. Stubbornly, she stays true to her word. Years later, Jennifer is spending the summer at sleepaway camp and Enid still addresses her letters to Sarah Pressman, much to Jennifer's annoyance.

Enid is also the source of one of Sandy and Norman's biggest challenges—their house in Plainfield, New Jersey. The couple bought it from Enid after Norman's father died. But the neighborhood is becoming predominantly Black and now Norman wants to sell it before property values plummet. The problem is, Enid won't let them sell her former home to a Black family. She has her own made-up epithet for Black people, too—*ductla*—which she uses instead of the Yiddish slur *schvartza*, claiming her version is sneakier. Enid's unapologetic racism aligns Sandy and Norman, although they come at the issue from different directions—Sandy is bothered by the moral implications, while Norman's concerns are financial in nature.

The Pressmans' all-white social circle is almost universally racist, and Plainfield's demographic transition gives them all plenty of opportunities to out themselves. "They're still different no matter how hard you try to pretend they're not," a woman at the club says of the Black families who are moving into the area. She warns Sandy: "I'd get out while the going's good and move up to the Hills." In another conversation, Gordon, Sandy's brother-in-law, takes it even further. "The natives are restless everywhere. It's only a matter of time before it really hits here," he says over dinner in the city. "Remember the riots in Newark in '67? Plainfield is next. You better get out before it's too late."

Beyond what these characters say, there's never any indication that Plainfield is roiling with civil unrest. Blume uses racism as a shorthand for this wealthy community's small-mindedness. Norman's scheme to unload the house without upsetting Enid—sell to a Realtor, who will then turn around and sell it to a Black family—makes him look deceptive, and cowardly, in Sandy's eyes. As she and Norman are signing the house over to Four Corners Realty Company, the representative assures them they'll be covert about flipping the property. "Don't worry Mr. Pressman, we're known for our discretion at Four Corners," he says. "We'll bring our clients in after dark, on nights when you and the family are out."

"Is that even legal?" Sandy interrupts.

"Damn right it's legal!" Norman answers.

Despite their differences and Sandy's sexual escapades, the couple stays together in the end, with all the security and sameness that entails. Even with her wandering heart, Sandy is still her mother's daughter, with a lifetime of good-girl conditioning that she's never quite able to shake. After Shep ends their affair, Sandy faces the truth—she was destined for suburban ennui, no matter what. "Marriage to him would have meant a life very much like the one I lead with Norman," she thinks to herself about Shep. "Yes, a house in the suburbs, kids, car pools . . . Okay, so [sex] would have been better but after a while, even with him, it would probably have become routine."

Neither Isadora Wing in *Fear of Flying* nor Bettina Balser in *Diary of a Mad Housewife* end up leaving their husbands, either. Isadora, after getting batted around like a cat toy by Adrian, shows up contrite in Bennett's hotel room. Bettina experiences a marital miracle when Jonathan confesses he's been talking to an analyst and has come to see himself, and not her, as the root of their problems.

Like Sandy, these women can still imagine happy endings alongside their spouses. They want versions of what their mothers had—intact families, material comfort—but better. Isadora recounts an argument she once had with her mom, Jude, who dressed in attention-grabbing getups and compulsively redecorated their Upper West Side apartment. The teenage Isadora pined for a less eccentric female role model. But as an adult, Isadora realizes that Jude's flair for unusual fashion wasn't really the issue. "When I think of all the energy, all the misplaced artistic aggression which my mother channeled into her passion for odd clothes and new decorating schemes, I wish she had been a successful artist instead," Isadora says. She goes on: "There is nothing fiercer than a failed artist. The energy remains, but, having no outlet, it implodes in a great black fart of rage which smokes up all the inner windows of the soul."

This sense—that previous generations of women had been victims of "misplaced artistic aggression," victimizing their daughters in turn—was foundational to the feminist movement.

Gloria Steinem wrote about it in her famous essay "Ruth's Song (Because She Could Not Sing It)." Ruth was Steinem's mother, once a headstrong and ambitious young journalist who, through most of Gloria's childhood, was painfully agoraphobic and addicted to tranquilizers. Gloria took care of Ruth, and it was only as an adult that she began to wonder about her mom's sad transformation. "She had been a spirited, adventurous young woman who struggled out of a working-class family and into college, who found work she loved and continued to do, even after she was married and my older sister was there to be cared for," Steinem writes.

Ruth quit her newspaper job after a nervous breakdown, which Steinem attributes to the simultaneous pressures of working, parenting, supporting her husband's dream of opening a lakeside resort, and doing housework. Immediately, the scope of Ruth's life shriveled. "The family must have watched this energetic, fun-loving, book-loving woman turn into someone who was afraid to be alone, who could not hang on to reality long enough to hold a job, and who could rarely concentrate enough to read a book," Steinem writes.

Steinem says her mother succumbed not only to the tragedy of her stifled creativity, but to the cultural forces that kept her from doing anything to regain it. Divorce and poverty, both of which Ruth had lived through, held her back and shoved her down with shame. Ruth had no strong female role models to pull her back up. She had admired her mother-in-law, Gloria's grandmother, who had been a suffragist, but at home she still deferred to the men in the family, treating her husband and her boys like the entitled kings of the castle. Circumstances doomed Ruth, and everyone, not just Gloria, lost out. "The world still missed a unique person named Ruth," Steinem concludes. "Though she longed to live in New York and Europe, she became a woman who was afraid to take a bus across town."

Activists hoped that experiences like Ruth's would subside with the work of feminism. In her essay, Steinem suggests that asking the question at all—*what really happened to Ruth?*—is an important start. But such questioning also grooved lines between mothers and daughters. Judy's mother, Essie, for instance, wasn't thrilled at the way moms came off in many of Blume's novels.

"My mother used to say, 'I'm very proud of you, but please leave mothers out of your books, everyone thinks it's me,'" Blume said at the Arlington Public Library event.

Judy patiently told her that wasn't possible. "I tried to explain that there would always be mothers in my stories and that none of them were based on her," she wrote in a 2004 introduction to *Wifey*. That didn't help, either. "She said it didn't matter, that everyone would think she was Sandy Pressman's mother anyway."

But when it came to the sexual content of the novel, Blume said that her mother was less concerned. Essie typed out many of Judy's manuscripts over the years and never said zip about the graphic scenes. She had learned a line from her former high school classmate, who happened to be Philip Roth's mom, Bess. They ran into each other on the street one day and Bess Roth offered Essie the wisdom she'd acquired from being a parent to the author of *Portnoy's Complaint*: the Oedipal, psychosexual 1969 literary sensation.

"When they ask how she knows all those things," Bess supposedly told her old friend, "you say, 'I don't know, but not from me!'"

## Chapter Sixteen

# Divorce

*"I don't think we could have
survived two more years together."*

Even before it was published in the fall of 1978, *Wifey* caused drama. The racy novel wasn't the right fit for Bradbury, which only handled books for children, so it was coming out with the Putnam imprint, under the eye of legendary editor in chief Phyllis Grann. Meanwhile, publicists at Blume's paperback publisher, Dell, worried that Blume's first book for adults would scare off her legions of loyal young readers. The trick was to herald *Wifey* properly but also make it very clear that this specific work was not intended for Blume's typical audience.

Judy wasn't concerned about professional fallout. She was confident that kids would have the good sense to avoid *Wifey*, or at least put it down as soon as they scanned a page or two and realized the book wasn't written for them. She brushed off any suggestions that she should publish it under a pseudonym. However, she was a little bit anxious about the impact the novel might have on her personal life. Since the story concerned a troubled marriage, she showed the manuscript to John before it came out, inviting his feedback. She assured him, "If there's anything that really bothers you, I'll change it," as she told *Bust* in 1997.

He handled it "brilliantly," Blume said. "He didn't say anything. He stayed out of it. I think that was really very smart."

As *Wifey*'s publication date approached, the reviews started rolling in. Immediately, it was clear that the novel hit a nerve with the critics. *Library Journal* augured success, with a caveat: "Adult readers will enjoy this light romance as much as their kids love Blume's best-selling juvenile novels, though they may not remember it a week later."

The reviewer from the *LA Times* praised Blume's abilities—"Blume has the enviable gift of good timing . . . she shares the same sense of proportion whether she's dealing with pathos, slapstick, romance or reverie"—then veered to the philosophical in her assessment of *Wifey*'s moneyed cast of characters. "Blume forces us to ask if we can only examine our 'inner needs' when we have material well-being and leisure," the reviewer wrote. "Or do those two factors magnify, or alleviate, our discontent?"

The *New York Times* was flattering, including *Wifey* in an article covering the "widespread trend" of feminist novels. The paper called Blume's take "a bawdy account of a suburban wife's rebellion against her unsatisfying marriage," and put it on a continuum with previous groundbreaking books, including *Fear of Flying* and *The Bell Jar* by Sylvia Plath, which didn't come out in the US until 1971, nearly a decade after Plath's death. But another critic, this one at the *Washington Post*, saw *Wifey* as derivative rather than innovative. Reviewer Sue Isaacs suggested, in a culturally prescient takedown, that the novel in question might as well have been penned by artificial intelligence. "Just for fun, imagine a computer which became bored with chess and war games. After a heart-to-heart with its programmer, it arranged to be fed every novel ever written about a stifled wife since the 1960s. Its lights blinked as it was fed *Diary of a Mad Housewife* and *Fear of Flying* . . . Then, it whirred for a microsecond or two, composing its own work which included all the ingredients of the genre."

That same reviewer took issue with Sandy's preoccupation with sex, summoning an accusation that had followed Judy since *Forever*—that she was intentionally using saucy scenes to sell books. "Sandy is a woman on the prowl, searching for Deep Meaning," Isaacs wrote. "But since even a computer knows that profundity is less marketable than sexuality, Sandy Pressman's search is more genital than cerebral." Ouch!

In fact, even before *Wifey*, Judy had earned a new nickname in the press: "The Jacqueline Susann of Children's Literature." *Newsday* attributed it to a librarian in Garden City, New York, who was trying to make sense of Blume's unmatched popularity among young book borrowers. *People* magazine used the phrase as part of the headline for a splashy feature on Blume, illustrated with photos of the forty-year-old author posing in a lacy camisole. "I cringe, even today, thinking of that article," Blume wrote in 2004.

*People*'s story emphasized Blume's slender and youthful appearance— "At 5'4" and 100 pounds ('103 on a fat day'), wearing T-shirt and jeans, Judy is always mistaken for a daughter when she answers the door"—as well as her cozy life of "family skiing, Scrabble and horseplay." By then, *Wifey* was a hit, and she and Tom had moved from Los Alamos to nearby Santa Fe, which was considerably more cosmopolitan. There, Judy settled in a bit, embracing Southwestern style: she lined the adobo house with colorful Navajo rugs and started wearing chunky silver jewelry. Tom commuted to Los Alamos, which was just over thirty miles away.

The move had been an attempt to save the marriage, but it hadn't worked. Judy and Tom still weren't getting along. They tried putting on a happy face for the media, letting photographers into their home to snap pictures of them with Judy's kids and the family cat, a fluffy calico named Chanelle. "We have a very nice family life," Blume told the *Chicago Tribune* in 1978. "I think kids are happy at home if they are living with people who are nice to each other and things are friendly and calm."

The *People* writer tried to position Blume's second marriage as her personal triumph, but a trickle of its challenges spilled through. "There is a problem for Judy in mixing family life and the long commute back to New York where her work really is," Kitchens told the reporter, in a rare interview. "They have to be cut apart, or one encroaches. Either role is demanding: the public would love to consume her, and of course, the family would too. There will always be a conflict."

And the undertow of her career was getting even stronger. *Wifey* made the *New York Times* bestseller list; by November 1979, there were a reported three million copies of the paperback in print. Judy had liberated herself artistically and financially. Now if only she could free herself from being a wife.

▪   •   •

She was concerned about her reputation, and her mother. She was especially worried about how another divorce would affect her kids. She had hoped to hold out until Randy and Larry went off to college, so at least they'd no longer be living at home when it happened. But she couldn't do it. "After three-and-a-half very painful years my second husband and I finally divorced," Blume wrote in *Letters to Judy*. "We had made a terrible mistake . . . I don't think we could have survived two more years together. Finally, I made the decision to take control of my own life."

But taking control wasn't easy. Unlike with her first divorce, Judy knew exactly how another marital fissure would destabilize Randy and Larry. They'd never really bonded with Tom and vice versa, so for them, losing him wasn't such a big deal. However, moving again would be a huge disruption. Although she preferred New York and the kids spent their summers there with their father, she decided to stay in Santa Fe for the time being so they wouldn't have to switch schools yet again. Everything felt unmanageable and Judy's guilt, for putting her family in this situation, was like a boulder she carted around, day in and day out. "I think divorce is a tragedy, traumatic and horribly painful for everybody," she told the *Chicago Tribune* a few years later, in 1985.

That perspective made its way into *Just as Long as We're Together*, a middle grade novel that Blume published in 1987. It covers similar ground as *It's Not the End of the World*, but this time, the breakup is messier and it takes more than her friendships to get Stephanie Hirsch, the seventh grader at the heart of the story, to feel better about it. She and her younger brother, Bruce, both experience difficulties as a result of their parents' separation. Bruce, age ten, suffers from ever-worsening nightmares about nuclear war. Stephanie starts binge eating, which causes bullies in her class to dub her El Chunko. Her self-esteem takes a hit. One night, she looks at herself in the mirror after a bath. "My breasts were growing or else they were just fat. It was hard to tell," Stephanie observes. "Maybe if I lost weight, I'd lose them, too. My glutes were pretty disgusting. When I jumped up and down they shook. The hair down there, my pubic hair, was growing thicker. It was much darker than the hair on my head."

The one-two punch of family drama and puberty propels Stephanie into a surly depression. She's nasty to her father's new girlfriend, Iris. She gets into fights with her friends. She's angry with her parents for keeping her and Bruce in the dark about their relationship status. She's ready to know if they're breaking up—or not. "I hate not knowing what's going to happen!" Stephanie yells at her mom after finding out her dad is moving back from Los Angeles, leaving Iris behind and taking an apartment close by, in New York. "I'd almost rather know you're getting a divorce. I want it to be settled one way or the other so I can get used to the idea, so I can stop thinking about it."

*Just as Long as We're Together* suggests divorce is never tidy. At the end of the book, we still don't know what's going to happen between Stephanie's parents. Stephanie's own "breakup"—a nearly two-month-long, silent treatment standoff with her lifelong best friend, Rachel Robinson—gets resolved when the two of them finally swallow their pride and talk it out.

Bruce's nightmares stop, too, not because things with the adult Hirsches improve, but because he wins second place in a "Kids for Peace" poster contest and realizes he's not the only person his age sitting up at night scared about nuclear weapons. The metaphor is easy to decipher. Divorce sets off a bomb in a family. Kids need the comfort of other survivors.

•    •    •

No matter what was going on in her personal life, Judy could take solace in one thing: that as an author, she genuinely connected with children. Her young readers had begun writing her letters to tell her so. First, just a few arrived; then they came in by the hundreds. By the mid-1980s, when she published *Letters to Judy*, she was receiving almost two thousand fan letters a month, all carefully handwritten and filled with children's deepest secrets, questions, and confessions.

They wrote about everything from friendships, to puberty, to arguments with their teachers and parents. Some of them reached out with darker problems. Most of the kids who contacted Judy received a mailer in return, complete with a signed black-and-white headshot and some jovial family photos: Randy smiling while her mom eats an ice cream cone; a floppy-haired Larry posing with Judy in front of a bus. It came with a cheery note typed on the back. "I wish I could write to you individually but then I would never have time to write another book," the message said. "The letters I receive from young readers are very important to me and the highlight of my day is sitting down to read my mail. Because writing is such lonely work, and I am really a people person, your letters remind me that I'm not alone," it went on, before offering up some breezy biographical details.

In fact, Judy did write back personal notes to a handful of her young correspondents, particularly those who shared they were suicidal or victims of incest or other physical abuse. She maintained an epistolary relationship with some of these children for years on end, becoming something of a lifeline for them. *Letters to Judy* is a mixture of memoir and samples of all kinds of letters. "Could you sort of be a second mother to me and tell me the facts of life?" an eleven-year-old named Camille wrote her after sharing that she felt she couldn't ask her own mom. A fifteen-year-old named Alisa sent Judy a letter about her battles with alcohol abuse, obesity, and depression. "Besides family and doctors you are the only person I've ever told this to," Alisa admitted. "You seem to understand teenagers so much that I figure you'd understand my problems."

Judy had become a mother figure to an entire country's worth of children, which was ironic, because at home she was struggling to raise her own pair of angry, rebellious teenagers. Randy and Larry didn't have the luxury of seeing their mom as some magnanimous, all-knowing guru. "With her own children, Judy Blume concedes, she's less a heroine than she is with all those other people's kids who write to her," Joyce Maynard wrote in the *New York Times*. "It can't always be easy, having for your mother this national expert on the private, and often sexual, feelings of teen-agers," she continued, with Randy tersely confirming: "Sometimes Judy and I disagree."

The entire world, it seemed, needed Judy's advice, yet her own kids wouldn't come to her, though at times their unhappiness was obvious. "During a particularly rough time for our family my daughter, Randy, confessed to someone else that she wasn't telling me the truth about how she was feeling because she sensed that I only wanted to hear that everything was wonderful," Judy wrote in *Letters to Judy*. "Well, everything wasn't wonderful and Randy found a way to let me know—by acting out her feelings."

By the late 1970s, Judy was a twice-divorced single mother stuck in a Southwestern city so that her children could graduate high school. She was also one of the hottest authors of her generation. Everything wasn't wonderful, but some things were. And even Judy couldn't deny that after four decades of people-pleasing, she was finally letting go.

## Chapter Seventeen

# ꟻame

*"One day, there's going to
be Judy Blume tampons."*

On the night of Friday, January 6, 1978, Judy became TV-movie
famous.

The screen adaptation of *Forever* aired on CBS. Set in idyllic San
Francisco instead of the East Coast suburbs, the cinematic version otherwise hewed closely to the novel: high school seniors Katherine Danziger
and Michael Wagner meet at a party and spend the months leading up
to graduation falling head over heels in love. Katherine was played by
Stephanie Zimbalist, the twenty-one-year-old daughter of Efrem Zimbalist Jr., a sixties-era small-screen star who helmed the detective shows
*77 Sunset Strip* and *The FBI*. A then-unknown actor, a Bay Area native
named Dean Butler, played Michael.

Butler, at the time a handsome, blond twenty-one-year-old, wasn't familiar with Blume or her books when he got the script. But once *Forever*
was on his radar he picked up a copy of the novel. "The book struck me
as incredibly candid," he said. "I mean, one of the big deals in the book
was what Michael's name for his male anatomy was. I had never seen

anything like that at twenty-one." He approved of the sequence where Katherine went to get a prescription for birth control. "My mother was on the board of directors of Planned Parenthood in the Bay Area. So I was completely in sync with that idea."

He and Zimbalist "felt safe with each other," Butler said, which was important because the script featured its fair share of love scenes. Unlike Blume's book, the movie was cautious around its presentation of teen sex and sparing in its language—this was for national television, after all. Butler and Zimbalist's Michael and Katherine engage in breathy, dimly lit, horizontal makeout sessions and exchange snippets of just-vague-enough dialogue.

"Oh come on," Michael says in an early sequence.

Katherine shakes her head no.

"Why not?" he goes on.

"Not yet," she answers.

Just like in Blume's book, Michael and Katherine are "good" kids: they're both college-bound and culturally fluent, bonding over Thoreau and Virginia Woolf. Their dates are sweet and age appropriate: dusky walks on the beach and goofing around with épées at a Renaissance Fair. Butler said the casting had a lot to do with how the young lovers come across on screen. Zimbalist—a lithe and wholesomely pretty brunette with thick, waist-long hair—"radiates a person with a good head on her shoulders," Butler explained. "And so, this wasn't some hot young teenager looking to go out and score. Stephanie's Katherine was in love and she wanted to do the right thing."

Butler said the set of *Forever* was comfortable with the exception of one awkward moment around the night Katherine loses her virginity to Michael. The castmates were shooting in a hot tub, with Zimbalist wearing a nude bandeau so that it looked like she was naked under the water. The music cue was "Right Time of the Night" by Jennifer Warnes—then a hit song with the lyrics *It's the right time of the night / For making love*—"So you sort of know what's going to happen there," Butler said. But Butler recalled that one producer suggested shooting "an alternate version" of the scene for potential release in Europe, where Zimbalist would be topless (Blume was not involved in the making of the film and was not on set). Despite the pressure of being a young woman surrounded by a crew full of men, Zimbalist refused, Butler said. "She was resolute about that," he remembered. "That's the only time that I really recall that there was a moment where this could have gone beyond what was going to be acceptable for television."

The final cut was prime time–friendly, with Katherine's eventual sexual awakening communicated in subtle, clever ways. On prom night, she surprises Michael by slipping off her dress and climbing under the sheets with a red flower, which she had been wearing in her hair, brandished in her mouth. The tone of the scene is silly, loving. Yes, the couple still breaks up in the end, but Butler's Michael handles it better than Blume's original character. Their final encounter in town, before they both head off for college, is more positive than awkward. The movie makes it clear that they've both learned something important from the experience.

Just like in the book, Katherine is surrounded by strong female role models. Her mother, played by Judy Brock, doesn't flinch when Katherine starts asking her questions about sex. However, in a later scene, she's firm about the fact that she doesn't approve of her daughter adjusting her college plans to stay closer to Michael. "I see a bright young girl with a full life ahead of her," she explains patiently. "And she's rearranging it to follow a man around."

Katherine's grandmother, played by Romanian actress Erika Chambliss, ultimately supplies the film's intended takeaway in a scene between her and Katherine, in which Katherine expresses regret about the breakup. "You didn't ruin anything," her grandmother reassures her. "You found out something about yourself. About men. About life. Think how much more you'll know the next time. You'll be a woman of the world."

In the language of the movie, a woman of the world isn't a literal traveler. She's taking in the landscape—as Katherine and her grandmother are at that moment—with kind and intelligent eyes, sharpened by her experiences. She's open to love, but responsible with her heart and her body. She's strong enough to walk herself into Planned Parenthood, but still soft with the people she keeps closest to her.

Judy loved the adaptation—of course she did! She got to see her progressive ideas about young men and women pumped out into people's living rooms by way of the small screen. Unlike the literary Michael, the movie's male protagonist ultimately forgives Katherine for breaking up with him, proving that he was worthy of her all along. And Butler said he enjoyed every minute of filming it. The movie didn't change his life but it opened doors in the industry, and he nabbed a starring role on *Little House on the Prairie* less than a year later. He said no one stopped him on the street after *Forever* premiered, but his dad's reaction to seeing it was particularly memorable.

"I remember my father looking at me afterwards and saying, 'Boy, I wish I had your job,'" he said.

•   •   •

When it came to pop culture in 1978, there was very little that felt off-limits. That year the film *Pretty Baby*, which serves up a doe-eyed eleven-year-old Brooke Shields as a child prostitute on an actual platter, landed in theaters. The same spring, audiences flocked to see Paul Mazursky's *An Unmarried Woman*, where a newly divorced woman named Erica, played by Jill Clayburgh, discovers her inner strength through a series of sexual and romantic affairs. National Lampoon's manic, raunchy campus comedy *Animal House* commanded rave reviews from serious critics including Roger Ebert and Frank Rich. Disco—glittering, sticky, breathless, gender-bending—was having an honest-to-God *moment* all over the country.

Quickly, Judy's face and name got aligned with this version of America, where sexuality came out of hiding to stay. But outside of movie theaters and nightclubs and beyond magazine covers, a new conservative movement was bubbling. Phyllis Schlafly, a Missouri-based mother of six and attention-grabbing anti-feminist activist, had already founded the Eagle Forum, a political interest group that promoted "traditional" family values. Prominent Baptist minister Jerry Falwell Sr. had been traveling the country for years promoting his fundamentalist vision of Christianity, which was anti-abortion, anti-gay, and anti-premarital sex. And in California, a charismatic former actor turned politician had made a name for himself on a national stage as a popular governor. Ronald Reagan helmed the Golden State for two terms, from 1967 to 1975. In that time, he reneged on his campaign promise to cut taxes—the state still had a deep bench of Democratic elected officials in place—but made it known that he wished to slash spending on public education and welfare. Reagan also made a number of new appointments to the state board of education, resulting in a bid to downplay the teaching of evolution in schools, requiring that Darwinism was always described in the classroom as a theory, not a fact, and that the religiously inflected idea of Creationism was given equal credibility.

Blume, still living in Santa Fe, wasn't terribly burdened by any of this. The burgeoning Religious Right still seemed fringe, nothing that she and her friends would have to take very seriously. Instead, she was working on an emotional new young adult novel, which she'd been calling "After the Sunset." It was about a fifteen-year-old girl living in Atlantic City when her beloved father is shot to death in a robbery at his 7-Eleven. A mourning Davis "Davey" Wexler then moves with her mother and younger brother to Los Alamos, New Mexico, where her aunt and uncle live. The book eventually got renamed *Tiger Eyes*.

Judy was also writing *Superfudge*, the long-awaited sequel to *Tales of a Fourth Grade Nothing*. In 1972, she'd published *Otherwise Known as Sheila the Great*, but that was more of a spin-off, centering on Peter's neighbor and often classroom rival Sheila Tubman. The book was well received but it didn't satisfy the hunger for a new story about the brothers Hatcher. Over the years, she had reached for another Fudge-focused storyline, but nothing persuaded her to sit down at her typewriter.

Suddenly, it hit her one day in the shower: the Hatchers should have another baby! And they'd leave the city for a while, testing out suburban life by renting a house in Princeton. *Superfudge* is even sillier than *Tales*, and introduces another zany animal plot when Fudge gets a French-speaking mynah bird named Uncle Feather. The bird's side-splitting, kid-pleasing catchphrase is "Bonjour, stupid!" Of course, he has a knack for saying it at inappropriate times. "I love to make kids laugh, and I laugh a lot myself when I'm writing," Blume told *Newsday* in 1980. "And so I'd be sitting there typing away [at *Superfudge*] and laughing my head off."

Fudge was already so popular with young readers that Blume received a reported $500,000 advance for *Superfudge* (over $2 million in today's dollars). By then, Judy Blume wasn't just a writer, a woman, a mom, she was a hot commodity: *JudyBlume*. Her name alone, spoken all in one quick exhalation, made children bounce up and down with excitement. And would-be entrepreneurs outside of the publishing world had caught on.

They wanted her to slap her name—*THE JudyBlume!*—on all sorts of products, from T-shirts to training bras. A rep for Jordache jeans got in touch about developing a range of Blume-themed denim (Judy gave them a vehement no). She was particularly annoyed by the board game someone pitched her called Growing Up with Judy Blume. "I am NOT a product," she insisted to the *Boston Globe* in 1981. "You wouldn't believe the tacky stuff I've been asked to endorse—like a Judy Blume board game with cards that read 'Your parents get divorced—move back six spaces' and 'You get your period—move ahead eight spaces.'"

Larry liked to tease her about it. "One day, there's going to be Judy Blume tampons," he told her.

She did lend her name to *The Judy Blume Diary*, which Dell put out in 1981. The rainbow hardcover featured quotes from her books, artsy black-and-white snaps of real children taken by young aspiring photographers, and plenty of room for writing. Judy pledged the royalties from the diary, which cost $6.95, to the KIDS Fund: her own newly established charity devoted to encouraging better communication between kids and their parents.

It's no wonder that people wanted to cash in on Judy's name—she was a legitimate publishing phenomenon.

In December of 1980, six of her books topped the bestsellers list at B. Dalton, then one of the country's largest book retailers with over seven hundred stores, most of them in shopping malls (in a nod to the store's premillennial ubiquity, a B. Dalton storefront shows up in the background of Kevin Smith's 1995 *Mallrats*). *Tales of a Fourth Grade Nothing, Otherwise Known as Sheila the Great, Blubber, Are You There God?, Iggie's House,* and *Freckle Juice* dominated the top ten, with *Then Again, Maybe I Won't* coming in at number thirteen. Young readers couldn't get enough of Judy's books.

She was everywhere, suddenly representing something much bigger than herself. For children, left-leaning parents, and educators, *Judy-Blume* signaled honesty and freedom. But for a growing contingent of conservatives, Blume's brand stunk of the rot at the heart of the culture.

America's favorite children's book author wasn't prepared for what came next.

## Chapter Eighteen

# ⸙Gatekeepers

*"Perhaps the best thing to do with
Ms. Blume would be to ignore her altogether."*

Here's what Judy knew going into her protracted public shaming: the literary establishment hadn't embraced her. Reporters were downright snide about her popularity, with the *Washington Post* describing her books in 1981 as "a scatological and soft-porn *cinema verité* of childhood, of puberty, of growing up." In the same article, she maintained that these kinds of criticisms didn't bother her all that much. "What is literature?" Blume asked her interviewer. "I don't care what they say as long as the kids are reading it, and as long as they're identifying, or in some way emotionally involved."

Then, she stopped herself. "Well, I *do* care," she admitted. "I care, but that's not what's most important . . . I don't get as angry about any of it as I used to. I'm 'mellowing out' as my kids say."

She had come to expect certain kinds of dismissive reviews, like the one *School Library Journal* gave *Forever*, where it negatively remarked on the novel's "quality." In 1980, the *Hartford Courant* echoed this sentiment in an article about Blume, asserting that she "may never win any prizes for literary quality."

The *Horn Book*, a go-to resource for school librarians, had also never been impressed with her writing. But Dick Jackson assured Judy that delighting young readers was far more important than winning over judgmental grown-up gatekeepers. They were in it together, Peter Silsbee recalled. "He really hated stuffy children's books," Silsbee said of Jackson. The *Horn Book*, he continued, "had very high ideals of what children should read. And so he was always sort of thinking, that's what I don't want to do. I don't want to write books for teachers, I don't want to write them for adults, I want to write them for the audience they're intended for."

But Jackson and Blume must have been surprised when the *Horn Book* came out with a nonfiction collection by the British young adult author David Rees, called *The Marble in the Water: Essays on Contemporary Writers of Fiction for Children and Young Adults*. Published in January 1980, the book contained an article called "Not Even for a One-Night Stand: Judy Blume." From the very first paragraph, Rees, who taught English Lit classes at the prestigious boarding school Exeter, sets the tone of his assessment. "Perhaps the best thing to do with Ms. Blume would be to ignore her altogether," he writes. "She is so amazingly trivial and second-rate in every department—the quality of her English, her ability to portray character, to unfold narrative—but that is impossible; she is 'controversial' on both sides of the Atlantic and her work is read and discussed not only by the young but by those adults who have serious concerns about children's literature."

What follows is a scathing assessment of Blume's body of work that arguably crosses the line to mean-spirited. Rees was punching up—Blume was more famous than he was, although he'd won awards in the UK for his novels—but nevertheless, his takedown goes so far as to suggest that the cadence of her prose is equivalent to that of a "shopping list ... entirely forgettable, drab, flat." He calls *Are You There God?* a "very bad book . . . a bore and an embarrassment, a complete waste of one's time." Fudge, according to Rees, is "wretched . . . a character the author clearly finds very appealing but who comes over to the reader as extremely tiresome."

Rees saves his harshest words for *Forever*, a novel he simultaneously disregards as unintentionally humorous while also getting charged up about its contents. Michael and Katherine's love story, complete with fumbling sex scenes, is absurd, he says: "The reader's reaction is laughter—anything from an embarrassed snigger to falling out of a chair with hilarity—when he ought to be moved or excited or enthralled." Rees goes on to recommend reading the "excruciating" pages "aloud to family or friends so that they can all join in the fun."

But the book, he explains, isn't just goofy—it's offensive to its intended audience. Over and over again Rees makes the point that Blume's coming-of-age plots are reductive and lacking in perspective and nuance. Blume is "doing the youth a great disservice," Rees writes, by suggesting that "falling in love is not a matter of complex emotions . . . but that it is simply a question of should one go on the pill or not, swapping partners quite heartlessly, and whether one is doing it right in bed." He goes on: "To serve them up the kind of stuff of which *Forever* consists is to underestimate totally their ability to think and to feel, not only about themselves but about the whole complexity of living that goes on around them."

Blume's oeuvre, he concludes—in language so decisive and spicy that it would likely go viral in today's literary landscape—is nothing short of an insult to the craft. "Judy Blume's novels are the ultimate in the read-it-and-throw-it-away kind of book," he announces halfway through the article. "In other words, they are not only short-changing the young; they are short-changing literature." Damn, David!

Reading the Rees essay now, a note of sexism stands out among the piece's more aggressive flavors. He takes issue with Blume's preferred topics, which also happen to be things that pertain to young girls. "What sort of picture would a being from another planet form of teenage and pre-teenage America were he to read 'Are You There God? It's Me, Margaret' and 'Forever'?" Rees asks. "He would imagine that youth was obsessed with bras, period pains, deodorants, orgasms, and family planning; that life was a great race to see who was first to get laid or to use a Tampax; that childhood and adolescence were unpleasant obstacles on the road to adulthood." Rees sounds a bit like the alien being himself here, as if he's never in his life interacted meaningfully with a female middle schooler.

But according to Roger Sutton, former editor in chief of the *Horn Book* (though not at the time *Marble in the Water* came out), Rees was simply representing the publication's point of view on most commercial children's fiction at the time. "In children's books, since they became a thing at the beginning of the twentieth century as a separate market of book publishing, there's always been this battle between what kids want to read and what an adult thinks is good," Sutton explained. "Always. And David Rees was expressing what at the time was a real *Horn Book* point of view, which is [that] high literary quality trumps everything. That's what matters."

Blume, he went on, is "not literary," thanks to a mixture of her preferred subject matter, the simplicity of her prose, her use of casual dialogue, and her avoidance of highly textured descriptions. ("I absolutely can't write descriptive prose," Blume acknowledged to Samantha Bee in 2015. "I can do characters and relationships and dialogue, but don't make me describe anything.") There was a sense in the late 1970s that when it came to books, giving children what they wanted to read was akin to feeding them soda and french fries—empty calories, lacking in real nutrients. But what if kids gravitated toward Blume's books because they contained unexpectedly nourishing ingredients that couldn't be found elsewhere?

"Dick, he once said to me, 'We're writing sugar-coated bitter pills,'" Silsbee remembered. "Judy's books—I don't think of them as bitter, but I think of them as sometimes teaching hard lessons that nobody will talk to you about, like [about] God." The sweetness, the girlishness—Blume's novels aren't worthwhile *in spite of* these attributes, but there's no doubt that these attributes tended to distract from their worth.

•    •    •

Then the bans started, first with a trickle.

In the mid to late 1970s, the public conflict about children's books started to shift from what kids should be reading to what they should be allowed to read at all. There's a difference. The first is a debate about the benefits (if any) of spending time with certain novels, while the latter concerns access.

In 1976 in Levittown, Long Island, the conflict came to a head when the school board voted to remove eleven books—including *Slaughterhouse-Five* by Kurt Vonnegut Jr., the anonymous drug diary *Go Ask Alice*, *The Fixer* by Bernard Malamud, *Black Boy* by Richard Wright, and *The Best Short Stories by Negro Writers*, a collection edited by Langston Hughes—from the school district's library shelves. At the time, five high school students pushed back and ultimately brought the board to court with the help of the ACLU (American Civil Liberties Union). The case was headed up by a then-seventeen-year-old high school senior named Steven Pico, who argued that the decision to remove the books violated young readers' First Amendment rights.

The publicly elected school board in the all-white district of Island Trees had determined that the offending titles were "anti-American, anti-Christian, anti-Semitic and just plain filthy," according to a press release quoted in the *New York Times*. But Pico, as the president of the student council, disagreed. He felt that the challenges were targeted, unjustly pointed toward minority voices. "Two of the authors banned in

Island Trees were among the most important Jewish-American writers, Bernard Malamud and Kurt Vonnegut," he said over email. "Half of the books banned in Island Trees were written by and about Black writers, among them two who were Black and gay: James Baldwin and Langston Hughes."

As Pico told CNN in 2022, the board was acting unilaterally, without wider community input. Right before the controversial books were un-shelved from all four high school libraries in the district, Pico said that board members had traveled upstate to attend a conference hosted by the conservative group Parents of New York United. The list of "objec-tionable" titles came directly from there. "They [the members] did not read the books in their entirety," Pico explained. "They used a handful of excerpts, a handful of words, a handful of vulgarities to make these books look bad."

Pico, who was lead plaintiff, was deeply invested in the case, but aside from his four co-plaintiffs, his peers weren't nearly as moved by the issue. The vast majority of his classmates were more concerned about getting into college than they were in taking up the anti-censorship mantle. Even his own family "had a lot of doubts," he told CNN. "They were not particularly supportive of the lawsuit because they thought it was per-ceived as troublemaking and that I might not get into college."

But Pico felt like the suit was a calling. He did, in fact, get accepted to Haverford College. And over the next few years, he appeared on Phil Donahue's show and spoke on panels with Vonnegut and Alice Childress, whose 1973 novel *A Hero Ain't Nothin' but a Sandwich*, about a thirteen-year-old getting hooked on heroin, was also being challenged. Initially, a federal district court ruled in favor of the board's prerogative to remove books on moral or political grounds. Then, the US Court of Appeals for the Second Circuit reversed that decision. The issue went all the way up to the Supreme Court in the early 1980s, with Pico shoring up continued legal support from the New York chapter of the ACLU. In June 1982, the

Supreme Court ruled for Pico, with the 5-4 majority arguing that elected school boards do not have the authority to remove books from circulation simply because they dislike them.

After that, Long Island officials bickered about how exactly to reinstate the titles; board members tried out a system where the books in question were returned to the libraries but stamped with red ink that said "Parental notification required." The New York attorney general disagreed with that practice, too, stating that it violated protections around the confidentiality of library records. In the meantime, Pico graduated and took a job in New York with the National Coalition Against Censorship, which was founded in 1974.

Ultimately, in January 1983, the school board relented and voted to return the books to shelves without restrictions. But they weren't happy about it. "Until the day I die, I refuse to budge on my position," board member Christina Fasulo told the *New York Times*, representing the minority opinion in the proceedings. "Since when is it demeaning to take filth off library shelves?"

•    •    •

The Island Trees school board didn't go after Judy Blume's books, but around the same time, in Loveland, Colorado, her novels caught the attention of another group of motivated conservative parents. In the fall of 1980, Karen Fleshman was a sixth grader at Mary Blair Elementary School when she heard the news that her favorite author had sparked concern among community members and was at risk of being purged from the school library.

Fleshman, then an eleven-year-old "voracious reader" with glasses, braces, and a short feathered blond haircut, was furious at the thought that kids like her were going to be denied the chance to read her best-loved Blume books, including *Are You There God? It's Me, Margaret* and *Starring Sally J. Freedman as Herself.* She came home one day and vented about it to her father, Roger. "He was a real nonconformist and he was someone who believed in standing up for yourself," said Fleshman, who was fifty-three and living in San Francisco at the time we spoke. "So when I told him all of this, he was like, 'Why don't you do something about it?'"

Fleshman took his advice, explaining that Blume's novels were so important to her because they "really gave me a sense of community, gave me a sense of identity and permission to just be who I am." She felt out of place in homogeneous Loveland, which had a history as a Sundown town, meaning it used discriminatory practices to maintain an all-white population. "By the time I'm growing up, it's a big hotbed of the John Birch Society. And like literally, everyone is blond and blue-eyed and everyone goes to Church on Sunday . . . [and is] super into football. It's that kind of place."

What it wasn't was the kind of place that supported kids reading stories about puberty and masturbation. And so Fleshman went to the children themselves, asking them to sign a petition to present at an upcoming board of education meeting. Unlike Pico's classmates, Fleshman's peers eagerly rallied around her cause. "I'm talking to everyone," Fleshman remembered. "I'm talking to the first graders." Ultimately, she collected signatures from ninety-three students and one adult.

Then came the meeting of the local board of ed, where Fleshman pleaded her case. To her shock, the board voted unanimously to keep Blume's books in the elementary school library, persuaded by Fleshman's advocacy and some additional pressure from the local independent bookstore, The Open Book. After Fleshman's campaign was successful, the store's owners wrote letters to the governor of Colorado and to Judy Blume herself, telling them what Karen had done. Fleshman received a letter of appreciation from the governor and—far more memorably—a thank-you note and a signed copy of *Sally J. Freedman* from Judy Blume. On the inside cover, Blume wrote: "For Karen, a brave young woman and a real friend."

"Oh my God, I just couldn't believe it," Fleshman said about seeing the inscription. All these years later, she's an anti-racist activist who has a background working with immigrants and preparing young men and women of color for corporate careers. She said her work in social justice all started in October 1980, when the board of ed sided with her. "This was my formative activist experience," she said. If it hadn't worked out, she confessed, it would have been "crushing." But instead, the experience was positive, with her being celebrated and featured in the local newspaper. As Fleshman put it, "It really gave me confidence the rest of my life."

## Chapter Nineteen

# Allies

*"Democracy is exhausting."*

Pico and Fleshman were successful, but the storm was still coming. By the spring of 1980, book challenges were prevalent enough that another popular children's book author, Betty Miles, used them as a starting point for a young adult novel. In *Maudie and Me and the Dirty Book*, eleven-year-old Kate Harris finds herself at the center of a town-wide controversy when she signs up for a new program to read aloud to the students in a first-grade classroom. After meeting one of the boys and hearing him rave about his new pet puppy, Kate carefully chooses a picture book that she hopes will appeal to her pint-sized listeners.

*The Birthday Dog*—a story that Miles invented—is about a little boy named Benjamin who wants a puppy for his birthday. The neighbor's dog Blackie is pregnant. Just when Blackie is about to give birth, the neighbor calls over Benjamin and his father to watch. Benjamin gets to pick out a puppy from her litter and names it Happy, for making his birthday wish come true.

The kids love the book, just as Kate anticipated. They're particularly excited by the page, and the picture, where Blackie starts popping out her pups. "Just then, Blackie gave a little moan, and her stomach began to ripple," Kate reads to her rapt audience. "A small, wet shape began to come out of Blackie . . . She pushed hard again, until all of it was out."

After the story is finished, the kids are bursting with questions. "How did the puppy get in there . . . inside his mommy," one child asks Kate, who nervously eyes the teacher to see how she should answer. When the teacher gives her an encouraging nod, she carefully begins to explain things. "Before the puppy begins, the father dog and the mother dog mate," Kate says. "And this little tiny thing called a sperm goes into the mother—"

"Into her *vagina!*" another child shouts, before the kids erupt with chatter about their body parts.

At the end of their allotted time together, Kate leaves the classroom feeling sheepish but proud of how she handled herself. The teacher, Mrs. Dwyer, reassures her. "Kids this age can be embarrassingly frank! But I don't want them to think there's anything wrong with their natural curiosity."

Kate continues on with her week, unaware that she's just set off a firestorm. The following Monday, she's called into the principal's office to discuss the incident. Her principal tells her that the elementary school received a number of calls from concerned parents, saying that they were unhappy with the topic of dogs mating being brought up with their children. A community-wide standoff ensues. Parents flock to the local library, trying to take out *The Birthday Dog*. Kate learns that one mother confronted the librarian, telling her that "it was a crime to spend public funds on smut like that!"

Kate finds it funny, at first. After all, the title in question is just a picture book about a little boy who wants a new pet. But the angry faction won't back down. They write letters to the editor of the local newspaper, slamming a world where "innocent sixth-grade children [are] being required to describe reproduction." They camp out in front of the grocery store and urge townspeople to join their new coalition, called Parents United for Decency. "You've probably heard," the ringleader tells Kate's mother, unaware of her connection to the incident, "that only last week the little first-grade children at Concord School were subjected to a book that displayed a birth scene in explicit detail."

Maudie, who is Kate's friend and co-volunteer in the first-grade classroom, convinces Kate to stand up for herself at an upcoming school board meeting. "I'm Kate Harris," she announces in front of the board and a packed audience. "I'm the one who read that book to the kids at Concord. I'm not ashamed of it," she goes on. "I think everyone in this room should read the whole thing before they criticize it . . . it's not dirty . . . It's educational!"

Kate's speech sways the tide of the meeting. The board votes unanimously to allow the reading project to continue, and the Parents United for Decency group eventually dissolves. "*Democracy* is exhausting," Kate determines after she gets home from the meeting. Still, it's well worth it, the novel implies.

*Maudie and Me and the Dirty Book* isn't the subtlest story, but it speaks directly to young readers about an issue that was becoming more and more prevalent in the early 1980s. In publishing it, Miles was fighting back.

•    •    •

Betty Miles—who also had a hit book about friendship and divorce called *The Trouble with Thirteen*—and Blume had a good pal in common: the novelist Norma Klein. "Norma Klein was my first writer friend," Blume told Terry Gross in an interview on *Fresh Air* in 2023. "And the two of us were banned together. Always. Norma and Judy, Norma and Judy." Early after the inception of Banned Books Week by the American Library Association in 1982, their headshots both appeared on a poster with black lines covering their mouths. The other silenced authors? Maya Angelou, Aleksandr Solzhenitsyn, and William Shakespeare, among other greats.

Klein was a New York native who grew up in Manhattan and never learned to drive. Her parents had been communist activists when they were younger and her father worked as a Freudian psychoanalyst. When Judy lived across the bridge in New Jersey, she and Norma would meet for long lunches. After Judy moved out west to New Mexico, they maintained their relationship via long, intimate letters.

A reserved brunette, Klein got her start publishing short stories in the 1960s, before she penned two successful books for children: *Mom, the Wolf Man and Me*, a YA novel, and *Girls Can Be Anything*, a picture book for younger readers. *Wolf Man*, which came out in 1972, is about Brett Levin, an adolescent girl growing up with an artistic single mother, who takes Brett to protests and lectures her about feminism. In an amusing role reversal, Brett wishes her mom was more conventional and sets her up on dates, hoping she'll settle down and get married.

*Girls Can Be Anything* has a more obvious agenda. In the 1973 book, two children named Marina and Adam bicker about the roles they get to inhabit in their games of pretend. Adam bosses Marina around, telling her that because he's a boy and she's a girl, *he* gets to be the doctor while she has to be the nurse. He's the pilot, she's the stewardess, according to Adam. He's the president and she's first lady.

In between their playdates, Marina tells her parents about Adam's demands and they assure her that he's wrong. "Well, that's just plain silly!" her father says when Marina shares that Adam told her women can't be doctors. "Why, your Aunt Rosa is a doctor. You know that." Bolstered by her family, Marina bravely stands up to Adam. "Adam, you know, *you* can be a pilot or a doctor . . . I'm going to be the first woman President!"

Adam is skeptical. "It seems like according to you girls can be anything they want," he says.

"Well, that's just the way it is now," Marina answers before they work it out, each giving their presidential talks and celebrating with a dinner of potato chips, lollipops, and marshmallows.

Klein, who died in 1989 at the age of fifty, dedicated the book to her daughter. "To Jenny," it reads, "who, when she grows up, would like to be a painter, join the circus, and work at Baskin-Robbins, making ice cream cones."

Jenny is Jennifer Fleissner—not an acrobat or an ice cream vendor but today a gender studies professor at Indiana University Bloomington. Fleissner said that like Judy, her mother didn't set out to be shocking with anything she wrote. "She was a very strong feminist," said Fleissner, who is the older of Klein's two daughters. "I think she would have said that the primary thing she was interested in writing about was writing honestly about sexuality and trying to do so in a way that was not shaming."

In her 1976 novel *Hiding*, Klein does just that. The novel is about an eccentric aspiring ballet dancer named Krii, who is struggling with how she wants to be a woman in the world. At eighteen, she moves to London ostensibly to attend a dance academy, but also to get away from her unusual family. Her mother and father are still together but live apart on separate continents, tethered by their children and what sounds like an open marriage. Her older sister lives on a commune and keeps popping out babies. "Here is Mother with her Planned Parenthood meetings. And there is Paula with the six kids . . . living in the kind of cheerful squalor I had only read about in books," Krii says. She describes herself as "the silent, clinging, frightened one. I always knew, from the time that I had any thoughts on the subject, that I would never marry and never have children."

Yet Krii's offbeat, enigmatic vibe proves irresistible to Jonathan, a handsome redheaded choreographer. She loses her virginity to him soon after they start dating—she's not burning with desire for him exactly, but she's definitely curious about sex. She's also aware she has anxiety about intercourse and wants to get past it. "I was afraid of the potential for failure and humiliation," she tells the reader. "At least with masturbation you can't disappoint anyone."

She gives her body to Jonathan and then is miffed when it seems as if he wants access to her inner life, too. "Where are you when we make love?" he asks her one morning. Krii is offended. "What am I guilty of? It's true I don't shriek out four-letter words when I come. I probably move tentatively and slowly. I don't have to be wiped off the ceiling afterward." Despite Jonathan's attempts to crack her open, Krii won't— or can't—climb out of her shell. They break up and Jonathan quickly marries her outgoing classmate, seemingly on a whim. Krii is hurt but she has trouble expressing that, too. "People say: Take off your mask," Krii explains. "But beneath that mask is another mask and beneath that another. They want to think it can be done by one simple gesture of abandon, but I'm afraid that in my case that won't work."

*Hiding* isn't an upbeat novel, but it is truthful. The ending implies that Krii is making peace with her mother and father and might let herself open up after all.

"I think she wanted to take the pleasure of girls seriously," Fleissner said of Klein. "I think she also just felt that usually the exploration of sex by young people was a kind of fumbling, awkward, complicated scenario and just wanted to show it to people, warts and all, as just sort of a part of human life."

Klein explained that mission in a 1977 article called "Growing Up Human: The Case for Sexuality in Children's Books." Published in the journal *Children's Literature in Education*, the first-person essay argues against the popular belief that kids are not ready to read about certain topics, such as sex. Klein begins by sharing that in her personal life, she's as conventional as they come. Married to Erwin Fleissner, a biologist and cancer researcher, and living on the Upper West Side, she writes that she "sometimes fear[s] that my husband and I will be hauled off to the Museum of Natural History to be put on display as one of the last examples of the happily monogamous middle class couple." She goes on to say that, nevertheless, she's drawn to stories about nontraditional families: "the kinds of complex family situations that exist now and that perhaps did not exist in quite the same way ten or thirty years ago."

Unlike these nontraditional setups—same-sex parents, for instance, or mothers and fathers with openly open marriages—sexuality is not new. Sex, she argues, is a core part of the human experience, but has been lumped into the crowded category of topics that adults prefer to hide from their children, probably because mothers and fathers don't feel comfortable talking about them. She says she's happy that books have started doing the work of promoting these conversations, and the criticism that authors are exposing young readers to unnecessarily difficult subject matter is nothing short of naive.

"Some of the things we are writing about today are being written about in children's books for the first time. Therefore I think we sometimes make the mistake of thinking these things didn't happen before," Klein writes. "In fact, for decades, even centuries, people have been getting divorced, men and women have been realizing that heterosexuality may not be suitable for them, little children and babies have been lying in their cribs exploring their bodies, girls have been getting their periods, boys have been having wet dreams."

Klein then writes that she's compelled to offer an alternative to what she calls the "and so she turned to" books—stories in which kids turn to sexual expression as a way of coping with unpleasant stuff that's going on at home. "All of these books are setting up what to me is a false and even dangerous premise, namely that sexual activity of any kind is only something children 'turn to' as a result of a negative experience." She echoes Blume's point that she hopes to see more novels where teenagers experiment with sex and don't lose their way because of it. And not just that; "I would like, most of all, books about young girls discovering, not in the 'will I get invited to the junior prom?' sense, what it is to be young and female in this new and sometimes bewildering age of ours."

Klein and Blume were clearly in lockstep, exchanging ideas as they spent time together; Jennifer Fleissner remembers Judy coming by their apartment back when she was a teenager and playing an REM song for her mother's famous writer friend. In 1979, when Judy was still living in Santa Fe, Klein wrote her a long letter in which she confessed, good-naturedly, that she was terribly jealous of *Forever* because she thought it was terrific, and also because she had wanted to be the first author to write so frankly about teen sex. In the same letter, she admitted that she hadn't liked *Wifey* and thought Judy had shortchanged Sandy by having her stay with Norman. Fleissner laughed at this and concurred that yes, her mother could be blunt. "It's funny, she could be very shy with people that she didn't know. She was definitely not shy in print. I would say she was not at all shy with people she was close to," she said.

If Klein—who published over thirty novels during the course of her career—felt any friendly competition with Judy, it likely fueled 1977's *It's OK if You Don't Love Me*, which is her version of *Forever*. The narrator is Jody Epstein, a rising high school senior who meets green-eyed, unassuming Lyle Alexander over the summer when they're both working as techs at Sloan Kettering. Unlike Jody, Lyle is new to New York City, having moved from Ohio to live with his sister and brother-in-law after his parents died in a car accident. Where Jody is outgoing, Lyle is quiet and reticent. Their romance blossoms over tennis.

Jody, who is Jewish, recognizes herself as a "type" that's nonetheless exotic to Midwesterner Lyle. "In New York girls like me are a dime a dozen," she tells him. When he asks her to elaborate, she flippantly describes herself as "sort of aggressive, but insecure. We'll all end up being doctors and lawyers and being analyzed for nine million years." Jody is nothing at all like Krii, except that they both come from complicated homes. Jody's parents are divorced, and her dad lives in Scarsdale with his new wife and their young children. She lives with her brother, her mother, and her mom's on-again-off-again boyfriend Elliot, who is still technically married to his ex. The closest thing Jody has to a fond father figure is her mother's second husband, Philip, a physicist who teaches at Columbia. Philip is who she calls when she needs a nonjudgmental ear.

Like *Forever, It's OK if You Don't Love Me* hits on a range of taboo topics: premarital sex, contraception, rape, and abortion. But Klein's most innovative spin on the teen romance novel lies in Jody and Lyle's dynamic—she's sexually experienced and he isn't. Because Lyle is a virgin, he takes sex more seriously than she does, at least initially. As Jody tells us, she's made out with boys before "out of sheer horniness," and she lost her virginity with her previous boyfriend. But Lyle wants his first time to be special, for both of them. One night, when they're lying in bed, he admits to Jody that he doesn't want to have intercourse yet because he doesn't know if he's in love with her.

"That's okay. I'm not sure I'm in love with you," Jody says.

"That's what I mean," Lyle answers.

"I don't care if you love me or not," Jody continues.

"You should," Lyle responds. Then: "It's your birthright to be loved."

Jody wonders about this but is understanding with Lyle, especially when he brings up the death of his parents in the context of feeling overwhelmed. The next week in school, Jody's English Comp teacher asks the students to write stories based on their previous Saturdays, in an effort to get them to tackle real subjects. Jody ends up sharing about her night with Lyle and the teacher reads her story aloud to the class—anonymously, of course. Her classmates argue that the piece is not, in fact, realistic. "First, most of the boys couldn't believe that there was a boy who wouldn't sleep with a girl who was willing to sleep with him," Jody says. "Then, the girls started in and they all latched onto the line about Lyle having said it was my birthright to be loved by someone. They all said they couldn't understand a girl 'stooping so low' as to be willing to sleep with someone she knew didn't even love her."

Jody doesn't take the comments too much to heart; she's generally pretty confident, and her teacher assures her that she shared the story with the class because she thought it was "poignant." Having been raised in a sex-positive household, Jody is a direct product of the feminist movement and the sexual revolution. Klein's novel is a study in what happens when a teenage girl is physically comfortable with herself but more fearful of genuine intimacy. The morning after she and Lyle have sex for the first time, they make breakfast together. "There was just this very peaceful, contented feeling," Jody explains. "I don't intend to get married for years, maybe ever, but it was the way you wish being married could be, without people yelling and ending up saying they can't stand each other."

Right around her eighteenth birthday, Jody's father calls to invite her to spend the weekend at his house in Westchester. He tells her she can bring her boyfriend, too. The very idea of introducing Lyle to her semi-estranged father twists her stomach into knots. "To take Lyle along and have him meet Daddy would, for me, be an act of trust that would go beyond practically anything I can think of," she says. "There's not a sexual act on earth that would come anywhere close." Ultimately, she decides to bring him for "moral support" and the trip goes almost exactly how she anticipated it would—her father disappoints her. Less predictable: Lyle gives her her very first penetrative orgasm.

It's not all happily ever after from there. Jody slips up and has a one-night stand with her ex. She picks a fight with Lyle's ultrareligious older sister. The pair break up but in the end they both take a leap of faith—Lyle invites her to play tennis again and Jody lets herself really *feel* something. "I wish I could be looking back ten years from now so I could know if Lyle will be someone important, someone who's still there, or someone whom I'll just remember because he was the first," she says. "Not the first in one sense, but the first in terms of being all-out in love."

All-out love, for Jody, is far more vulnerable than sex. Even though the novel is explicit about lovemaking, *It's OK if You Don't Love Me* is about a young woman setting her heart free. But for a vocal contingent of readers, all they could see was the body parts. And these body parts, they argued, didn't belong in school libraries.

## Chapter Twenty

# ᴄ̃ensorship

*"I willed myself not to give in to the tears*
*of frustration and disappointment I felt coming."*

The temperature was unusually mild the day of January 20, 1981, in Washington, DC. For the first time ever, the inauguration was set to take place on the Capitol's west front, facing the National Mall and providing more room for spectators. There, the newly elected president of the United States stood to take his oath of office. The onetime governor of California placed his left hand on the Bible and repeated after the then–chief justice of the Supreme Court, a white-haired Warren E. Burger. "I, Ronald Reagan, do solemnly swear that I will faithfully execute the office of president of the United States and will to the best of my ability preserve, protect and defend the Constitution of the United States, so help me God," he said.

Reagan then went on to kiss his wife on the cheek—an impeccable Nancy Reagan dressed in a matching red Adolfo dress coat and pillbox hat—and delivered his inaugural address. "As great as our tax burden is, it has not kept up with public spending," Reagan announced, his folksy, Midwestern rhythms burnished by the years he'd spent as an actor in

Hollywood. "For decades we have piled deficit upon deficit, mortgaging our future and our children's future for the temporary convenience of the present. To continue this long trend is to guarantee tremendous social, cultural, political, and economic upheavals."

His hair pomade-slick, Reagan was the picture of the elder statesman. "I believe we, the Americans of today, are ready to act worthy of ourselves," he went on, in response to a quoted passage from the Massachusetts physician Joseph Warren, a Founding Father. The faintest smile played at Reagan's lips during an otherwise somber delivery. "Ready to do what must be done to ensure happiness for ourselves, our children, and our children's children."

That afternoon, the country's fortieth president made his aims clear: "to reawaken this industrial giant, to get government back within its means, and to lighten our punitive tax burden." This approach aligned with the philosophy of his Republican supporters; Reagan's suggestion that "with God's help we can and will resolve the problems which now confront us" called out to the evangelical Christians who helped put him in office.

The government's priorities were shifting dramatically from the liberal approach of Reagan's predecessor, President Jimmy Carter. Judy Blume would later cite this as the day that everything changed.

"When we elected Ronald Reagan and the conservatives decided that they would decide not just what their children would read but what all children would read, it went crazy," Blume told the *Guardian* in 2014, of the challenges against her books that began in the early 1980s. "My feeling in the beginning was wait, this is America: we don't have censorship, we have, you know, freedom to read, freedom to write, freedom of the press, we don't do this, we don't ban books. But then they did."

The tide against her turned practically "overnight," as she explained while she was on tour promoting *In the Unlikely Event*. And it wasn't just Blume. In December 1981, almost exactly a year after Reagan ascended to office, the *New York Times* reported that challenges against books had "shot up" since the late 1970s. Moreover, instead of requesting that access to certain books be restricted, complainants insisted that titles should be removed from public libraries altogether. "The reason would-be censors give most often is that a book is unsuitable for minors because of its vulgarity or its descriptions of sexual behavior," the *Times* explained. "But the censors also condemn the depiction of unorthodox family arrangements, sexual explicitness even in a biological context, speculation about Christ, unflattering portraits of American authority, criticisms of business and corporate practices, and radical political ideas."

Among the books being called out were Blume's novels—the *Times* described her provocatively as "a best-selling author of sexually explicit books for children and young adults"—as well as *Portnoy's Complaint*, Avery Corman's 1977 divorce novel *Kramer vs. Kramer*, *Our Bodies Ourselves*, and *Stuart Little*, E. B. White's adventure starring a natty mouse. The article attributed the rise in book challenges to conservative organizations such as the Heritage Foundation, Phyllis Schlafly's Eagle Forum, and the Moral Majority, which Jerry Falwell Sr. had recently founded in 1979. These groups were empowered by Reagan's election, and they were efficient. Once leaders set their sights on certain titles, they were able to drum up passions among their supporters and encourage them to voice their grievances.

Peter Silsbee recalled being on the receiving end of written complaints aimed at Bradbury about Judy's work. "We began to get letters from these people . . . It was Jerry Falwell [spearheading it], who had just sort of come on the scene." Silsbee said it was obvious that the objectors were all following a script. "We came to understand that a lot of the letters were very much the same. It felt to us like it was a campaign that was all across the United States." Sending angry letters was just one way that these fired-up folks would operate, Silsbee continued. "They'd go after school librarians, they'd go after teachers, and disrupt school board meetings and PTA meetings."

They accused certain books of promoting Secular Humanism, a once-obscure philosophy that became a conservative buzzword in the 1980s, much like Critical Race Theory today. Dating back to the nineteenth century, Secular Humanism hinged on the notion that humans are capable of behaving morally without the scaffold of religious or theistic dogma. But in the mouths of the Moral Majority and other right-wing groups, the term evolved to mean blatantly anti-religion and anti-God. "Thanks to Jerry Falwell and his Moral Majority I went from being called a 'Communist' to being labeled a 'Secular Humanist,'" Blume wrote in a 1993 essay for the *New York Law School Review* called "Is Puberty a Dirty Word?" According to her new Christian fundamentalist critics, Judy's books were not only "undermining of parental authority"—as she put it in the same article—but undermining the sovereignty of Jesus Christ as well.

•      •      •

You'd think the decision in *Island Trees School District v. Pico* would be enough to defang today's most ban-thirsty elected officials and parents. But the Supreme Court's ruling on that case didn't go far enough, even according to the lawyer who argued it. "We didn't create the law that we would have liked," Pico's legal rep Arthur Eisenberg told WNYC in 2022. At the time, the Supremes argued that a political or ideological objection to a title isn't a good enough reason to evict it from schools. Looking back, Eisenberg said he wished that they'd been able to legally enshrine curatorial power over libraries to the librarians. "Just as academic judgements should be left to the academics . . . decisions about the content of library collections should be left to the librarians."

Without that, the decision in *Island Trees v. Pico* still leaves room for the idea that certain books are too *objectively* vulgar or offensive or obscene for the eyes of children. Governor Ron DeSantis defends his stance on book removals in precisely this way: "In Florida, pornographic and inappropriate materials that have been snuck into our classrooms and

libraries to sexualize our students violate our state education standards,"
he says on his official website.

In the 1980s, book challenges weren't coming from government officials like they are now. But in the fall of 1982, one book was effectively
banned by the federal government. It was called *Show Me!*, and it was a
Germany-imported sex ed publication that came out in the US in 1975.
It billed itself as "A Picture Book of Sex for Children and Parents" and
consisted of black-and-white photographs and captions by an American named Will McBride, along with educational passages by European
doctor Helga Fleischhauer-Hardt. Covering it for the *New York Times*,
reviewer Linda Wolfe described paging through *Show Me!* with a mounting and palpable sense of alarm. "The photographs reveal the world of
sex through the eyes of two exquisite noble savages of about 5 years of
age," she writes. "We puzzle with them over their bellybuttons and the
fact that he has a penis and she a vagina. She turns bottoms-up so he can
see close-up what she's got, and he shows her how he 'pees' and 'poops.'"

Up until this point, Wolfe says, she still believed the book could be
an asset to families. Then, it got weirder. "But soon these children are
pondering the sexual behavior of their adolescent siblings. The boy has
seen—and we see through his eyes—his teenage brother and a barely
pubescent girlfriend having intercourse. The girl has watched her older
sister rub her clitoris, and we see that, too."

The prose is tempered but it's clear that Wolfe is so repulsed by *Show
Me!* that the effect is borderline humorous. "One begins to suspect that
the photographer enjoys scaring children," she writes. "And throughout
the book one grand and erroneous impression about sex in our society is
conveyed: it is that sex is something which happens in public."

Wolfe was not alone in her impression of *Show Me!* Although the title
was lauded in Germany, even SIECUS hesitated to recommend it. The September 1975 issue of the *SIECUS Report* opens with a cover story reiterat-
ing its position of sex education as a basic human right. But just pages later,

Dr. E. James Lieberman's review of McBride's book implies that, human rights notwithstanding, there is still such a thing as *bad* sex ed. "This book poses a problem for enlightened parents and sex educators because those who oppose it presumably wear the black hat of sexual repression," Lieberman begins. Yet he goes on to argue that in this case, negative reactions to *Show Me!*—with its explicit, close-up photos of everything from fellatio to childbirth—are probably justified. "There is no need to hustle children into an appreciation of adult sexuality, any more than we need to introduce caviar or Kantian philosophy at an early age," he writes. "This delicious-*looking* book is indigestible, an oxymoronic oddity of rawness overdone: it is blandly erotic, childishly adult, somberly silly, elegantly gross."

Almost as soon as it was published in the States, *Show Me!* was challenged and subject to claims of obscenity. But it wasn't until 1982, when the Supreme Court voted unanimously to uphold a New York State law barring child pornography, that St. Martin's Press, the book's US publisher, decided to withdraw it. In the *New York Times*, St. Martin's then-president Thomas McCormack stated that they were doing so to protect themselves as well as the booksellers who could get in trouble for stocking it. "Until the Supreme Court decision of July, it was not against the law to sell the book," he explained. "Now, the court has said in so many words that it is."

Which is to say, the accusation that it was in poor taste wasn't the death knell for *Show Me!* However, once the federal government confirmed that it was illegal to show minors engaged in sexual acts on film, in pictures, or on stage, the book—which at that point had sold about 150,000 copies in the US, according to a *New York Times* story about it—was effectively banned. Today, you can buy a copy of *Show Me!* from a specialty online bookseller for upwards of $700, but you can't get it from Barnes & Noble or Bookshop.org or even the New York Public Library. As a culture, we've decided that the First Amendment doesn't protect child pornography, and the vast majority of people agree this is the correct stance. But what counts as pornography isn't always instantly apparent.

"I distinguish pornography in terms of intent," Cory Silverberg said. "Pornography is material that is intended to sexually arouse someone. That is the point of it, so that's why *Forever* is not pornography, because that's not why she wrote the book."

Silverberg's definition dovetails with the existing legal one, established by the Supreme Court in 1973. Before that, the closest thing America had to a definition amounted to a gut check. In 1964, Justice Potter Stewart delivered his famous but ultimately unhelpful line about hard-core pornography: *I know it when I see it*. Then came *Miller v. California*. The case started when a restaurant owner in Newport Beach received a number of sexually graphic brochures in the mail. The pamphlets were traced to Marvin Miller, who sent them out to drum up interest in his mail-order porn store.

Miller's case found its way to the Supreme Court, which ultimately ruled against him, determining that the First Amendment did not protect the distribution of obscene material. As part of their decision, the judges created the "Miller Test" for obscenity, which is still used today. In order to qualify as *legally* obscene, a product has to fit all three of these criteria. One: that the average person would say it "appeals to the prurient interest," according to contemporary standards. Two: that it depicts or describes sexual or excretory behavior—in other words, crude bodily functions. Three: that it lacks "serious literary, artistic, political or scientific value."

That last bit is pretty subjective, don't you think?

*     *     *

In 1981, the tenor of conversation around children's books was getting so heightened that for the first time in her career, Judy got pushback from her own publisher about a sexually inflected passage in one of her drafts. The original version of *Tiger Eyes* included a short scene where Davey—awakening from an oppressive grief after her father's murder—masturbated.

The scene took place right after a sequence that made it into the published novel. Davey spends an unpleasant night out with her new friend in Los Alamos, Jane. They meet up with two boys in a parking lot, and Jane and the guys pass around a bottle of vodka. Davey doesn't drink, so she's still completely sober when Jane and one of the boys start drunkenly making out. After a little while, Jane throws up on a car, and Davey has the unfortunate job of walking her sloppy friend home. With Jane passed out in her bed, Davey nods off on a nearby bedroll. She dreams of an older guy who she met while out hiking, named Wolf.

In the draft, Davey wakes up and starts touching herself. Her climax unleashes her tears about the night, about Los Alamos—everything. But that's not how it goes in the finished book. Instead, the section reads like this: "I get Jane undressed down to her shirt and her underpants, pull the covers up around her, then climb into the bedroll her mother has set out for me. I fall asleep quickly and dream about Wolf. About the two of us together in our cave. It's not the first time I have dreamed about him."

When Judy arrived at Bradbury to consult with Jackson about her pages, he had the masturbation passage circled. Jackson, her longtime friend and collaborator, put down his pencil and looked her straight in the eye. He told her that from a character perspective, the scene made perfect sense, and as a writer she'd handled it gracefully. But he thought she should take it out.

"We want this book to reach as many readers as possible, don't we?" Jackson said.

Judy was shocked. After all, this was the same editor who had published *Are You There, God? It's Me, Margaret, Deenie,* and *Forever.* Aside from his decision to market the last as a novel for adults, he'd never expressed reservations before about the sexual content in her writing. She tried to explain why the moment belonged in *Tiger Eyes.*

Jackson listened sympathetically, then argued that times had changed. "If you leave in those lines, the censors will come after this book," Blume recalls him saying in a 1999 essay published in *American Libraries* magazine. "Librarians and teachers won't buy it. Book clubs won't take it. Everyone is too scared."

His words hit Judy hard. "I felt my face grow hot, my stomach clench," Blume wrote. "I willed myself not to give in to the tears of frustration and disappointment I felt coming."

In his interview in 2001 with *School Library Journal*, Jackson admitted that yes, he did keep the difficulties of book challenges in mind when he edited his authors. He didn't mention Blume but described an incident with another writer where he convinced her to change the word "devil" to "imp" in her work in progress. "Why deprive kids in some parts of the country of what is, essentially, a story of a dog who cleverly helps her master," he said of making the choice to "sidestep the religious issue." The writer agreed, begrudgingly. "So, is this censorship? One might say it's making an adjustment to reality," he went on, while admitting that this specific reality was one he wished he didn't have to accommodate.

But he was right that by the time *Tiger Eyes* was on his desk, the political climate had become untenable for books that acknowledged teen sexuality. In January 1981, the *New York Times* published a long polemic by journalist Marie Winn, called "What Became of Childhood Innocence?" Winn's piece was expansive, railing against everything from television to X-rated movies to working mothers to *Mad* magazine to Kentucky Fried Chicken. All of these things, she claimed, contributed to a tasteless, extravagant culture where children were growing up too quickly. "Without a doubt, the upheavals of the 1960s—from divorce and the breakdown of the family to women's liberation and increased employment—weakened the protective membrane that once sheltered children from precocious experience and knowledge of the adult world," she wrote.

Winn's take on the past was suspiciously rosy; she described medieval child labor as a folksy prelapsarian dream. "Children's integration into adult work in the past becomes understandable when one remembers that the work, in those preindustrial days, often consisted of those very arts and crafts offered today . . . for children's amusement: spinning, weaving, pottery, basket making." She pined for the moment in history that she called "The Age of Innocence . . . [when] children really believed that all adults were good, that all Presidents were as honest as Abe Lincoln, that the adult world was in every way bigger and better than their own world."

She name-checked Blume, Norma Klein, and *My Darling, My Hamburger* author Paul Zindel as writers whose success was caused by the phenomenon of shrinking childhoods. Winn implied that their popularity was not altogether desirable, but that was understandable given the zeitgeist. "Today, parents often forget that, despite the end of the Age of Innocence, some children remain vulnerable longer than others," she wrote. "In avoiding the past excesses of secrecy and overprotectiveness, adults in our society often abdicate their responsibilities for dealing with children's special needs."

The editorial was a call to arms. Winn challenged adults to speak out and save children from a sad state of affairs where mothers were too busy working to provide home-cooked dinners and deferred responsibility for teaching important life lessons to the likes of *JudyBlume*. And Judy was beginning to understand that this was the way an increasingly vocal contingent was beginning to think of her.

So, she gave in to Jackson. She took the masturbation scene out of *Tiger Eyes*. "Ultimately, I was not strong enough or brave enough to defy the editor I trusted and respected," she wrote.

But did she believe it was the right decision? All she had wanted was to write honest books for kids and there she was, dropped into the deep end of the culture wars. She went on: "I've never forgiven myself for caving in to editorial pressure based on fear, for playing into the hands of the censors."

# Chapter Twenty-One

# ᴄMorals

*"They call her a Pied Piper
leading kids down the wrong path."*

ackson was right that the censors had it out for Judy. They were mobbish and rough, demonstratively flashing their pitchforks. Phyllis Schlafly's Eagle Forum circulated a pamphlet called "How to Rid Your Schools and Libraries of Judy Blume Books."

Another Texas-based conservative group, called the Pro-Family Forum, created a flyer with the frightening title "X-Rated Children's Books," about mature themes—sex, drugs, and divorce—snaking their way into fiction for young adults. The handout mentions *The Outsiders* and V.C. Andrews's haunting 1979 novel *Flowers in the Attic,* but it really goes in on Blume, denouncing *Forever* for the explicit scenes between Michael and "Kathy" (a repeated mistake that suggests whoever drafted the primer didn't actually spend a lot of quality time with Blume's characters).

"X-Rated Children's Books" walks readers through the process of challenging these books, with the intention of getting them removed from public libraries as well as privately owned bookstores. It encourages concerned citizens to investigate their local libraries and shopping malls, and bring any inappropriate titles to the attention of public school teachers and principals, whose salaries rely on tax dollars, as the leaflet points out. It also suggests that aspiring book vigilantes buy copies of the flyer, at a price of three for a dollar, and distribute them within their communities. Other mounting threats, according to the Pro-Family Forum, include the role-playing game Dungeons & Dragons and the creep of Atheism.

The moral center dropping out of everyday life was an important idea among book banners. In February 1980, a complaint from an upset parent prompted an elementary school library in Montgomery County, Maryland, to remove *Blubber*, Blume's 1974 YA novel about fifth-grade bullying, from the shelves.

*Blubber* is narrated by Jill Brenner, an average student who is suddenly swept up in some nasty social dynamics after her classmate Linda Fischer gives an oral report on whales. Linda is nervous and chubby, and when she mentions that the giant sea creatures are encased in a thick layer of fat called, yes, *blubber*, the popular girls in class seize on it.

"Blubber is a good name for her," Wendy, the queen bee, writes in a note to Jill.

Wendy, her sidekick Caroline, and Jill start relentlessly taunting Linda. "School isn't as boring as it used to be," Jill says after the entire class catches on to the game, egged on by a list that Wendy circulates titled "How to have fun with Blubber." Suggestions include pushing her, tripping her, and telling her she stinks. The kids make Linda say "I am Blubber, the smelly whale of class 206" before she can eat lunch, drink from the water fountain, or use the bathroom. Jill has moments of ambivalence about what's happening, but there's no denying she's on board. For Halloween, she ditches her witch costume of three years running to dress up as a flenser: someone who strips blubber from whale carcasses. She's proud of the cruel inside joke and annoyed when she doesn't win the school's costume contest.

Jill eventually gets her comeuppance, not from an authority figure—the fifth-grade teacher, Mrs. Minish, has been checked out for months—but from Wendy herself. The class submits Linda to a mock trial after she's accused of tattling on Jill for pulling a Halloween prank on a grumpy neighbor. Jill isn't sure Linda's actually guilty, but she's enthusiastic until Wendy, who has appointed herself the judge, refuses to assign Linda a lawyer. Jill stands up for her: "If we're going to do this we're going to do it right, otherwise it's not a real trial," she says. An argument ensues and Wendy turns on her. The next day at school, everything is worse. Linda has teamed up with Wendy, and Jill—freshly dubbed B.B. for Baby Brenner—is the new classroom pariah.

Wendy never faces any consequences. Still, Judy was surprised when she heard that *Blubber*, of all her books, was ruffling feathers. Unlike many of her other novels, *Blubber* makes zero references to sexuality.

The whole thing started in Maryland with a mom named Bonnie Fogel, who called up her daughter's public school after her seven-year-old, named Sarah, checked *Blubber* out of the library.

As Fogel told the *Washington Post*, she was half listening as the second grader read aloud from the book at the dinner table, until one line stopped her in her tracks.

"That teacher is such a bitch," Sarah said.

Instantly, Fogel asked to see the book and was "shocked" when she spied the offensive word spelled out on the page. *B-I-T-C-H*. In a book for children?! She flipped ahead and wasn't reassured. *Blubber* was brutal. "What's really shocking is that there is no moral tone to the book," she told the *Post*. "There's no adult or another child at the end who says, 'This is wrong. This cruelty to others shouldn't be.'"

Fogel spoke to the school superintendent, who decided to pull *Blubber*, along with two other books he'd received negative feedback about, including *It's Not What You'd Expect* by Norma Klein. (Klein's novel tells the story of fourteen-year-old twins who, while struggling to make sense of their parents' divorce, find out that their older brother has gotten his girlfriend pregnant and wants her to get an abortion.) A spokesman for the superintendent told the *Post* that he'd decided these stories were better suited to high schoolers. Meanwhile, although Montgomery County's schools were reconsidering *Blubber*, the local public library had just ordered 110 copies.

"It's not a great piece of literature," librarian Ann Friedman said at the time, echoing long-standing criticisms of Blume's work. "But I feel we have an obligation to be responsive to what kids are reading . . . I have great faith that kids will figure out what's the right thing to do without having a moral lesson spelled out."

Fogel vehemently disagreed. "I think adults have an obligation to steer young children away from cruelty," she said. "Not introduce them to more."

Asked to comment on the controversy, Blume stood up for her novel. "The fact that it is not resolved is the most important part of the book," she said. "*Blubber* is a tough book, but I think kids are awfully rough on each other. I'd rather get it out there in the open than pretend it isn't there."

In light of the situation in Montgomery County, other Maryland schools were also reassessing the book's suitability for young readers. But given the novel's intended audience, the *Post* chose to give Sarah— the only young reader whose voice appears in the article—the final word on the matter.

And Sarah loved it. "*Blubber*, she told her mother, is 'the best book I ever read.'"

•     •     •

Hardly anything exemplifies the high-speed shift in the public's understanding of Judy Blume like two profiles in the *Christian Science Monitor*, published less than two years apart. The first, headlined "Writing for Kids Without Kidding Around," came out in May 1979 and described a pleasant visit with Blume at her new home in Santa Fe, where she had just moved from Los Alamos with Tom Kitchens, Randy, and Larry, who were seventeen and fifteen at the time. Beyond Blume's own mention in passing of the "sensational" responses to her novels, the tone of the story is warm and admiring.

"Blume's books are sympathetic stories of ordinary children, suffering from a bossy sibling, confusing sexuality, or a disintegrating family," the reporter wrote. "Blume brings humor, affection and order to the often bewildering complexities of being a child today."

The second article, however, reads like it was published on a different planet. "Judy Blume: Children's Author in a Grown-Up Controversy" came out in the *Christian Science Monitor* in December 1981, almost a year after Reagan's inauguration. Gone were the coolheaded and complimentary hat tips to Blume's writing. Instead, the focus had shifted to her critics. "A growing number of iconoclasts are out to take the bloom off the Blume books," reporter Gay Andrews Dillin wrote. "They call her a Pied Piper leading kids down the wrong path. They don't like her tune and charge that she plays to the prurient interests of her adolescent audience."

Once again, Blume forcefully defended her work. She offered what would become her go-to line on censorship: parents have a right to control what their own children read but cannot unilaterally make those decisions for other families. She blamed the swell of outcries against her books on the Moral Majority. However, Cal Thomas—an evangelical Christian and then the vice president of communication for Jerry Falwell's organization—deflected responsibility. "They're trying to use us to sell more of their books," he told the *Christian Science Monitor* dismissively. "It's the old 'Banned in Boston' scam. Too often the Moral Majority is used generically to mean any group that is right-wing or conservative."

That might very well have been true, but further down the page, Thomas made his stance on Blume's novels abundantly clear. He said it was "intellectually indefensible" to insist that kids were already talking about sex, so it couldn't hurt for them to read about it, too. "It's the writers and advertisers who are the ones putting it before us every day," he said.

Thomas ran with this line of thought a few years later, when he published an op-ed in the *Philadelphia Daily News* called "In Kids' Books, Guess What 'Honest' Means." The headline makes it sound like he's describing an entire genre, but his opening lines reveal the narrowness of his target. "Judy Blume writes what she calls 'honest' books for children," Thomas began. "Others call them just short of kiddie porn."

He continued by bringing up a recent case in Peoria, Illinois, where Blume's books had been removed from elementary school shelves. "Critics label as 'lunatic' the Peoria decision to remove the Blume books from the school libraries," Thomas wrote derisively. But to him, it was equally crazy to suggest that the books should be freely available to kids just because they reflected a new "reality." "Why is it that chastity until marriage and caring enough for another person not to engage in premarital sex are not considered reality?"

Thomas contended, as many other religious and right-leaning people have over the years, that children don't always know what's good for them. He said that adults had a responsibility to provide moral guidance and that Blume—twice divorced herself, as he pointed out—wasn't the right person to do it.

He concluded by comparing her books to the crunchy, salty, sticky-sweet snacks kids would gobble down if their parents weren't around to stop them. "Arguing that Blume is just giving kids what they want is no argument at all," he wrote. "Many schools have banned junk food vending machines as unhealthy to children's bodies." Thomas wanted kids ingesting the literary equivalent of broccoli. "In public schools, kids will learn far more from studying the classics than from the mental junk food dished out by Judy Blume."

Thomas's argument that parents and role models should act as correctives in an out-of-control culture extended well beyond the realm of children's fiction. In 1981—the same year that Charles and Diana got hitched in London and MTV premiered with an infectious *oh ah oh* in "Video Killed the Radio Star"—sex education was under attack as well. There was a widespread political agenda to reroute the way kids were being taught to think about their bodies, steered by people who believed America, thanks to the civil rights and women's movements, had taken an abrupt wrong turn in the 1960s. Too many adults, they thought, had been corrupted by their appetites, with activists and atheists spoon-feeding them crap. But kids—kids were still movable. The Right wanted to get back in the driver's seat, escorting boys and girls toward traditional, Christianity-approved pairings: monogamous, heterosexual, breadwinner/homemaker relationships.

In 1981, the Reagan administration quietly pushed through the Adolescent Family Life Act (AFLA), which provided federal funding to programs that promoted abstinence-only sex ed. It was the first bill of its kind and was passed as part of the new president's Omnibus Budget Reconciliation Act of 1981, aimed at making good on Reagan's campaign promise to cut down on government spending. AFLA's purported goal was to solve the fiscal crisis of teen pregnancy by teaching high schoolers that the only safe sex before marriage was no sex at all. This, supporters argued, would scale back on government handouts, because teen moms were almost always on the take.

Really? Here's how that logic went. Young women who gave birth out of wedlock grew up to be "welfare queens"—a racially coded epithet for mothers who had more and more children in order to live off the taxpayers by vampirically extending their benefits.

While family life classes had always been designed to underscore the primacy of heterosexual marriage, the abstinence-only model went a step further by stressing that state-sanctioned male-female unions were the *only* appropriate context for sexual activity. This is just another angle on the pro-censorship argument, really; the thinking goes that if you can't read or learn about it, it doesn't exist. Once again, teens were being told that until they grew up and made it to the altar, they'd simply have to control themselves. Masturbation, contraception, and homosexual experimentation were not presented as ways to explore safer sex. The religious undertones in this approach were unmistakable. AFLA denied funds to programs that offered abortions or abortion counseling, according to Jeffrey Moran, the author of *Teaching Sex.* "Congress soon passed the so-called squeal rule," he wrote, "which required federally funded family planning clinics to inform parents if their teenage children were seeking contraception or an abortion."

The controlling Republican Party was prepared to punish teens for getting pregnant by condemning them to poverty. Conservatives were trying to legislate girls like Katherine Danziger—bright, feminist, sexually empowered from a relatively young age—out of existence. If Judy Blume was the Pied Piper, as the *Christian Science Monitor* wrote, then the Reagan administration and its champions were trying to barricade the gates to Hamelin. But they didn't account for the fact that making a big show of locking her out only amplified her music.

## Chapter Twenty-Two

# ❦Notoriety

*"Isolated and alone"*

In 1984, Judy appeared on an episode of CNN's *Crossfire*, then a two-year-old entertainment news show hosted by Tom Braden, a former CIA operative and liberal journalist, and Pat Buchanan, a former advisor to the Nixon White House and leading voice in conservative Christian politics. As the guest, Blume was seated between them, the set sparse with three stately leather armchairs against a black backdrop. She was dressed stylishly in a green sweater, khaki skirt, and tan knee-high boots, a patterned green and purple scarf looped around her neck. Her curly hair was cut into a flattering long shag. She smiled nervously at the camera as an announcer introduced her as "award-winning writer of children's books Judy Blume."

Buchanan, his hair slicked into a camera-ready comb-over, glanced at her warmly. "Ms. Blume looks like a very nice lady," he began, "and what I wanted to ask you, I looked through three of your books, what is this preoccupation with sex in books for ten-year-old children?"

Judy raised her eyebrows and blinked a few times while he continued.

"I have looked through several of these, Ms. Blume. One of them talks about masturbation, another one talks about a little boy who is window-peeping on his neighbor, a little girl, another one talks about somebody throwing up."

She tilted her head to interrupt him. "Throwing up is sex?"

"Well, it has to do with bodily functions," Buchanan said. "What is all this doing in a book for ten-year-olds?"

"There is no preoccupation with sex," Blume countered quickly. "Did you read the whole book or did you just read pages that were paper clipped?"

The question didn't ruffle Buchanan. The tenor of the conversation heightened as he started reading passages aloud to Blume from her own novels. "Why can't . . . you write an interesting, exciting book for ten-year-olds without getting into a discussion of masturbation?" he asked.

Judy threw him a skeptical look, her mouth tightening. "First of all, *Deenie* is not about masturbation, it's about a girl with scoliosis," she corrected.

Buchanan was literally shaking her book at her. Judy looked like she was going to pop. "Are you hung up on masturbation?" she asked him, an uncomfortable laugh catching in her throat.

"You are! You're hung up about this stuff," Buchanan insisted.

"One scene in one book," Blume said, barely letting him finish.

Blume came off as tough. She held her own—more than that, she got in a good shot against Buchanan in his camel suit jacket and brown-striped tie, giving a face and a voice to the yearslong right-wing onslaught. But inside her, it was a different story. Inside, she was dissolving, her eyes revealing just a glint from that hidden puddle.

•     •     •

Judy was suffering. She felt "isolated and alone." The years of being scru-tinized, of being called a bad influence and a pornographer, had chipped away at her. And it wasn't just sexual themes that her critics had issues with. "I had letters from angry parents accusing me of ruining Christmas forever because of a chapter in *Superfudge*, called 'Santa Who?,'" she wrote in her essay for *American Libraries*, referring to a sequence where Peter and Fudge acknowledge that Santa isn't real. (This is still a thing! Librarian Lauren Harrison said when elementary schoolers check *Superfudge* out of the library, she taps out a quick email to the parents warning them that "there's a whole chapter that blows up Santa Claus.")

Other moms and dads tossed off angry notes to Judy about her language. "Some sent lists showing me how easily I could have substituted one word for another. *Meanie* for *bitch*, *darn* for *damn*, *nasty* for *ass* . . . Perhaps most shocking of all was a letter from a nine-year-old addressed to *Jew*dy Blume telling me I had no right to write about Jewish angels in *Starring Sally J. Freedman as Herself.*"

Blume couldn't help but take the criticisms personally, even though she knew other authors—from Norma Klein to canonical writers, including John Steinbeck and Anne Frank—were being targeted, too.

Unlike Blume, Klein mostly found the whole thing amusing. In the summer of 1982, *Publishers Weekly* came out with a list of the most banned writers in America, which included Solzhenitsyn, Ernest Hemingway, William Faulkner, and D. H. Lawrence. "Judy Blume and I were the only women writers on the list, as well as the only authors of books for children," Klein wrote in an essay for the American Library Association called "On Being a Banned Writer." "My first thought was: I'll never be in such good company again," she joked, before calling it "Perhaps the proudest moment of my literary career."

As her daughter Jennifer Fleissner confirmed, Klein was "happy to be a quiet pioneer." It helped that she, like Judy, received letter after gushing letter in the mail, "mostly from girls who were just so thankful for the books and felt . . . it was this window into another world and another way of thinking that was very important to them," Fleissner said.

Also like Judy, Klein hadn't set out to be a renegade. But Norma wasn't afraid to step into that role. "Once she realized that people did see the books as blazing this trail, then I think that was a mantle that she was willing to take on," Fleissner said.

Klein's most challenged book was *It's OK if You Don't Love Me*, according to a count put together by Arizona State University professor Ken Donelson and published by the University of North Carolina Press in 1990. Donelson tallied up protests against books as reported by the Office for Intellectual Freedom between 1952 and 1989. His list included a number of familiar, widely celebrated titles along with the supplied justifications for their removal from public spaces. Judith Guest's *Ordinary People* was described by a woman in West Virginia as "absolutely filthy, dirty, vulgar." In Baton Rouge, Louisiana, a school board member said of Vonnegut's "book of dirty language" *Slaughterhouse-Five*: "I've been told the author is a great writer. He may have boo-booed on this one." (The earnestness of this phrasing—ha!)

Claude Brown, a Black writer who published the autobiographical novel *Manchild in the Promised Land* about growing up in Harlem, was subjected to a particularly memorable critique. In Old Town, Maine, a member of a school committee objected to the book as well as the elective course it was being taught in, called "The Nature of Prejudice." The protestor noted that because there were no Black people in Old Town, "prejudice was no problem."

Topping Donelson's list was J. D. Salinger, with *The Catcher in the Rye* challenged seventy-one times. Blume followed with fifty-seven objections against a number of her books: *Forever* led the pack with eighteen challenges, followed by *Deenie*; *Then Again, Maybe I Won't*; *Are You There God? It's Me, Margaret*; *Blubber*; and *It's Not the End of the World*. Steinbeck came in third with forty-seven total complaints, mostly against *Of Mice and Men* and *The Grapes of Wrath*. "There's an obvious drop-off after Steinbeck," Donelson wrote. "Whatever authors we add beyond, the point is clear—Salinger and Blume and Steinbeck lead all the rest by a wide margin." Donelson also argued that Blume, not Salinger, deserved the top spot "since several of Blume's books are on the hit parade . . . while Salinger has only one." He mused that the book banners were actually undermining their own agendas by keeping Salinger's book front and center. "How many adolescent readers would read about Holden Caulfield's life if they weren't frequently reminded by censors how dreadful and immoral *Catcher* is?"

*Go Ask Alice* was the subject of thirty-one incidents—ironic, as the tragic diary was eventually revealed to be a cautionary tale fabricated by a staunchly anti-drug Mormon homemaker named Beatrice Sparks. Norma Klein had been called out fourteen times, mostly for *It's OK if You Don't Love Me* but also for *Mom, The Wolf Man, and Me*, along with a handful of other titles.

In "On Being a Banned Writer," Klein took the high ground when it came to anybody's issues with her own books, but also expressed real concerns about living in a world where demonizing the written word was considered fair game. She called the 1980s-era hankering for book bans "a deadly and frightening thing to observe, especially after the fifties and McCarthyism and the toll such denial of freedom of speech took on an entire generation." Klein went on: "Having heard about this era from my parents, I am horrified to see my own teenage daughters come of age at a time when the books to which they have access in libraries and schools are being scrutinized in a way we would deplore were it described as taking place in the Soviet Union."

◦　　•　　◦

Far from the Soviet Union was the town of Peoria, Illinois, where in the fall of 1984 the local school district removed three of Blume's books— *Then Again, Maybe I Won't*; *Deenie*; and *Blubber*—from the school library's shelves. Despite the increased frequency of book challenges across the country, this particular one made national headlines, perhaps due to the city's reputation as a bellwether of Midwestern tastes and tolerances. The *New York Times* followed the story closely, reporting that the town's associate superintendent, Dennis Gainey, approved the decision, regardless of his own personal view that Blume's books were "excellent."

Gainey told the press that the district had determined the books were not appropriate for readers younger than seventh grade, which put officials in a bind, because the school library was open to students of all grades, from kindergarten to eighth. The offending titles were plucked out for their sexual content—*Deenie* and *Then Again, Maybe I Won't* of course being the infamous masturbation and wet dream books—and for strong language (once again, *Blubber*'s use of the word "bitch" got Blume in trouble). In the *Times*, Richard Jackson called the decision "lunatic," given that the titles were still available at public libraries and bookstores. But Peoria's officials had carefully considered the issue, they said. When it came to these three novels, Blume's work just didn't play there.

Or so the city thought. After news of the bans spread, school board secretary Winifred Henderson started receiving letters and calls in response to the bans. Some of them were supportive—"99 percent" of callers outside of Peoria agreed with the decision to remove the books, Henderson told the *Times*—while the city's constituents were more evenly split.

But at the end of November, the school board also received one extremely notable dissension from a number of high-profile signers. The letter came on behalf of the Authors League and made the case that pulling books from school libraries teaches kids "the wrong lesson, one of intolerance, distrust and contempt" for the First Amendment, which protects "not only the freedoms to write, publish and read but also the freedom to decide what to read." The eight names on the note were impressive, all belonging to influential children's book authors: Madeleine

L'Engle; Natalie Babbitt, who wrote *Tuck Everlasting*; Caldecott Medal-winning picture book writer Uri Shulevitz; and cartoonist William Steig, among others.

By early December, the school board had agreed to reconsider the issue. On Monday, December 3, the board convened and voted 5-2 in favor of reinstating Blume's novels. However, it was a qualified victory, with the library setting up a new system where these books would only be available to older readers, and to younger ones with parental consent. One local mother, who'd spoken out against the bans, told reporters she was satisfied with this outcome. "This is what I first suggested as a compromise," she said. "I feel that the action they took will address the rights of children and all parents."

The rhetoric of parental rights animated both sides of the conversation, with would-be book banners arguing that they had license to control what their kids were reading at school. That's what happened in Gwinnett County, Georgia, in August 1985, when a local mom named Teresa Wilson asked to see the new book that her nine-year-old daughter, Naco, had borrowed from the school library. That October, she told the *Chicago Tribune* that she flipped *Deenie* open and immediately, she was disgusted. "The first page I opened to talked about masturbation," she explained to a reporter. "That's when I got involved."

Wilson described herself as a homemaker who had "never been involved in anything like this before." Nonetheless, she sprung to action, contacting Naco's school, the county school board, and—in a way that closely mirrored the fictional events described in *Maudie and Me and the Dirty Book*—founded a group called Concerned Citizens of Gwinnett. As is often the case when even just one parent challenges a book, local officials hurried to remove *Deenie* from the shelves. But that wasn't the end of the story. Another committee, called the Free Speech Movement of Gwinnett, came together to fight the decision. It was led by George Wilson (no relation to Teresa).

Gwinnett County is just outside Atlanta, and at the time it was home to twenty-three thousand elementary school students—all potential readers of novels by Judy Blume. George Wilson told the *Tribune* that both he and his ten-year-old daughter Katherine had read *Deenie* and he had no problem with it: "No one is obligated to read this book, but I want my child to have the option to go into the school library and pick out any book she wants, without someone else's parent dictating what she can read." He felt so strongly about the issue that he got the Georgia chapter of the ACLU involved. It went ahead and filed an appeal to the state school board.

But that didn't scare Teresa Wilson, who had also enlisted help from the Freedom Foundation—a conservative think tank—and the Moral Majority. Beyond that, she had connected with a Texas couple named Mel and Norma Gabler, whose organization Educational Research Analysts was devoted to ridding public schools of textbooks that conflicted with their fundamentalist Christian values. Wilson told the *Tribune* that with challenging *Deenie*, she was just getting started. "I'm hearing about all kinds of other books in our schools that I'd object to," she said, including those that "sympathize with communism, encourage premarital sex or experimenting with drugs, take pro-abortion positions and stress evolution without teaching creationism, too."

George Wilson said that this was exactly why he rallied a team to fight on behalf of *Deenie*. His opponent's point of view put her "in the same boat with fascism," he argued. "If you give them Czechoslovakia, they'll come back for Poland later."

The ACLU agreed. In December 1985, the *Chicago Tribune* published a follow-up that included results from a national survey showing an uptick in book challenges across the South, as well as data from affected librarians suggesting that more often than not, these challenges resulted in the books being removed altogether. A spokesperson for the American Library Association's Office for Intellectual Freedom added that while book banning efforts in the South tended to be more organized, the problem was bad in the Northeast, too. By then, the Gwinnett school board had agreed to restore *Deenie* to elementary school libraries, but only if it lived on a restricted shelf that students would have to avoid unless they had written permission from their parents. The ACLU didn't like that so-called resolution, either.

The Gwinnett case dragged on—as we know from recent national elections, Georgia is deeply divided when it comes to politics and its citizens are passionate. In 2006, an evangelical Christian mother of three landed Gwinnett back in the news when she demanded that the school system remove the Harry Potter books from libraries on account of their "evil themes, witchcraft, demonic activity, murder, evil blood sacrifice, spells and teaching children all of this." The *Gwinnett Daily Post* covered the situation, noting that "book appeals have been fairly rare in the Gwinnett school system." The article noted that before the Potter furor, the last challenge had been back in 1997, when some parents fought to remove two books: *Ghost Camp* by middle grade horror writer R.L. Stine, and Judy Blume's *It's Not the End of the World.*

The school board examined these titles and voted to keep them on the shelves. And even the *Deenie* episode proved that book challenges had a tendency to backfire. In September 1985, a month after Teresa Wilson first set her sights on *Deenie*, the Associated Press reported that Gwinnett's bookstores were experiencing an unprecedented run on the novel.

"That's what happens when they start banning books," Bobbie Setzer, a local bookstore manager, told the AP. "Everyone wants to read them."

•    •    •

It was at least a partial victory for Blume—and by then, she commanded a cavalry. She donated money to the National Coalition Against Censorship in the early 1980s and by spring of 1983, she had joined their advisory council. In June 1984, she received a letter from a board member requesting a more substantial donation and offering a face-to-face meeting with Leanne Katz, NCAC's executive director. Judy wrote back, saying yes, she would very much like to sit down with Katz as soon as she was back in New York.

"My life changed when I learned about the National Coalition Against Censorship . . . and met Leanne Katz, the tiny dynamo who was its first and longtime director," Blume wrote in 1999, just two years after Katz died of cancer at the age of sixty-five. "Leanne's intelligence, her wit, her strong commitment to the First Amendment and helping those who were out on a limb trying to defend it, made her my hero."

NCAC had started as an offshoot of the ACLU, where Katz was working at the time, but quickly became its own entity. The Coalition—made up of dozens of nonprofit groups, ranging from Planned Parenthood to PEN America to the National Council of Jewish Women to the United Methodist Church—was created specifically to fight against bans. Katz herself believed wholeheartedly in the primacy of the First Amendment, the worthiness of art, and the rights of citizens to access information, even about subjects that were controversial or complicated. She was also a staunch feminist. "The intense battles around the control of sexuality have always been fought on the terrain of women's bodies," she wrote in the *New York Law School Review* in 1993. "Women have long been barred from access to knowledge and information on sexuality, including reproduction, and have been excluded even from viewing or creating representations of their own bodies."

Women were *barred from access to knowledge*. Think about that. Katz did; she saw book challenges as just another way for the Right to control female bodies and minds. At this point, Katz and Blume were completely aligned. Connecting with Katz opened a valve for Judy, releasing years of pent-up pressure. She could finally exhale. "I used to feel so alone when I heard my books were being challenged and even banned," Blume wrote in "Is Puberty a Dirty Word?" "I had nowhere to turn . . . Today, when I get a message from my publisher that a distressed teacher or librarian or parent or group of students is trying to defend one of my books, I put them in touch with Leanne Katz at the NCAC and from that moment we all work together, not just to keep my books available, but to assure readers of all ages that they will continue to have the freedom to choose."

In the same essay, Judy once again talked about the letters she received from children and adults whose exposure to her books turned out to be life-changing for them. She quoted a forty-one-year-old fan. "My periods began just before my twelfth birthday," the woman wrote, "and for six months I suffered untold agonies that I was dying. I hid the evidence for fear it was something bad I had done." The woman went on to say that she'd been raised in a home where even if Judy's books had been available at the time, she probably wouldn't have been allowed to have them. "I have two daughters, ages eight and eleven, and I promised myself that I won't make the mistakes my own mother made with me. But because of my sheltered upbringing, I still don't know what is normal and what is not," she confessed.

Blume also talked about the letters she received from victims of incest and sexual abuse. These children reached out to Judy not because she was an authority on the subject, but because they trusted her and didn't know where else to turn. "While the censors are looking for obscene passages in my books and others, I'm hearing from kids like this," Blume wrote, before quoting a letter from a girl who talked about being raped by her father. "Dear Judy, I just graduated from eighth grade, and I need an adult's advice," the missive started. "I have a problem, which concerns my father and myself. It started when I was in fourth or fifth grade and it still continues. It is incest. I feel tremendously guilty, like I led him on."

How could Blume stop fighting when she was being let in on such horrors? Some children were lost—it was heartbreaking but also not inevitable. And Judy, with the help of NCAC, was found again.

## Chapter Twenty-Three

# ℘Daughters

*"I gave you a lot of shit
this year, didn't I, Mother?"*

What a whirlwind the past twenty years had been for Judy. She had gone from a Betty Draper type letting off steam with a metaphorical shotgun in her backyard, to the frantically flapping avian target, to something else, like a tree—grown-up and grounded, even approaching peaceful. Yes, she had taken her kids on the journey and she felt bad about that. But she never, ever stopped trying to make their lives better.

In 1981, she bought an apartment on Manhattan's Upper West Side, which meant she could go back and forth between New York, her all-time favorite city, and Santa Fe. And even New Mexico had started to feel more like home, thanks to a man she'd met. A friend, actually his ex-wife, had set them up in the winter of '79. As tough as the early Reagan years had been, Judy knew things would have been a thousand times worse without him.

George Cooper was a Columbia Law professor with a graying beard, shaggy hair, and glasses. He had a twelve-year-old daughter named

Amanda—when Judy and George met, Amanda had heard of Judy Blume but he hadn't. For their first date, on a Sunday, they went to dinner. The next night they got tickets to see *Apocalypse Now*. On Tuesday, Judy had a date with another guy. George came over afterward and as Judy likes to put it in interviews, he never left.

In her 2004 introduction to her adult novel *Smart Women*, Blume writes of getting to know George: "Falling in love at forty (or any age) is *s'wonderful*, just like the song says. But this time around you bring all that baggage with you, not to mention your kids, who might not think it's as romantic as you do."

*Smart Women*, first published in 1983, covers exactly this territory. Margo is a divorced mother of two teenagers, raising them as a single mom in Boulder, Colorado. Over the past few years, her children, Michelle and Stuart, have transformed from her sweet little buddies into rough, prickly strangers, banging around the house. After spending the summer in New York with their conservative father, Stuart comes back west as Dad's preppy clone with a tidy haircut, piles of Polo shirts, and a newfound passion for tennis. Meanwhile Michelle is consistently hard on Margo. "She did not understand how or why Michelle had turned into this impossible creature," Margo says early on in the novel. "Margo would never voluntarily live with such an angry, critical person. Never. But when it was your own child you had no choice."

In the introduction, Blume explains that because some details from her personal life overlapped with Margo's, everyone assumed *Smart Women* was about her and her family. Even Randy, she says, "believes that Michelle is based on her (when she was that age) and maybe she's right." Judy goes on to say that "all the characters in the book (okay, except for some parts of Michelle) are fictional," admitting that Michelle is closest to her heart. "Michelle is my favorite character in the book . . . I love her for giving her mother a hard time because she cares about her and can't bear to see the family painfully disrupted again."

The novel is told from four different perspectives: Margo's, Michelle's, Margo's friend B.B.'s, and that of B.B.'s twelve-year-old daughter Sara. B.B. (whose real name is Francine) is also a divorced forty-year-old who is newish to Boulder. She and Margo meet at work and hit it off. But their burgeoning friendship gets complicated when B.B.'s ex-husband, Andrew, sublets the house next door to Margo's for three months. One balmy August night, he calls over the fence and invites himself over for a drink and a hot tub. The flirtation revs up.

Andrew, a journalist, is rakish and charming. He earnestly tells Margo that she "look[s] like the girl on the Sun-Maid raisin box." For their first official date, Margo calls him and tells him she's leaving for *Apocalypse Now* in a few minutes, and would he like to join her? He would. He brings two boxes of raisins to the theater and they eat them before holding hands. When Margo nods off because she doesn't like the movie, she snuggles up to Andrew's shoulder.

Margo has casually dated around since her divorce. Her ex wanted "a Stepford Wife . . . a plastic princess," she explains, and she isn't eager to get married again. But after turning forty, she resolved to find herself a "steady man."

"No more affairs going nowhere," she reminds herself early in her and Andrew's courtship. "From now on she was only interested in men who wanted to settle down . . . He would have plenty of experience with women, her steady man, and with life, so that settling down with her would be a pleasant relief."

When Andrew's sublet is up just a few months after they've been dating, Margo invites him to move in. She knows it's quick but as soon as the words are out of her mouth, she's excited. "She tried to think reasonably, but she couldn't," she says. "She wanted to jump up and shout, *Yes, move in with me* but a mature adult did not react solely on an emotional level. A mature adult thought things through, considered both sides of the issue." So Margo checks herself. "There would be a million complications," she admits.

Good-naturedly, Andrew agrees, but they resolve to go on the adventure anyway. The complications are real, and they include B.B., Sara—who openly wants to *Parent Trap* her mom and dad—Stuart, and, topping the list, Michelle. Michelle is horrified that her mother is letting Andrew move in with them, and she isn't shy about telling her so. Ten days after Andrew has officially become the new roommate, Margo throws a dinner party with a few friends. Everything is rolling along smoothly until a conversational lull, when Michelle seizes on the chance to chat up Andrew in front of the group. "Did you know when we first moved to town my mother joined Man-of-the-Month club?" she asks sarcastically, before rattling off the names of Margo's former lovers.

Margo is mortified but Andrew takes it in stride. "Oh, those were just alternative selections, Michelle," he jokes. "They don't count." Soon, we find out that Michelle is hazing Andrew as a way of protecting her family. "Michelle had set out to test Andrew as soon as he'd moved in, because it was better to find out now if he could take it, and if he couldn't, to get rid of him quickly, before she got to know him and like him." As she confesses to Stuart, Michelle is tired of riding her mother's emotional roller coaster, sick of being ignored when Margo is happy and getting dragged down with her when she's miserable. "I'm the one who has to suffer through it every time one of her love affairs fizzles," Michelle tells her brother defensively, after he scolds her for being obnoxious at dinner. "Me . . . not you!"

We learn that Michelle is harboring quieter resentments, too, ones she doesn't admit to Stuart. Michelle writes poems that she'd like to show to Margo but she talks herself out of it. "One day, Margo would be sorry," Michelle says. "Sorry that she'd had a daughter and hadn't bothered to get to know her."

This sequence complements a handful of passages from another book, published sixteen years later by a different author: Randy Blume. After graduating from Wesleyan in 1983, Randy's professional life took

an unexpected turn. She fell in love with flying planes and set out to become a pilot. She worked in commercial aviation for years and in 1999,
she wrote *Crazy in the Cockpit*, a comic novel about a young female pilot
trying to break into the male-dominated world of air travel. The book
was edited by Dick Jackson, who by then had sold Bradbury and had set
up his own imprint elsewhere.

Kendra is *Crazy in the Cockpit*'s protagonist, the only child of a respected academic who chairs the sociology department at Princeton.
Early on in the book, Kendra tells us that her mother, Rachel, was distressed when she learned Kendra had no intention of attending Princeton herself: "You've become so self-absorbed that you probably never
even considered what my life would be like without you!" Rachel said at
the time. Kendra's college roommate, a psych major, has diagnosed their
mother-daughter bond as "'acutely neurotic' and wanted to use it as a
case study for one of her research papers."

Rachel hates that Kendra wants to walk away from her journalism
training and pursue flying. When Kendra arrives home for Thanksgiv-
ing break, she anticipates a thorough guilting from her mom. But that's
not what happens. "It turned out my mother wouldn't have noticed if
I'd flown an airplane through the living room," Kendra says. "She was
too busy with Norman, her new boyfriend, who I found comfortably en-
sconced in our town house." (Is the name "Norman" an Easter egg reference to *Wifey*?)

Christmas break, at a rental house in Key West, brings more of the
same. "My mother and Norman got up early every morning to bike,
snorkel, or sail, and I sat by the pool with my books and Jennifer, Norman's sullen twelve-year-old daughter, who was angry because she'd
been dragged away from her friends in Phoenix to a place that didn't
even have a decent mall," Kendra explains. Throughout the novel, Rachel functions as a mixture of annoying adversary, conscience, and comic
relief. When Kendra gets a flying job in Guam, Rachel visits and brings

her anxiety with her. "How could she have let me come to this intellectual and cultural wasteland," Kendra says, aping her mother's point of view, "this *paved rock* in the middle of the Pacific? What if, God forbid, I ever needed emergency surgery?" (Randy was clearly grateful for her real mother's well-earned appreciation of the differences between fact and fiction, and dedicated her one and only book to Judy, "who always believed I would write—even when I was too busy flying.")

In *Crazy in the Cockpit*, the mother-daughter plot is a high-strung counterpoint to the much bigger story of Kendra's coming-of-age drama, played out against the clouds. But in *Smart Women*, the relationship between Margo and Michelle—not Margo and Andrew—provides the book's emotional center. The novel takes some wacky turns, like when teenage Michelle starts dating an older guy who secretly used to sleep with Margo. Thorny, for sure, but the pair work things out. *Smart Women's* last chapter sees Michelle heading off for a summertime trip to Israel with Stuart and their father. The family has found a cautious balance, and Michelle has surprised herself by developing a big-sisterly fondness for Sara.

In a clever bit of symbolism, Michelle, who has smoothed out a bit, asks Margo to take care of a cactus in her absence. "I gave you a lot of shit this year, didn't I, Mother?" she asks. Margo doesn't argue, and is touched when Michelle asks her for a goodbye kiss. Margo tells Michelle that she loves her. "I love you too," Michelle says as they embrace. "You know something, Mother . . . for a while I had my doubts, but you've turned out okay."

Her words please Margo immensely and after Michelle is gone, she cries heavy tears of relief, in recognition of all they've been through. The deep emotional release is akin to surrendering to something sublime in nature, like a perfect sunset, Margo tells us. "She felt a pouring out of motherly love, followed by an enormous sense of pride in herself and her children. She had made a lot of mistakes, but they had come through it together," Margo thinks with satisfaction.

"Is there any relationship more complicated than mothers and daughters?" Blume asks rhetorically in the introduction to *Smart Women*. Any close-knit, strong-willed mother-daughter duo would recognize the truth, the heat, and the humor in this question. The feminist movement didn't ease generational tension among these pairs—if anything, it made it worse at times. Divorce, dating, and consciousness-raising meant that mothers grew up clumsily in front of their daughters. Girls, born native to the language of freedom, watched their mothers stumble and didn't understand why they couldn't just soar. Moms wanted the world for their female children, but then resented the bigness of their dreams, their easy entitlement. Hopefully we'll do it better, whispers every generation of parents. Hopefully next time we'll get it right for our kids.

## Chapter Twenty-Four

# ℒibraries

*"It's really scary being
a librarian right now."*

There's still work to do. The Equal Rights Amendment—which, along with *Roe v. Wade*, was supposed to be the crowning achievement of Second Wave feminism—still hasn't passed. It went through Congress and the Senate, but then died at the state level in 1979 thanks to a swell of conservative activism led by Phyllis Schlafly. As any parent of an elementary school–aged child can attest, the breadwinner/homemaker model of marriage is still "super baked in" to our legal and school systems, Suzanne Kahn said, which means that, arguably, traditional gender roles are, too. Regardless of any political lip service, universal child care still sounds like a progressive pipe dream. The tide of right-wing support that got Reagan elected is once again overtaking local and state governments.

While book challenges certainly slowed down by the end of the 1980s, they continued through the 1990s, and in some extreme cases ruined peoples' careers in the process. That's what happened when Wisconsin guidance counselor Michael Dishnow took on his school principal, who wanted to ban *Forever* in the early nineties. As Dishnow tells it, the principal at Rib Lake High School, where he worked, saw a girl reading *Forever* in the hallway and snatched it out of her hand. "Of course, [he] opened it initially to the perfect page with the sexual intercourse, and confiscated the book," Dishnow remembered.

Dishnow was married to the school librarian at the time, who had described Judy Blume to him as "the best of the best." Dishnow, a mustached former Marine and a onetime school principal himself, thought it "just wasn't right" that the principal "didn't go through any process" when he decided to take the student's book away from her and subsequently ban it from the school library. They argued over it, and Dishnow recalled that "at one point I made a statement to the effect, I used a curse word, I said something about the 'damn principal' and this 'damn school' or whatever." (The judge's ruling on the case quoted him as having referred to the "God damned administration" at a faculty meeting.)

The well-liked guidance counselor said he was a rare liberal in a conservative town, where the school's less-is-more approach to sex ed struck him as naive, given "the realities I knew having been in the Marine Corps overseas, various places, especially when it came to sexual issues." Dishnow wrote a column in the local newspaper, Medford's *Star News*, where he mused about things that came across his desk as a guidance counselor—mostly uncontroversial topics, like college applications and job hunts. But after the principal "unilaterally" banned *Forever*, he used his "Counselor's Corner" platform to sound off on the situation.

Dishnow said that was probably the last straw. "They fired me . . . for being insubordinate," he alleged. He'd had a successful twenty-five-year career working as a school administrator in Alaska before moving to Wisconsin, and felt the blow to his reputation was unjustified. He sued the Rib Lake school district, arguing that he had been let go in retaliation for exercising his First Amendment rights. "I was a gadfly, no doubt about it," Dishnow said, "[but] they're not going to take my rights away from me, so I fought it."

The case went on for three long years, during which Dishnow looked for another position but claims he was kneecapped by the very public details of his dismissal, and the fact that he couldn't get a letter of recommendation from his former employer. A jury agreed, awarding him $400,000 in damages (that number was reduced to approximately $180,000 in subsequent appeals, according to Dishnow). Dishnow eventually took the one and only employment offer he received, in another small town in Wisconsin, where he still resides, at a significantly lower salary from the already modest one he was making at Rib Lake. "But I wasn't in it for the money to begin with," Dishnow said. "Nobody else would touch me at that point. It was a long time ago but it was a pretty trying experience."

He is still in contact with some former colleagues at Rib Lake High School and they told him that to this day, *Forever* remains on a restricted shelf in the library. Dishnow's campaign seems to have done nothing to change the principal's mind about the book, but he did get one high-profile shoutout for his efforts. In *Places I Never Meant to Be*, Blume mentions Dishnow among a number of examples of people who stood up to book bans and experienced dire personal and professional consequences. "Guidance counselor Mike Dishnow was fired for writing critically of the board of education's decision to ban my book *Forever*," she notes. "Ultimately, he won a court settlement, but by then his life had been turned upside down."

* * *

For a while, it looked like the culture wars over children's books had been diffused. Two blockbuster series took over bookstores in the mid-1980s: The Baby-sitters Club and Sweet Valley High. Ann M. Martin, who created the Connecticut band of business-minded babysitters, had them talk about serious issues—diabetes, divorce and remarriage, cultural differences, death—but left the puberty stuff to Blume. Sweet Valley High, about a pair of pretty blond twins, was straight fluff. Fleissner said her mother hated those books, which crowded out complex novels like hers: "From my mom's point of view and the other seventies-era writers, it was such a step backwards, to this much more 1950s sanitized version of like, 'Oh, who's dating who?' Little high school dramas."

Parents and politicians argued over Satanism, rap lyrics, *Beavis and Butt-Head*, and whether or not it was cool that Britney Spears dressed like a sexy schoolgirl. But now, book challenges are back—and they're more cutthroat than ever.

In April 2023, Blume told the BBC that the current movement to ban books is "so much worse than it was in the '80s," because instead of being stoked by grassroots movements, it's driven by the politicians themselves. She cited her adopted home state of Florida as a place where "bad politicians who [are] drunk with power, who want to get out there" are using extreme talking points and legislation to do so. "It is so frightening," Blume told British journalist Laura Kuenssberg. "I think the only answer is for us to speak out and really keep speaking out, or we're going to lose our way."

Arlene LaVerde, who has spent three decades working for the New York City Department of Education, said that Blume's novels aren't challenged nearly as often now, in part because they aren't as ubiquitous as they were in the 1980s, and also because the bull's-eye of conservative grievance has moved. Now the young adult books that are most often under attack are ones with LGBTQ+ themes. Of the top thirteen most banned books in 2022 according to the American Library Association's list, seven contain LGBTQ+ subjects and/or characters, including *Gender Queer*, *All Boys Aren't Blue*, the award-winning graphic novel *Flamer* by Mike Curato, and transgender writer Juno Dawson's *This Book Is Gay*.

LaVerde said that thanks to the brouhaha over Critical Race Theory, books that speak openly about race—even straightforward history books—are under fire, too. "Critical Race Theory is not taught in K–12 education," insisted LaVerde. "But it's a term that people grab on to and use because they feel like it's indoctrination. Indoctrinating what? Indoctrinating that in the United States, more than half of the country had slaves? And that it was legal?" She went on: "It's a shameful part of our history, yeah. But it's a part of our history and we should learn about it."

In New York City, a book would never get removed from a school library if just one parent or educator complained about it, LaVerde explained. A complaint initiates a formal process, wherein the first step is requesting that the challenger read the book from cover to cover (many parents who balk at certain titles do so because "they looked over a kid's shoulder and, excuse my language, they saw the word 'fuck.' Or they saw the word 'sex,'" she said). If they're still unhappy after that, they can fill out a challenge form, which then prompts the school to put together a committee of readers, consisting of a school administrator, a representative from the DOE's library system, and the librarian. If it's a high school, some students will be invited to sit on the committee as well. The group then meets to discuss the book, its merits, and whether it actually belongs in the building. If the committee votes in favor of retaining the title, it cannot be challenged for another two years.

With such a robust system in place, few books end up getting removed—but librarians still absorb strong feelings from parents when they disagree with the reading material that's been selected for their children. At the time we spoke, Lauren Harrison had worked as an elementary school librarian at a public school in the West Village for seven years. She said she stocked her shelves with the popular titles of the moment—all the Dog Man books, The Baby-sitters Club updated graphic novels—as well as inclusive picture books for early readers, like *My Own Way: Celebrating Gender Freedom for Kids*; *Our Skin: A First Conversation About Race*; and *Antiracist Baby*. Given the demographics of the families who attend her school, Harrison said she was surprised when she received feedback from a mom that her book selections were "too gay." She recalled getting an angry email after reading the picture book *Our Subway Baby*—based on author Peter Mercurio's real-life experience of finding an abandoned baby on the New York City subway and ultimately adopting him with his husband—aloud to the students. Harrison dismissed the email as "ridiculous," with her principal's blessing. "I loved that book, the kids loved it, they fought over who got to borrow it," she said. "It's offensive to me that that book's offensive to you."

Harrison's mother, Carol Waxman, is also a librarian and has worked in the Connecticut public library system for almost forty years. She had a harrowing experience after she helped plan West Hartford's first drag queen story time in the summer of 2022.

Waxman was enthusiastic about hosting the event as part of a larger local Pride celebration, especially given the town's "very active Pride community." But as soon as the story time was scheduled, the blowback started. "Well, it ended up being so controversial and difficult. Letters, phone calls, people came in to see me, furious," Waxman remembered. She was shaken up by it, "because some of the letters to me were threatening. 'This is on you, your career is at stake, you're gonna throw everything away because of this,'" people were telling her. The town's mayor and manager also received rage-filled correspondences, all from older citizens who stressed that they'd never, ever let their grandchildren attend an event hosted by drag queens. Reluctantly, officials made the decision to move the reading outside, in light of the threats of violence and vandalism against the library. And when it became clear that the event might need a rain plan, a nearby Barnes & Noble stepped up and offered to absorb it. "I went over to see it and it was packed," Waxman said.

She noted—as Blume has, too—that this moment's increased appetite for censorship isn't coming exclusively from the Right. Blume experienced this firsthand in April 2023 after expressing solidarity with J.K. Rowling, who has borne the brunt of major social media pile-ons due to her outspoken anti-trans views. Public response was so negative that Judy issued an aggrieved statement on X (then Twitter) clarifying that "I wholly support the trans community. My point, which was taken out of context, is that I can empathize with a writer—or person—who has been harassed online."

Then there were the sanitized versions of Roald Dahl's books that struck up a frenzy in the winter of 2023. That February, UK conservative broadsheet the *Telegraph* reported that "Augustus Gloop is no longer fat, Mrs. Twit is no longer fearfully ugly, and the Oompa Loompas have gone gender-neutral in new editions of Roald Dahl's beloved stories." Dahl's publisher, with the blessing of the Dahl estate, had scrubbed potentially offensive descriptions and passages from his famous books, presumably to appease today's more sensitive readers, with Gloop going from "enormously fat" to just "enormous," and the Cloud-Men in *James and the Giant Peach* becoming Cloud-People, for instance. But the response was mixed at best; PEN America criticized the move, and oft-censored author Salman Rushdie tweeted that Puffin Books and Dahl's descendants "should be ashamed." Puffin later announced that it would continue to publish "classic" versions of Dahl's novels, giving contemporary readers a choice between the two.

Waxman said that she keeps her collection up to date, which at times means retiring titles that no longer fit in with cultural norms. She said any children's books that depict guns—which used to be unremarkable—are now "taboo, completely taboo" in the age of mass shootings. Same goes for illustrations that show adults smoking cigarettes. Waxman also mentioned Lois Lenski, an author and illustrator who published award-winning children's books in the 1930s and 1940s. Waxman would "never" recommend them for young readers today, she said, because of their outmoded depictions of gender roles within families. "The mother is always home, never works, always wearing a dress, always home cleaning the house," Waxman said. "I'm very aware of those books now, not that anybody is going to tell me to ban them, but they're just not in good taste."

(People have compared this process, called "weeding" in the library biz, to banning books but it's a false equivalency. Weeding is about unshelving titles that have been rendered irrelevant by the culture. Banning is about cutting off access to books that are contributing to current cultural conversations in the hopes that these conversations will stop.)

"It's really scary being a librarian right now," LaVerde confessed, given high levels of polarization and the aggression with which citizens express and defend their personal views. "It's really scary being an educator," she went on, "which is weird, because it's something I would never in my entire career of thirty-plus years think I would say." LaVerde conceded that "honestly, in New York, we're luckier. But I think about my colleagues in Florida, in Texas, who are being threatened, not only to lose their certification, their license, their pensions, their careers, but they're being threatened with bodily harm." Politics, religion, and the concurrent racial justice and transgender rights movements have all crashed together in a shockingly painful collision over . . . books, of all things. But LaVerde thinks stories for kids are so contentious not only because they tend our children's nascent moral fibers but also because they uproot our deepest fears as parents—that in being exposed to increasingly mature topics, our kids will become independent and leave us to lead their own lives.

"Parents don't want to admit that their children are growing up," she said. "It hurts."

Nevertheless, she's strongly opposed to book bans and believes that reading about our differences—whether they're cultural, racial, or involving sexual orientation—actually builds empathy by reminding us that we all share the same human experiences. "Your struggles are a little bit different [than a character's] but you know what? The kid in rural Mississippi is fighting with his mom to go to a sleepover, and me in New York City, I'm fighting with my mom, she's not letting me go to a sleepover, either," LaVerde said, channeling a young reader's point of view.

School librarian Julia Loving said that she makes a priority of re-minding her students that access to a wide range of books is a privilege, even in the age of social media, where kids often tell her that reading takes too long and is "boring."

Loving recently responded to this sentiment by sharing her own history with them—about her parents, who migrated to New York City from the Jim Crow South because they wanted their chil-dren to have better opportunities than they had. About her great-great-grandparents, who Loving found out could read and write when she dug into her genealogical roots. That surprised her. She told her upper schoolers that literacy was rare among Black people in Virginia in the late nineteenth century. She asked the students if they had any idea why that might be.

"They said, 'Well, they couldn't read or write because maybe many of them had been enslaved, right? Because that was something that was illegal to do, educate enslaved people,'" Loving recalled someone saying. "And so I asked them, 'Out of all things in the world, why would someone want another human being not to know how to actually read and write?' And one of the kids said, 'Well, you keep them from power, you strip them of their power.'"

Knowledge is power, *reading* is power, and for the first time since the 1980s, today's kids are caught up in a multidirectional adult power-play over the kinds of books they should be allowed to slip into their backpacks and quietly enjoy in their bedrooms. Loving said her personal share made a visible impact. "I always say, the reason [to have] inclusiv-ity and diversity in our collections, and definitely having our kids have access to books, is because of the power that can be gained from them," Loving explained. "They can take you places that you've never been, can teach you how to do this or that . . . in those scenarios, why would you *not* want to read? Because you have to realize that there's something to this reading thing."

## Chapter Twenty-Five

# Legacy

*"We didn't have the internet; we didn't have any places where we could find the answers."*

In the 1981 *Christian Science Monitor* article, there's a quote about Blume that feels kind of ridiculous now. It came from Mary Burns, then a professor of children's literature at Framingham State College in Massachusetts. Burns told the reporter that "in every age . . . there are books that answer the needs of the moment, and Judy Blume's books seem to be fulfilling that need. But you can't equate popularity with quality, nor quality with popularity. The question that needs to be asked now is: will Judy Blume's books be as popular 20 years from now?"

Okay, it sounds silly in hindsight, especially given the flash flood of love and gratitude that has washed over Blume these past few years. But Burns wasn't *entirely* off base. Kids aren't reaching for Blume's novels as frequently as they were in the 1980s and 1990s. Julia Loving noted that while she keeps all the Judy Blume books in her library, they don't circulate nearly as much as they used to. Carol Waxman agreed. These days, she said, it's mostly parents of young children who are checking out Blume's books, wanting to share beloved characters like Fudge and

Margaret and Deenie with the next generation. Less often, it's the kids themselves who are plucking them off the shelves. They're reaching instead for graphic novels and Captain Underpants.

But whether Blume's work stands the test of time is an entirely different conversation. You only need to spend a few hours reading *Superfudge* with a second grader to appreciate the perennial appeal of her writing. "Bonjour, stupid!" still unleashes a tiny bellyful of giggles. Also, the challenges kids face remain largely unchanged. Parents are still getting divorced. Elementary schoolers still get diagnosed with scoliosis and require intervention. Bullies terrorize their classmates; best friends laugh and sob and struggle. The competitive friendship dynamics between Margaret and Nancy remain true to life, with or without the intrusion of iPads and cell phones.

And we, the pre-internet generation, genuinely needed Judy Blume. She was dropping nuggets of truth and wisdom that kids couldn't get anywhere else at the time. Yes, if we were lucky, we had some sex ed in school, and yes, a fifth grader could steal her parents' copy of *The Joy of Sex* and smuggle it into a birthday party the way a classmate of mine did in 1992 (she was caught and everyone got reprimanded and sent home). But it wasn't the same. "The way that sex education is usually done is to put up one picture of a female body and one picture of a male body, which already scientifically is not enough," Cory Silverberg said of the heteronormative approach to sex ed that dominated the twentieth century. That's something, but it's not gender- or orientation-inclusive and it's not meeting children at their level.

It's just another spin on the eggs and moon talk Judy got in the 1950s from her dad.

What's still missing from a lot of contemporary sex ed is an exploration of the way sex intersects with relationships, experts say. Even today, very few parents and educators are prepared to discuss the way dynamics of care and safety and vulnerability all contribute to true intimacy, which is crucial for a satisfying love life. That's what Judy innately understood how to do. She taught us about our bodies and our hearts through her stories. Periods are something that happens to a whole friend group. First teenage love affects the entire family. Boys experience heartbreak, too! Truly safe intercourse requires talking and planning. *You can't go back to holding hands.*

Sex educator Shannon Dressler brings this perspective to the classroom in her own work with middle- and high school–aged kids. Consent, desire, pleasure, respect—these are all parts of a successful partnership, and children need to be taught what that looks like. "It's really helping [students] learn how to have healthy relationships, where you're feeling good about the relationships and connections you have with others," she said of ideal sex ed curriculums. The Netflix show *Sex Education*, featuring fictional British teens discovering their passions, peccadillos, and hang-ups, does this well. It's all about bringing context to the body and the bedroom. That's what Blume did for her readers back in the day. "We didn't have the internet; we didn't have any places where we could find the answers. Her books were certainly a beginning point," Dressler said.

Now kids have the opposite problem—they're glutted with information.

"These kids have access to so much," Dressler continued. By pretending that there's only one right way to have sex, within the realm of heterosexual marriage, abstinence-only programs just leave kids and teens with more questions. Then, when they "try to find the answers on their own," they get lost "in spaces and places that actually aren't giving them the right information," Dressler explained, alluding to the maelstrom of free porn swirling on the web. OnlyFans and Pornhub are quite a bit less wholesome than *Deenie* and *Forever*—not that they're doing remotely the same thing. Kids today have quicker access to graphic sexual images and videos than any previous generation, and just like in the wake of the sexual revolution, adults have a responsibility to confront this challenge head-on. The right kind of education, Dressler said, actually helps inoculate children from the virus of a hyper-sexed culture: "These are all protective factors that we need to put in place in young people as early as possible as they move through the complexities of life."

Proper sex education needs to start early, and it's not necessarily about explaining the mechanics of reproduction, Silverberg agreed. "I get why parents don't want to talk about where babies come from, because they don't want to talk about intercourse with their four- and five-year-olds. Why are we talking about intercourse with four- and five-year-olds? If a four- or five-year-old wants to know how a sperm and egg meet, that's fine, it's not harmful to them, but it's also not in any way relevant to them." What is relevant to them—or will be so much sooner than conception—is what it feels like to have a body that's constantly in flux, in a world where allusions to sex are all around, all the time, in songs, on billboards, in television commercials, and on YouTube. "Kids are [watching] movies and have feelings about things. Kids overhear other older siblings listening to music. Kids know about advertising. They hear other kids say stuff about gender," Silverberg said.

They need to learn how to process all these stimuli through their own eyes and not through the eyes of a pedantic adult, Silverberg went on. "We're figuring out ways to help young people learn, in their own way, in their own path, in a way that honors all the things that they already know," Silverberg said of their colorful comic-style books with artist Fiona Smyth. "When you're seven, you've lived a lifetime in your seven-year-old body and nobody knows what that's like other than you."

Judy Blume understood that. She got it, instinctively, and was able to authentically channel a pre-teen's perspective better than anyone else could. That was the thrust and the sparkle of her talent.

Her genius, if you will.

•    •    •

The literary gatekeepers finally started to recognize Blume's unique contribution. Ironically, the relentless attacks on her books in the 1980s served to put her in a category with the world's finest writers. In 1989, after Ayatollah Khomeini issued his fatwa against Salman Rushdie, authors gathered at the Atlanta-Fulton central library to read aloud from *The Satanic Verses*, as well as other frequently banned books, including Henry Miller's *Tropic of Cancer* and Blume's novels.

Before that, in November 1987, the then-forty-nine-year-old Judy was dubbed a Library Lion by the New York Public Library, among a class of fellow honorees that included Raymond Carver, Mary McCarthy, and Harold Pinter. On a Wednesday night, Blume flitted among the city's literati—and its stylish upper crust—for a decadent dinner of beef Stroganoff in the ornate Stephen A. Schwarzman Building's Special Collections room, heralded by trumpets. The author of popular children's books, who had been dismissed for so long as a purveyor of addictive, junky pseudo-literature, accepted a gold medallion strung from a red ribbon around her neck. Fashion designer Bill Blass chaired the event; Jacqueline Onassis, Brooke Astor, and Oscar de la Renta were among the posh crowd, cheering her on.

Judy had something else to celebrate that night: she was a newlywed. Before they tied the knot, she and George had lived together for the better part of a decade. They'd sold the house in Santa Fe and moved back to New York City, buying a country home in western Connecticut.

She had been wary of marriage given her past experiences, but by then she was sure about George. On June 6, 1987, just a week after his fiftieth birthday, the longtime couple gathered their family and friends for an informal wedding on their Upper West Side terrace. A female judge, a friend, performed the nuptials. The rings came from a street fair on Broadway. Larry bought his mother a mixed bouquet of white flowers to hold.

Essie Sussman lived to see her daughter get married again but died that August of pneumonia, at the age of eighty-three. In *Presenting Judy Blume*, Judy said that she was grateful her mom was there to witness her exchanging vows with George. "She always said, 'I should only live to see this wedding,'" Blume said. "And she did."

By the time she turned fifty herself in February of 1988, the most difficult years of Judy's life were behind her. It also marked the end of a roiling, tumultuous, wildly productive stretch when Blume wrote the books she'd be best known for. "I used to think that when my kids grew up, then I could really focus on my writing," she said at an event in 2015. "Instead, it's kind of been the opposite. You know, I got happy. And writing comes of angst," she explained, before quickly assuring the audience: "I can still conjure it up, don't worry."

Judy got happy. She called up her angst when she had to, for work, but she unleashed her joy into many other things—marriage, friendship, a midlife passion for tap dancing. In the early 1990s, Randy gave birth to a baby boy and Judy became a besotted grandmother. She took up water sports at Martha's Vineyard, and later, she and George fell in love with Key West, Florida, where they'd eventually live full-time and invest in a bustling bookstore.

Committed feminist that she was, she never stopped talking publicly about puberty, or menstruation, or sex. As the now-octogenarian Blume likes to point out, the pleasurable things we can do with our bodies are an integral part of our human existence. And shouldn't we all be making the most of our short time on earth, delighting in these amazing and awkward physical forms? Judy has written as she has lived: wholeheartedly. Chasing, embracing, pinning down experience—and gathering it up again, so very full.

# Acknowledgments

T hank you to David Halpern, who is the best agent I could ask for and an even better friend. Thank you to my editor, Julia Cheiffetz, who I've been lucky to work with twice and who is one of my all-time favorite collaborators. Thank you to Nick Ciani, Abby Mohr, Hannah Frankel, and Joanna Pinsker at One Signal for believing in this book and helping me bring it out into the world. Thank you to Laywan Kwan for the gorgeous cover design. Thank you to my longtime pal and production editor Liz Byer for taking such good care of the manuscript.

Thank you to the people who generously shared their time and their thoughts, making this a sharper, more nuanced project than anything I could have done on my own: Dean Butler, Michael Dishnow, Shannon Dressler, Michelle Fine, Jennifer Fleissner, Karen Fleshman, Lauren Harrison, Suzanne Kahn, Arlene LaVerde, Rachel Lotus, Julia Loving, Peter Silsbee, Cory Silverberg, Roger Sutton, Carol Waxman, and Jonathan Zimmerman.

Thank you to Mary Ellen Budney, John Monahan, and the entire staff at Yale's Beinecke Rare Book and Manuscript Library for helping me navigate the Judy Blume papers. Thank you to the many other librarians and archivists who pitched in along the way, especially Aimee Fernandez-Puente at the Elizabeth Public Library, Maribeth Fisher at the Scotch Plains Public Library, Greg Guderian at the Newark Public Library, Demetrius Watson at *School Library Journal*, and John Wright at the Fulton County Library.

Thank you to Chris St. John and Rebecca Santiago for taking the time to read an early draft and offering invaluable feedback that made blurry ideas click into focus.

The story of this book is not complete without acknowledging the health challenges that shaped the entire editorial process. I would not have been able to put together a decent sentence, let alone a book proposal, during a global pandemic were it not for my village, the other parents in my childcare pod: Frank Boudreaux, Suzanne Dikker, Megan Gaffney, Matt Kebbekus, Lauren Portada, Sarah Rockower, and Hans Maarten Wikkerink. Thank you to them, and also to our beloved babysitters Rizzo Klotz and Zoe Tanner, who treat our kids like family.

Thank you to all the friends and family who supported me when my own medical crisis hit while I was still writing the book's first draft. In particular, thank you to Neal Dusedau for a perfectly timed cross-country visit, to Gwen Schantz for being my art-viewing buddy, and to Jess Lattif for the fun and diverting phone conversations. To my parents—Annette Bergstein, Jay Bergstein, Pauline Bergstein, and Jeff Wilson—my sisters—Allison Bergstein and Deanna Smetanka—and my in-laws—Herb Rosenberg and Jean Rosenberg—thank you for loving me in sickness and in health, no matter what I do for a living.

Thank you to Judy Blume, for writing books that truly changed the world.

Thank you to The West coffee shop, for providing such a lively creative hub for the neighborhood and for being an extension of my office.

Thank you to Henry, my furry companion of fifteen years who never fails to warm laps, hearts, and manuscript pages (my son would be very indignant if I left out the cat).

Most of all, thank you to my most cherished guys, Andrew and Curtis, who fill our home with joy, laughter, great conversation, and silly dance moves. You show me every day what life is really about.

# Notes

For biographical information about Judy Blume, I am most indebted to three books: *Judy Blume's Story* by Betsy Lee (New York: Dillon Press, 1981), *Presenting Judy Blume* by Maryann N. Weidt (New York: Dell Publishing, 1990), and *Letters to Judy: What Kids Wish They Could Tell You* by Judy Blume (New York: Pocket Books, 1986). I also visited the Judy Blume Papers at Yale University (General Collection, Beinecke Rare Book and Manuscript Library) twice, first in April 2022 and again in May 2022. In deference to the conditions governing use of this collection, I have not quoted directly from any of the materials that I saw during that time. I spent the afternoon of June 28, 2022, at the Elizabeth Public Library's main branch in Elizabeth, New Jersey (Blume's hometown), where I viewed clippings related to her life and career. I've consulted hundreds of articles and interviews with Judy Blume, published between 1969 and the present day. Specific citations are below.

## Epigraph

vii *"But here she had / no children"*: Sharon Olds, "Visiting My Mother's College," *The Wellspring* (New York: Knopf, 1999), p. 3.

ix *"The word police can fuck off"*: Vanessa Grigoriadis, "Madonna Talks 'Fifty Shades of Grey' ('Not Very Sexy'), the Pope and Why the 'Word Police Can F— Off,'" Billboard.com, February 13, 2015. Accessed online: https://www.billboard.com/music/music-news/madonna-interview-rebel-heart -50-shades-of-grey-pope-word-police-6472671/.

## Preface

xv Stephanie is into hunks: Judy Blume, *Just as Long as We're Together* (New York: Orchard Books, 1987). I worked from the 2013 reprint from Delacorte Press, p. 1.

xvi *"The Judy Blume Renaissance is upon us"*: Nicole Sperling, "How Judy Blume Finally Got a 'Yes' from Hollywood," *New York Times*, March 7, 2023. Accessed online: https://www.nytimes.com/2023/03/07/business/media/judy -blume-hollywood.html.

xvi *"We Need Judy Blume Now More Than Ever"*: Cindy White, "We Need Judy Blume Now More Than Ever," A.V. Club, April 28, 2023. Accessed online: https://www.avclub.com/we-need-judy-blume-now-more-than-ever-185 0384851.

xvi *according to the American Library Association*: From the ALA's "Top 13 Most Challenged Books of 2022." Accessed online: https://www.ala.org/advocacy /bbooks/frequentlychallengedbooks/top10.

xx *"The fact is that to women born after 1920"*: Betty Friedan, *The Feminine Mystique* (New York: Norton, 1963). I worked from the 1983 reprint by Dell Publishing, p. 100.

xx *"When the ballot was won"*: Kate Millett, *Sexual Politics* (New York: Doubleday & Company, 1970), pp. 83–84.

## Chapter One
## Housewife's Syndrome

1 *"I went in the closet and I cried"*: Quoted from an interview Blume did with *CBS Sunday Morning* (original airdate May 17, 2015). Accessed on YouTube: https://www.youtube.com/watch?v=_KAAIschIBc.

1 *John Blume was a promising law student*: Lee, *Judy Blume's Story*, p. 56.

1 *her single most important ambition as "college"*: From the 1956 Battin High School yearbook, accessed at the Elizabeth Public Library's main branch (1 South Broad Street, Elizabeth, NJ 07202) on June 28, 2022.

2 *Judy framed her college diploma*: Mentioned in a 2007 commencement

speech Blume gave at her alma mater, New York University. Box 122 of the Judy Blume Papers at Yale University's Beinecke Rare Book and Manuscript Library. Accessed May 10, 2022.

3 *"Those women weren't even shopping"*: Weidt, *Presenting Judy Blume*, p. 13.

3 *"the problem that has no name"*: Betty Friedan, *The Feminine Mystique* (New York: Norton, 1963), p. 15.

3 *"The American housewife—freed by science and the labor-saving appliances"*: Ibid., p. 18.

3 *"I feel as if I don't exist"*: Ibid., p. 20.

4 *The "housewife's syndrome" or "housewife's blight"*: Ibid., pp. 20–21.

4 *"If you want to know about my illnesses, read Wifey"*: Weidt, *Presenting Judy Blume*, p. 118.

4 *"It was another side of my life that I wanted to share"*: Ibid., p. 117.

4 *"Ten days later it returned, but much worse"*: Judy Blume, *Wifey* (New York: Berkley Books, 1978). I worked from the 2004 reprint, p. 12.

5 *made fun of her for being jumpy*: Lee, *Presenting Judy Blume*, p. 4.

5 *volunteered in town as an air-raid warden*: Ibid., p. 5.

5 *Bloomingdale's agreed to stock them and they sold for $9 apiece*: John Neary, "The 'Jacqueline Susann of Kids' Books,' Judy Blume, Grows Up with an Adult Novel," *People*, October 16, 1978. Accessed online: https://people.com/archive/the-jacqueline-susann-of-kids-books-judy-blume-grows-up-with-an-adult-novel-vol-10-no-16.

6 *She wrote one story, called "You Mom, You?"*: Box 116 of the Judy Blume Papers at Yale University's Beinecke Rare Book and Manuscript Library. Accessed April 28, 2022.

7 *She started carrying around a green-gray three-ring binder*: Box 121 of the Judy Blume Papers at Yale University's Beinecke Rare Book and Manuscript Library. Accessed May 10, 2022.

7 *Wyndham likely empathized with Judy*: "Lecturer Reveals Secrets of Writing Stories—Even Her Own 'Lucky Break,'" *Post-Standard*, Syracuse, New York, August 21, 1981, p. 9.

8 *For another story, called "The Ooh Ooh Ahh Ahh Bird"*: Weidt, *Presenting Judy Blume*, p. 10.

8 *"He thought it was better than shopping"*: Ibid., p. 13.

8 *"All I have to do is buy Judy some paper and pencils and she's happy!"*: Lee, *Judy Blume's Story*, p. 64.

8 *At one point, John sent a few of her drafts to his friend*: Box 118 of the Judy Blume Papers at Yale University's Beinecke Rare Book and Manuscript Library. Accessed May 10, 2022.

9 *"Larry's mother is crazy!"*: Lee, *Judy Blume's Story*, p. 65.

9 *the pair danced across the lawn together*: Ibid.

9 *The publisher matched Judy with an artist*: Hannah Torain, "Mom Keeps Busy Writing Books for Little Children," *Courier News*, Central New Jersey, October 10, 1969, p. 15.

9 *"The more I write, the more controversial I'm getting"*: Ibid.

## Chapter Two
### Kiddie Lit

10 *"It was the best $5,000 we ever spent"*: Weidt, *Presenting Judy Blume*, p. 11.

10 *When he moved to New York and his acting career flopped*: Neil Genzlinger, "Richard Jackson, Who Had an Ear for Children's Books, Dies at 84," *New York Times*, October 13, 2019. Accessed online: https://www.nytimes .com/2019/10/13/books/richard-jackson-dead.html.

10 *"These two guys sort of considered themselves pirates"*: Interview with Peter Silsbee in Brooklyn, New York, May 27, 2022.

11 *"Books about real kids for real kids"*: Ibid., May 27, 2022.

12 *the original manuscript for* Iggie's House *"wasn't very good"*: Ibid., May 27, 2022.

12 *"The day he called and said he'd like to meet me"*: Diane Roback, "Dick Jackson Remembered," *Publishers Weekly*, October 17, 2019. Accessed online: https://www.publishersweekly.com/pw/by-topic/childrens/childrens-authors/article/81494-dick-jackson-remembered.html.

12 *She took a pill to try to settle it*: Lee, *Judy Blume's Story*, p. 66.

13 *he was "a stunningly beautiful man"*: Sarah Larson, "Judy Blume's Unfinished Endings," *The New Yorker*, April 25, 2023. Accessed online: https:// www.newyorker.com/culture/persons-of-interest/judy-blumes-unfinished -endings.

13 *Jackson confessed he wasn't sure about publishing* Iggie's House *yet*: Lee, *Judy Blume's Story*, p. 67.

14 *"Don't be so bugged about being a greaser"*: S. E. Hinton, *The Outsiders* (New York: Viking Press, 1967). Accessed electronically via New York Public Library.

14 *"*Harriet the Spy *was transgressing all over the place"*: Telephone interview with Roger Sutton, June 10, 2022.

15 *Shyly, Beth Ellen confesses that she doesn't "want to be anything at all"*: Louise Fitzhugh, *The Long Secret* (New York: Harper & Row, 1965). I worked from the March 2002 reprint from Yearling Books, pp. 44–45.

15 *Later in* The Long Secret, *Beth Ellen is acting grumpy*: Ibid., p. 94.

15 *"Now, you know the baby grows inside a woman, in her womb, in her uterus?"*: Ibid., p. 97–98.

15 *one popular Victorian-era nickname for the uterus was "mother room"*: Joan Jacobs Brumberg, *The Body Project: An Intimate History of American Girls* (New York: Vintage Books, 1997), p. 36.

15 "The Long Secret, *moreover, observes in so many words"*: Carolyn Heilbrun, "And More for Young Readers," *New York Times*, November 21, 1965, sec. B, p. 56.

16 *the finished book still "wasn't up to what became her standard"*: PS to RB, May 27, 2022.

16 *"the bumbling, besieged liberal at age eleven"*: *Kirkus Reviews*, April 1, 1970. Accessed through the New York Public Library.

16 *In an afterword to a recent edition of the novel*: Judy Blume, *Iggie's House* (New York: Simon & Schuster, 2014). The afterword is called "Judy Blume

Talks About Writing *Iggie's House.*" The original book was published by Bradbury Press in 1970.

17 *"Judy was in my office one day"*: Weidt, *Presenting Judy Blume*, p. 63.

## Chapter Three
## Pre-Teen Girls

18 *"Always in love"*: William Leith, "Teen Spirit," *The Independent*, July 18, 1999, pp. 11–13. Accessed through the New York Public Library.

18 *Letters to Jackson from 1969 reveal*: Box 115 of the Judy Blume Papers at Yale University's Beinecke Rare Book and Manuscript Library. Accessed April 28, 2022.

19 *"In* Margaret, *I decided I'm going to write about"*: Beverly Solochek, "Plotting the Real Teen Scene," *Daily News*, September 3, 1976, p. C9.

19 *Judy thought of him as a natural philosopher*: Box 34 of the Judy Blume Papers at Yale University's Beinecke Rare Book and Manuscript Library. Accessed April 28, 2022.

20 *Blume described it in her 1977 autobiographical novel*: Judy Blume, *Starring Sally J. Freedman as Herself* (Englewood Cliffs, NJ: Bradbury Press, 1977). I worked from the 2014 reprint published by Simon & Schuster, p. 57.

20 *"Are you there God? It's me, Margaret," she begins*: Judy Blume, *Are You There God? It's Me, Margaret* (Englewood Cliffs, NJ: Bradbury Press, 1970). I worked from the 2014 reprint published by Simon & Schuster, p. 1.

20 *Sally has the same fear in* Sally J. Freedman: Blume, *Starring Sally J. Freedman as Herself*, pp. 147–48.

20 *"I made bargains with God"*: Judy Blume, *Letters to Judy: What Kids Wish They Could Tell You* (New York: Pocket Books, 1986), p. 134.

21 *once, he got sent home from kindergarten*: Lee, *Judy Blume's Story*, p. 35.

21 *"a lovely, gay, blissful society almost untouched by war"*: Maureen Kudlik, "Teen-Age Girls: They Live in a Wonderful World of Their Own," *Life*, December 11, 1944, pp. 91–99.

22 *"Loafers, but no socks," Nancy says solemnly*: Blume, *Are You There God? It's Me, Margaret*, pp. 14–15.

22 *"Well then, I'll just have to suffer"*: Ibid., p. 29.

22 *In sixth grade, she also belonged to a club, called the Pre-Teen Kittens*: Lee, *Judy Blume's Story*, p. 26.

22 *with the members adopting feline identities*: Box 110 of the Judy Blume Papers at Yale University's Beinecke Rare Book and Manuscript Library. Accessed April 29, 2022.

23 *"We must—we must—we must increase our bust!"*: Blume, *Are You There God? It's Me, Margaret*, p. 85.

23 *"But it doesn't work," Blume joked*: Interview with HuffPost Live, June 10, 2013. Accessed on YouTube: https://www.youtube.com/watch?v=XgTIUa2y7gY.

23 *"I pretended to be really busy reading a book"*: Blume, *Are You There God? It's Me, Margaret*, pp. 45–46.

23 *"It's not so much that I like him as a person, God"*: Ibid., p. 74.

24 *"A really fast kiss!"*: Ibid., p. 106.

24 *"make-out parties . . . you invited a group of boys and girls"*: William Leith, "Teen Spirit," *The Independent*, July 18, 1999, pp. 11–13. Accessed through the New York Public Library.

24 *"When you're that age, everything is still there in front of you"*: Weidt, *Presenting Judy Blume*, p. 62.

25 *which she plunked out on her typewriter in a wildly creative six-week burst*: Lee, *Judy Blume's Story*, p. 69.

25 *"I ripped the card into tiny shreds and ran to my room"*: Blume, *Are You There God? It's Me, Margaret*, p. 116.

25 *Instead, he wondered—is Nancy telling the truth?*: Box 115 of the Judy Blume Papers at Yale University's Beinecke Rare Book and Manuscript Library. Accessed April 28, 2022.

26 *"It was the voice, the absence of adult regret, instruction or nostalgia"*: Pat Scales, "Natural Born Editor," *School Library Journal*, May 2001, pp. 50–53.

26 *"He told me, 'This is the reason I got into doing children's books'"*: PS to RB, May 27, 2022.

## Chapter Four
## Menstruation

27 *"Someday, it will happen to you"*: Judy Blume, *Letters to Judy*, p. 164.

28 *which took its iconic name from a typist*: Weidt, *Presenting Judy Blume*, p. 63.

28 Kirkus *gave* Are You There God? *a mixed review*: *Kirkus Reviews*, October 1, 1970. Accessed through the New York Public Library.

28 New York Times *described it as a "funny, warm and loving book"*: Dorothy Broderick, "The Young Teen Scene," *New York Times*, November 8, 1970.

28 *That same day, the* Times *included* Are You There God?: "Outstanding Books of the Year," *New York Times*, November 8, 1970.

28 *"That was the first time I felt 'I can really do this'"*: Lee, *Judy Blume's Story*, p. 70.

29 *"Communist!" the voice shrieked*: Judy Blume in conversation with Samantha Bee at an event at the 92nd Street Y on June 2, 2015. Accessed on YouTube: https://www.youtube.com/watch?v=l7svP4zqCc0.

29 *"When I was 17 I discovered one of my younger siblings"*: Mr Malky (@MrMalky) on X (Twitter), April 16, 2023: https://twitter.com/MrMalky/status/1647740739978244099.

30 *"looking at the problem [of unwanted pregnancy] from the wrong end of the telescope"*: Zoom interview with Jonathan Zimmerman, May 31, 2022.

31 *"Mary Calderone, despite what her enemies said"*: Ibid., May 31, 2022.

31 *"The plants and animals stuff was a way to try to teach"*: Ibid., May 31, 2022.

31 *"The sperm, which come from the father's testicles"*: Andrew C. Andry and Steven Schapp, *How Babies Are Made* (New York: Time-Life Books, 1968), no page numbers.

32 *"destroy the traditional moral fiber of America"*: As quoted in *Teaching Sex: The Shaping of Adolescence in the 20th Century* by Jeffrey P. Moran (Cambridge, MA: Harvard University Press, 2000), p. 182; see also Gordon V. Drake, *Sex Education in the Schools* (Tulsa, OK: Christian Crusade Publications, 1968), pp. 16–18.

33 *"You'll find out when you're thirteen"*: Judy Blume, *Letters to Judy*, p. 163.

33 *"There was something about eggs dropping down"*: Ibid., pp. 163–64.

33 *"that I once put a pin in my finger to draw blood"*: Lee, *Judy Blume's Story*, p. 28.

34 *"Today I was feeling brave"*: Judy Blume, *Are You There God? It's Me, Margaret*, p. 156.

34 *in a change originally suggested by Blume's British editor*: Judy Blume in conversation with Samantha Bee at an event at the 92nd Street Y on June 2, 2015. Accessed on YouTube: https://www.youtube.com/watch?v=l7svP4zqCc0.

34 *"I wanted to find out how it would feel"*: Judy Blume, *Are You There God? It's Me, Margaret*, p. 158.

34 *"You were never allowed to talk about [menstruation]"*: Telephone interview with Arlene LaVerde, October 12, 2022.

35 *Kotex became a status symbol among young, middle-class women*: Joan Jacobs Brumberg, *The Body Project: An Intimate History of American Girls* (New York: Vintage Books, 1997), pp. 44–45.

35 *by approximately 100 million American girls*: Sharra Louise Vostral, *Under Wraps: A History of Menstrual Hygiene Technology* (Lanham, MD: Lexington Books, 2008), p. 121. Accessed on Google Books: https://www.google.com/books/edition/Under_Wraps/PWAOyisYPnEC?hl=en&gbpv=0.

35 *"If the egg is impregnated"*: "The Story of Menstruation," Disney, 1946. Accessed on YouTube: https://www.youtube.com/watch?v=vG9o9m0LsbI.

36 *"The narrator of the film pronounced it menstroo-ation"*: Judy Blume, *Are You There God? It's Me, Margaret*, p. 111.

36 *"It was like one big commercial"*: Ibid., p. 112.

37 *"Everyone gets sex ed, all seven billion people"*: JZ to RB, May 31, 2022.

37 *The booklet, published in 1970*: Box 67 of the Judy Blume Papers at Yale University's Beinecke Rare Book and Manuscript Library. Accessed May 11, 2022.

## Chapter Five
## Bad Kids

38 *"Sometimes I am a mean and rotten person"*: Judy Blume, *It's Not the End of the World* (Englewood Cliffs, NJ: Bradbury Press, 1972). I worked from the 2014 reprint published by Simon & Schuster, p. 46.

39 *"I heard all about you and Moose Freed"*: Judy Blume, *Are You There God? It's Me Margaret* (Englewood Cliffs, NJ: Bradbury Press, 1970), p. 133.

39 *"My brother was so rebellious"*: V.C. Chickering, "A Judy Blume Interview from the *Bust* Archives," *Bust*, February 12, 2015, originally published in the 1997 Spring/Summer issue. Accessed online: https://bust.com/tbt-a-very-special -judy-blume-exclusive-from-our-bust-vault/.

39 *"My mother used to say, 'We never have to punish Judy'"*: Judy Blume, *Letters to Judy*, p. 15.

40 *"I wanted to say let me alone"*: Judy Blume, *Then Again, Maybe I Won't* (Englewood Cliffs, NJ: Bradbury Press, 1970). I worked from the 2014 reprint published by Simon & Schuster, p. 113.

40 *"the best looking girl I've seen in person anywhere"*: Ibid., p. 43.

41 *"When I read Joel's paperbacks, I can feel myself get hard"*: Ibid., p. 52.

41 *prompting some rigorous tête-à-têtes with Jackson*: Box 115 of the Judy Blume Papers at Yale University's Beinecke Rare Book and Manuscript Library. Accessed April 28, 2022.

41 *"You'll get a new one . . . from Rosemont Junior High"*: Judy Blume, *Then Again, Maybe I Won't*, p. 29.

41 Kirkus *said on October 18, 1971: Kirkus Reviews*. Accessed through the New York Public Library.

42 *"There are a number of different factors"*: Telephone interview with Suzanne Kahn, October 14, 2022.

43 she *"did considerable reading and six months of crying"*: Weidt, *Presenting Judy Blume*, p. 87.

43 *"I tried to reassure [Randy and Larry] but I really wasn't sure myself"*: Judy Blume, *Letters to Judy*, p. 90.

43 *"I felt tears come to my eyes"*: Judy Blume, *It's Not the End of the World*, p. 38.

43 *"I would rather have them fight than be divorced"*: Ibid., p. 42.

44 *"Sometimes I feel sorry for my mother and other times I hate her"*: Ibid., p. 108.

44 *"I stamped on it with both feet until there was nothing left"*: Ibid., p. 170.

44 *Early drafts of* It's Not the End of the World *show Blume*: Box 110 of the Judy Blume Papers at Yale University's Beinecke Rare Book and Manuscript Library. Accessed April 29, 2022.

45 *"I have discovered something important about my mother and father"*: Judy Blume, *It's Not the End of the World*, p. 180.

45 *And eventually, Jackson suggested that Bill's second marriage plot*: Box 110 of the Judy Blume Papers at Yale University's Beinecke Rare Book and Manuscript Library. Accessed April 29, 2022.

45 *"All you care about is yourself!"*: Judy Blume, *It's Not the End of the World*, p. 115.

## Chapter Six
## The Fourth Dimension

46 *"In my heart, I was out there marching"*: Judy Blume in conversation with Samantha Bee at an event at the 92nd Street Y on June 2, 2015. Accessed on YouTube: https://www.youtube.com/watch?v=l7svP4zqCc0.

46 *"a theory of patriarchy"*: Kate Millett, *The Second Sex* (New York: Doubleday & Company, 1970), p. 24.

46 *"Women who are employed have two jobs"*: Ibid., p. 41.

47 *During the 1960 race between Richard Nixon and John F. Kennedy*: Weidt, *Presenting Judy Blume*, p. 119.

48 *"Daddy and I just don't enjoy being together"*: Judy Blume, *It's Not the End of the World* (Englewood Cliffs, NJ: Bradbury Press, 1972), p. 85.

48 *"I had you when I was just twenty"*: Ibid., p. 102.

48 *"The children need you at home, Ellie"*: Ibid., p. 112.

48 *"It was like the bacteria, the bad bacteria was coming out"*: Judy Blume at the Arlington Public Library event on October 22, 2015. Accessed on YouTube: https://www.youtube.com/watch?v=PUDBcovfFjM.

49 *"My mother had many, many talents and much to offer"*: Lee, *Judy Blume's Story*, p. 78.

49 *"the hero, the cowgirl, the detective"*: V.C. Chickering, "A Judy Blume Interview from the *Bust* Archives," *Bust*, February 12, 2015, originally published in the 1997 Spring/Summer issue. Accessed online: https://bust.com/tbt-a-very-special-judy-blume-exclusive-from-our-bust-vault/.

49 *"She had a Roadster with a rumble seat"*: Ibid.

50 *Judy has said Dr. O was based on her father*: Judy Blume in conversation with Samantha Bee at an event at the 92nd Street Y on June 2, 2015. Accessed on YouTube: https://www.youtube.com/watch?v=l7svP4zqCc0.

50 *"After that, she'd reinvented herself"*: Judy Blume, *In the Unlikely Event* (New York: Vintage Books, 2015), p. 385.

51 *"in the feminine mystique, which defines woman solely"*: Betty Freidan, *It Changed My Life: Writings on the Women's Movement* (New York: Norton, 1976). I worked from the 1991 reprint from Dell Books, p. 38.

51 *"Women who work because of a commitment [to their vocation]"*: Ibid., p. 42.

51 *She endorses "a new kind of city living"*: Ibid., p. 53.

52 *"You never grew up! You're still Ruth's baby!"*: Judy Blume, *It's Not the End of the World*, p. 168.

## Chapter Seven
## Money

53 *"It's scary to think about my mother with no money to feed us or buy our clothes"*: Judy Blume, *It's Not the End of the World* (Englewood Cliffs, NJ: Bradbury Press, 1972).

53 *John controlled the family's finances and doled out cash*: Box 34 of the Judy Blume Papers at Yale University's Beinecke Rare Book and Manuscript Library. Accessed April 28, 2022.

53 *"The reason that divorce became the politicizing moment"*: SK to RB, October 14, 2022.

54 *"They were really sort of economically displaced"*: Ibid., October 14, 2022.

54 *"If there is any one thing that makes a feminist"*: Betty Friedan, *It Changed My Life: Writings on the Women's Movement* (New York: Norton, 1976), p. 414.

55 *"Women should be educated to do the work society rewards"*: Ibid., p. 409.

56 *"Our movement to liberate women and men from these polarized, unequal sex roles"*: Ibid., p. 414.

56 *"I don't think I'll ever get married," she says*: Judy Blume, *It's Not the End of the World*, p. 1.

56 *"My mother has no money that I know of"*: Ibid., p. 76.

56 *"Daddy can afford to"*: Ibid., p. 153.

57 *"self-help reading, a guide for those troubled by divorce"*: Lael Scott, "Divorce Juvenile-Style," *New York Times*, September 3, 1972.

57 *about a mother who is so worried about her son's meager appetite*: Box 116 of the Judy Blume Papers at Yale University's Beinecke Rare Book and Manuscript Library. Accessed April 28, 2022.

57 *It was a decision he'd eventually come to regret*: Pat Scales, "Natural Born Editor," *School Library Journal*, May 2001, pp. 50–53.

58 *who occasionally ate on the floor*: Weidt, *Presenting Judy Blume*, p. 96.

58 *"Oh no! My angel! My precious little baby!"*: Judy Blume, *Tales of a Fourth Grade Nothing* (New York: Dutton Books, 1972). I worked from the 2007 reprint from Puffin Books, p. 112.

58 *"Someday she'll grow up and go to school"*: Judy Blume, *Superfudge* (New York: Dutton Books, 1980). I worked from the 2007 reprint from Puffin Books, p. 28.

## Chapter Eight
## Mothers

59 *"One thing I'm sure of is I don't want to spend my life cleaning some house like Ma"*: Judy Blume, *Deenie* (Englewood Cliffs, NJ: Bradbury Press, 1973). I worked from the 2014 reprint published by Simon & Schuster, p. 44.

59 *"This 'flare-up,' as the doctors called it"*: Judy Blume, *Letters to Judy*, p. 74.

59 *"I never want to see Boston again"*: Lee, *Judy Blume's Story*, p. 55.

60 *"The thing that really scares me is I'm not sure I want to be a model"*: Judy Blume, *Deenie*, p. 4.

60 *"Deenie's the beauty, Helen's the brain"*: Ibid., p. 3.

60 *"Nobody expects much from my schoolwork"*: Ibid., p. 43.

61 *"they make your feet spread so your regular shoes don't fit"*: Ibid., p. 5.

61 *"She's really fussy about what I eat"*: Ibid., p. 15.

61 *"Most times I don't even think about the way I look"*: Ibid., p. 14.

61 *"This woman was falling apart"*: Weidt, *Presenting Judy Blume*, p. 103.

62 *"She was very open about her problem"*: Judy Blume, *Letters to Judy*, p. 81.

62 *"I felt like the world's biggest jerk"*: Judy Blume, *Deenie*, p. 149.

62 *"She's a nice kid," Deenie says*: Ibid., p. 175.

63 *"I always feel funny when I pass her house"*: Ibid., p. 16.

63 *"I wonder if she thinks of herself as a handicapped person"*: Ibid., p. 178.

64 *"You're not telling us Deenie's going to be deformed"*: Ibid., p. 63.

64 *"I expected Daddy to explain everything on the way home"*: Ibid., p. 64.

64 *"I had to fight to keep from crying"*: Ibid., p. 110.

64 *whose kids are grown up and "has nothing better to do"*: Ibid., p. 48.

65 *doing each other's hair like schoolgirls*: Ibid., p. 145.

65 *"I used to tell myself it didn't matter if I wasn't pretty"*: Ibid., p. 173.

65 *"I wanted better for you," she tells them*: Ibid., p. 174.

66 *"Ma says pigeons are dirty birds with lots of germs"*: Ibid., p. 141.

66 *"I looked out the window and no pigeons were on the ledge"*: Ibid., p. 152.

66 *Judy was quite proud of them, according to Dick Jackson*: Box 115 of the Judy Blume Papers at Yale University's Beinecke Rare Book and Manuscript Library. Accessed April 28, 2022.

## Chapter Nine
## Masturbation

67 *"I rubbed and rubbed until I got that good feeling"*: Judy Blume, *Deenie* (Englewood Cliffs, NJ: Bradbury Press, 1973), p. 169.

67 *"I have this special place and when I rub it I get a very nice feeling"*: Ibid., pp. 67–68.

67 *"If there were a Professional Masturbators League"*: Sherman Alexie, *The Absolutely True Diary of a Part-Time Indian* (New York: Hachette, 2009), p. 26.

68 *"The first time I slid on my back to the bottom of the tub"*: Melissa Febos, *Girlhood* (New York: Bloomsbury, 2021), p. 23.

68 *"Does anyone know the word for stimulating our genitals?"*: Judy Blume, *Deenie*, p. 105.

68 *"The hot water was very relaxing and soon I began to enjoy it"*: Ibid., p. 169.

69 *"There's a whole section on wet dreams and another on masturbation"*: Judy Blume, *Then Again, Maybe I Won't* (Englewood Cliffs, NJ: Bradbury Press, 1970), p. 104.

70 *In 1969, a group of women in their twenties and thirties*: Details about the making of *Our Bodies, Ourselves* come from the documentary *She's Beautiful When She's Angry*, released in 2014.

71 *"When the man and woman have been wriggling so hard"*: Peter Mayle, *Where Did I Come From?* (Secaucus, NJ: Lyle Stuart Inc., 1973), no page numbers.

71 *"There's some joy and fun in that book"*: Zoom interview with Cory Silverberg, October 26, 2023.

71 *"It is also comfortably frank about the preoccupations of young teen-agers"*: Judith Viorst, "Deenie," *New York Times*, November 4, 1973.

72 *"Instead of giving Deenie any personality or independent existence"*: *Kirkus Reviews*, September 17, 1973. Accessed via the New York Public Library.

72 *Judy dealt with bad reviews by scribbling*: Judy Blume at the Arlington Public

Library event on October 22, 2015. Accessed on YouTube: https://www.you
tube.com/watch?v=PUDBcovfFjM.

72 *"I had never heard the word masturbation when I was growing up"*: Judy
Blume, *Letters to Judy*, pp. 186–87.

72 *"I wrote the truth, what I knew to be the truth"*: Judy Blume in conversation
with Samantha Bee at an event at the 92nd Street Y on June 2, 2015. Accessed
on YouTube: https://www.youtube.com/watch?v=l7svP4zqCc0.

73 *she casually asks Helen to loan her her "sex book"*: Judy Blume, *Deenie*,
p. 176.

73 *"I know he was trying to feel me," she says*: Ibid., p. 164.

73 *"This time when he kissed me, I concentrated on kissing him back"*: Ibid.,
p. 183.

73 *"Maybe that's why my spine started growing crooked!"*: Ibid., p. 105.

74 *"It's very common for girls as well as boys, beginning with adolescence"*: Ibid.,
p. 106.

74 *"Family life education was the first time that American educators"*: JZ to RB,
May 31, 2022.

75 *"Those were called the 'Big Four'"*: Ibid., May 31, 2022.

75 *"Once a young man touched himself in that way"*: Jeffrey P. Moran, *Teaching
Sex: The Shaping of the Adolescent in the 20th Century* (Boston: Harvard University Press, 2000), p. 8.

76 *"girls who fell prey to self-abuse were clearly aberrant"*: Ibid.

76 *"For a long time there has been a certain ritual"*: Andrew Hacker, "The Pill and
Morality," *New York Times*, November 21, 1965.

76 *"If [the teacher] does that at PS3 down in the Village, she'll be teacher of the
year"*: JZ to RB, May 31, 2022.

77 *Professor and researcher Michelle Fine was "shocked"*: Zoom interview with
Michelle Fine, January 6, 2023.

77 *"This was about, 'you're a victim, bad things will happen'"*: Ibid., January 6,
2023.

77 *"I just think people can't say no if they can't say yes"*: Ibid., January 6, 2023.

78 *"unacknowledged social ambivalence about female sexuality"*: Michelle Fine,
"Sexuality, Schooling, and Adolescent Females: The Missing Discourse of Desire," *Harvard Educational Review* 58, no. 1 (February 1988): 29–53.

78 *"I still go into classrooms where I'll say the word 'masturbation'"*: Zoom interview with Rachel Lotus, November 8, 2023.

78 *"I don't think you'll talk to any sex educator who doesn't think that Judy
Blume"*: Ibid., November 8, 2023.

## Chapter Ten
## Virginity

79 *"Nice girls didn't go all the way"*: Judy Blume, *Letters to Judy*, p. 211.

79 *She gave Judy book ideas*: Lee, *Judy Blume's Story*, p. 77.

79 *She thought Tony carried the raincoat to cover his face*: Box 115 of the Judy Blume Papers at Yale University's Beinecke Rare Book and Manuscript Library. Accessed April 28, 2022.

80 *"In these books, the boys had absolutely no feelings"*: Weidt, *Presenting Judy Blume*, p. 50.

80 *"I set out to teach very few things in my books"*: Ibid., p. 51.

81 *"When I was growing up, we had very firm rules"*: Judy Blume, *Letters to Judy*, pp. 210–11.

81 *"years of kissing experience"*: Beverly Solochek, "Plotting the Real Teen Scene," *Daily News*, September 3, 1976, p. C9.

81 *Blume later elaborated in the* Independent: William Leith, "Teen Spirit," *The Independent*, July 18, 1999, pp. 11–13. Accessed through the New York Public Library.

81 *"My friends and I played sexual games, sexual games between girlfriends"*: Ibid.

83 *"We are exactly the same size"*: Judy Blume, *Forever* (Englewood Cliffs, NJ: Bradbury Press, 1975). I worked from the 2014 reprint from Simon & Schuster, p. 13.

83 *"He threatened that if I wouldn't sleep with him"*: Ibid., p. 15.

83 *"Let's save something for tomorrow"*: Ibid., p. 21.

84 *"In the old days girls were divided into two groups"*: Ibid., p. 37.

84 *"I've been thinking"*: Ibid., p. 30.

84 *"I've been doing a lot of thinking and have decided I don't want"*: Ibid., p. 184.

84 *"Sybil Davison has a genius IQ"*: Ibid., p. 1.

85 *"whole experience was more than she bargained for"*: Ibid., p. 184.

85 *"that a girl like Sybil might have a genius IQ"*: Weidt, *Presenting Judy Blume*, p. 50.

85 *"Were you a virgin when you got married?"*: Judy Blume, *Forever*, p. 83.

86 *"Sex is a commitment . . ."*: Ibid., p. 84.

86 *"The new ideology is that sex is good and good sex means orgasm"*: Richard V. Lepe, "What About the Right to Say 'No'?," *New York Times*, September 16, 1973. Referenced on pp. 111–12 of *Forever*.

86 *"Not that I don't identify with Katherine"*: Weidt, *Presenting Judy Blume*, p. 53.

87 *"be careful"*: Judy Blume, *Forever*, p. 37.

87 *"Sometimes it's hard for parents to accept the facts"*: Ibid., p. 119.

88 *"There were double standards then"*: Ibid., p. 83.

88 *Three years later in 1939, Tampax was featured*: Details about the Hall of Pharmacy found in the New York Public Library's digital World's Fair 1939 and 1940 collection. Accessed online: https://digitalcollections.nypl.org/search/index?utf8=%E2%9C%93&keywords=pharmacy#.

89 *"that a tampon took up no more room than a standard nozzle"*: As quoted in Joan Jacobs Brumberg's *The Body Project: An Intimate History of American Girls* (New York: Vintage Books, 1997), p. 161.

89 *"of the time that Erica taught me how to use tampons"*: Judy Blume, *Forever*, p. 129.

90 *In a TikTok from 2022*: https://www.tiktok.com/@singinraisin/video/71804 50325726285102.

90 *"This is really rough"*: Judy Blume, *Forever*, p. 27.

90 *"soft mattresses are good for making love"*: Ibid., p. 41.

90 *she's not "mentally ready . . . a person has to think"*: Ibid., p. 50.

90 *"If I didn't know better, I'd think you were a tease"*: Ibid., p. 51.

91 *"Sometimes I want to so much," she admits*: Ibid., p. 52.

91 *"I was thinking, I love you Michael"*: Ibid., p. 66.

91 *"I didn't tell them that with Michael and me it's different"*: Ibid., p. 91.

92 *"In my whole life nothing will ever mean more to me"*: Ibid., p. 134.

92 *they don't have to "do anything"; they can "just talk"*: Ibid., p. 96.

92 *"when we were naked, in each other's arms, I wanted to do everything"*: Ibid., p. 102.

92 *"I'm thinking about getting pregnant"*: Ibid., pp. 102–103.

92 *"Still, I can't help feeling let down"*: Ibid., p. 107.

## Chapter Eleven
## Pleasure

93 *"Can we do it again?"*: Judy Blume, *Forever* (Englewood Cliffs, NJ: Bradbury Press, 1975), p. 141.

93 *"Our old ethic is, like Venice, sinking imperceptibly into the sea"*: John Money, "Recreational—and Procreational—Sex," *New York Times*, September 13, 1975.

94 *which had more than doubled between 1963 and 1975*: U.S. Bureau of the Census, *Current Population Reports* Series P-20, No. 297, "Number, Timing and Duration of Marriages and Divorces in the United States: June 1975" (Washington, DC: U.S. Government Printing Office, 1976).

95 *she answers, "Does it matter?"*: Judy Blume, *Forever*, p. 120.

96 *"I'd rather take the Pill"*: Ibid., p. 128.

96 *"Katherine absolutely wants it and is in touch with her own desire"*: RL to RB, November 8, 2023.

96 *Michael describes his mom and dad as "a little stuffier"*: Judy Blume, *Forever*, p. 142.

96 *"We don't have to do anything . . ."*: Ibid., p. 136.

97 *he "use[s] more junk" than she does*: Ibid., p. 138.

97 *"Do you ever put it on your balls?"*: Ibid., p. 139.

97 *"I grabbed his backside with both hands"*: Ibid., p. 140.

97 *"I thought how nice it would be if we could go upstairs"*: Ibid., p. 143.

98 *"Any way you want," Michael answers*: Ibid., p. 174.

98 *"I thought, there are so many ways to love a person"*: Ibid., p. 175.

98 *"We both think you could use a change of scenery"*: Ibid., p. 151.

99 *"So they'll find out that separating us won't change anything"*: Ibid., p. 158.

99 *"What's forever supposed to mean?"*: Ibid., p. 187.

99 *"There's another guy, isn't there?"*: Ibid., p. 203.

100 *actually he "screwed [his] way around North Carolina"*: Ibid., p. 206.

100 *"I'll never regret one single thing we did together"*: Ibid., p. 208.


## Chapter Twelve
## Paperbacks

101 *"We'd all whisper and certain pages would fall open"*: Telephone interview with Lauren Harrison, October 25, 2022.

101 *"Labeling it an adult book . . . was our way of saying"*: Weidt, *Presenting Judy Blume*, p. 59.

101 *She told* School Library Journal *that seeing the book described that way*: Roger Sutton, "An Interview with Judy Blume, Forever . . . Yours," *School Library Journal*, June 1996, pp. 25–27.

101 *"Dick told me, 'Judy Blume is our big author'"*: PS to RB, May 27, 2022.

102 *"a kind of heroine to the kids who read and re-read her books"*: Best Seller List, *New York Times*, August 15, 1976.

102 *The paper of record's review of* Forever: "Forever," *New York Times*, December 28, 1975.

102 *Obviously it's not a quality book*: Review by Regina Minudri, *School Library Journal*, November 1975, p. 95.

102 *Kirkus was also dismissive*: *Kirkus Reviews*, October 1, 1975. Accessed through the New York Public Library.

102 *with whom Judy would eventually develop a warm relationship*: Box 26 of the Judy Blume Papers at Yale University's Beinecke Rare Book and Manuscript Library. Accessed April 1, 2022, over email.

103 *Pollack did not include* Forever *in her story*: Pamela D. Pollack, "Sex in Children's Fiction: Freedom to Frighten?," *SIECUS Report 5*, no. 5 (May 1977).

104 *"Being Black, I always assumed that Deenie was white"*: Telephone interview with Julia Loving, November 8, 2022.

104 *"There was a copy of* Forever *that was passed around in fifth grade"*: LH to RB, October 25, 2022.

104 *Maynard went to the "pretty, mostly white, upper-middle-class community"*: Joyce Maynard, "Coming of Age with Judy Blume," *New York Times*, December 3, 1978.

107 *"I read that book so many times," Silverberg said*: CS to RB, October 26, 2022.

107 *"I was fourteen and I remember reading [ Forever ]"*: JZ to RB, May 31, 2022.


## Chapter Thirteen
## Rebellion

108 *"He had married this little girl, and he was happy that way"*: Peter Gorner, "Tempo: The Giddy/Sad, Flighty/Solid Life of Judy Blume," *Chicago Tribune*, March 15, 1985, p. D1.

108 *She was holding his hand when he lost consciousness*: Lee, *Judy Blume's Story*, pp. 58–59.

108 *Before Judy and John told them, Judy had consulted a family counselor*: Judy Blume, *Letters to Judy*, pp. 90–91.

109 *"It was a nice marriage," Blume later said*: Lee, *Judy Blume's Story*, p. 73.

109 *"I wasn't terrible. I was responsible"*: Weidt, *Presenting Judy Blume*, p. 16.

110 *John blamed* Fear of Flying: V.C. Chickering, "A Judy Blume Interview from the *Bust* Archives," *Bust*, February 12, 2015, originally published in the 1997 Spring/Summer issue. Accessed online: https://bust.com/tbt-a-very-special -judy-blume-exclusive-from-our-bust-vault/.

110 *"What* was *marriage anyway?"*: Erica Jong, *Fear of Flying* (Fort Worth, TX: Holt, Rinehart & Winston, 1973). I worked from the 2003 reprint from New American Library, p. 14.

110 *"Was I going to be just a housewife who wrote in her spare time?"*: Ibid., p. 193.

111 *"Leaving Bennett was my first really independent action"*: Ibid., p. 390.

111 *"I was afraid of being a woman," she says*: Ibid., p. 407.

112 *"Why should I be disturbed by the sado-masochistic aspects of that relationship"*: Sue Kaufman, *Diary of a Mad Housewife* (New York: Bantam Books, 1967), p. 191.

112 *"Without a cent of my own, without a checking account"*: Ibid., p. 272.

112 *in which she has to be the "submissive woman"*: Ibid., p. 207.

112 *"Did Lisbeth think she was a mad housewife too?"*: Judy Blume, *Wifey*, (New York: Berkley Books, 1978), p. 79.

113 *"Have you been reading that book again?"*: Ibid., p. 188.

113 *"Just getting through the day was a real struggle for me"*: Judy Blume, *Letters to Judy*, p. 92.

113 *"That's what divorced women on TV always turn out to be—cocktail waitresses"*: Judy Blume, *It's Not the End of the World* (Englewood Cliffs, NJ: Bradbury Press, 1972), p. 101.

113 *"If I divorced him, I'd have to give up the house"*: Judy Blume, *Wifey*, p. 201.

114 *"He entertained them lavishly"*: Judy Blume, *Letters to Judy*, p. 94.

## Chapter Fourteen
## Mistakes

115 *"From the beginning, we fought"*: Judy Blume, *Letters to Judy*, p. 99.

115 *"My son and daughter thought he was a kid"*: John Neary, "The 'Jacqueline Susann of Kids' Books,' Judy Blume, Grows Up with an Adult Novel," *People*, October 16, 1978. Accessed online: https://people.com/archive/the-jacque line-susann-of-kids-books-judy-blume-grows-up-with-an-adult-novel-vol -10-no-16.

116 *"I could have had affairs, but instead I got married"*: Weidt, *Presenting Judy Blume*, p. 18.

117 *"I would say, 'Isn't he wonderful?'"*: Judy Blume, *Letters to Judy*, p. 107.

117 *Larry was having a particularly hard time*: Weidt, *Presenting Judy Blume*, p. 17.

117 *"It was very hard for me to get married again"*: John Neary, "The 'Jacqueline Susann of Kids' Books,' Judy Blume, Grows Up with an Adult Novel."

118 *"In spite of my vow to respect her privacy"*: Judy Blume, *Letters to Judy*, p. 151.

118 *"It is a town with very frustrated, resentful, talented women"*: Weidt, *Presenting Judy Blume*, p. 18.

118 *"You're the one who's making the bombs"*: Judy Blume, *Tiger Eyes* (New York: Bradbury Press, 1981). I worked from the 2014 reprint from Simon & Schuster, p. 163.

119 *Judy had two abortions during that time*: Nicole Sperling, "How Judy Blume Finally Got a 'Yes' from Hollywood," *New York Times*, March 7, 2023. Accessed online: https://www.nytimes.com/2023/03/07/business/media/judy -blume-hollywood.html.

119 The Career, *as she called it*: John Neary, "The 'Jacqueline Susann of Kids' Books,' Judy Blume, Grows Up with an Adult Novel."

119 *"I think I know who you are"*: Judy Blume, *Starring Sally J. Freedman as Herself* (Englewood Cliffs, NJ: Bradbury Press, 1977), p. 117.

119 *"They had to change cars," her mom explains*: Ibid., p. 69.

120 *"What would your mothers say if they knew what you'd been doing?"*: Ibid., p. 194.

120 *"While Ms. Blume's book is teeming with social value"*: Julia Whedon, "The Forties Revisited," *New York Times*, May 1, 1977.

121 *"Blume's approach will be resented as frivolous by many readers"*: As quoted in Weidt, *Presenting Judy Blume*, p. 67.

## Chapter Fifteen
## Monogamy

122 *"Oh Mother, dammit! Why did you bring me up to think that* this *was what I wanted?"*: Judy Blume, *Wifey* (New York: Berkley Books, 1978), p. 119.

122 *In April 1977, she penned a respectful note to Mercier*: Box 27 of the Judy Blume Papers at Yale University's Beinecke Rare Book and Manuscript Library. Accessed April 1, 2022.

123 *In the meantime, she scarfed down way too many glazed donuts*: Judy Blume, *Wifey*, Introduction, p. x.

123 Lisbeth *"explained it as Sandy's need to control her own destiny"*: Ibid., p. 16.

124 "What are you doing?": Ibid., p. 61.

125 *"I used to know that [sex scenes] were good"*: Brandon Sanchez, "Sex Between the Pages of the New Yorker Festival," *Vulture*. https://www.vulture .com/2023/10/new-yorker-festival-2023-book-sex-scenes-judy-blume .html#_ga=2.9118197.170374204.1701972221-1398311225.1701972221.

125 *"That's why I douche with vinegar . . . "*: Judy Blume, *Wifey*, p. 23.

125 *"I won't forbid you from seeing him, Sandy"*: Ibid., p. 88.

125 *"Make his interests your interests"*: Ibid., p. 60.

126 *"She wasn't sure. If he beat her, she could complain"*: Ibid., p. 190.

126 *"To me she'll always be Sarah"*: Ibid., p. 30.

127 *"They're still different no matter how hard you try to pretend they're not"*: Ibid., p. 42.

127 *"The natives are restless everywhere"*: Ibid., p. 107.

127 *"Don't worry Mr. Pressman, we're known for our discretion at Four Corners"*: Ibid., p. 212.

128 *"Marriage to him would have meant a life"*: Ibid., p. 247.

128 *"When I think of all the energy, all the misplaced artistic aggression"*: Erica Jong, *Fear of Flying* (Fort Worth, TX: Holt, Rinehart & Winston, 1973), p. 205.

129 *"She had been a spirited, adventurous young woman"*: Gloria Steinem, "Ruth's Song (Because She Could Not Sing It). Accessed as a PDF online: https://englishiva1011.pbworks.com/f/RUTHSONG.PDF.

129 *"The family must have watched this energetic, fun-loving, book-loving woman"*: Ibid.

129 *"The world still missed a unique person named Ruth"*: Ibid.

130 *Essie typed out many of Judy's manuscripts over the years*: Sarah Larson, "Judy Blume's Unfinished Endings," *The New Yorker*, April 25, 2023. Accessed online: https://www.newyorker.com/culture/persons-of-interest/judy-blumes-unfinished-endings.

130 *"When they ask how she knows all those things"*: Judy Blume, *Wifey*, Introduction, p. xii.

## Chapter Sixteen
## Divorce

131 *"I don't think we could have survived two more years together"*: Judy Blume, *Letters to Judy*, p. 125.

131 *Meanwhile, publicists at Blume's paperback publisher, Dell*: Email with Sarah Gallick, June 22, 2022.

132 *He handled it "brilliantly," Blume said*: V.C. Chickering, "A Judy Blume Interview from the *Bust* Archives," *Bust*, February 12, 2015, originally published in the 1997 Spring/Summer issue. Accessed online: https://bust.com/tbt-a-very-special-judy-blume-exclusive-from-our-bust-vault/.

132 *"Adult readers will enjoy this light romance"*: *Library Journal*, September 1, 1978.

132 *The reviewer from the* LA Times *praised Blume's abilities*: Marilyn Murray Willison, "Judy Blume Writes One for the Grown-Ups," *Los Angeles Times*, September 24, 1978, p. K8.

132 *"a bawdy account of a suburban wife's rebellion"*: Eric Pace, "Fictional Heroines with a Will," *New York Times*, November 22, 1979.

132 *Reviewer Sue Isaacs suggested, in a culturally prescient takedown*: Sue Isaacs, "Hello Grown-Ups, It's Me Judy," *Washington Post*, October 8, 1978, p. E5.

133 Newsday *attributed it to a librarian in Garden City, New York*: David Behrens, "Sugar—And a Little Spice," *Newsday*, March 1, 1978, p. 1A.

133 *"I cringe, even today, thinking of that article"*: Judy Blume, *Wifey* (New York: Berkley Books, 1978), Introduction, p. xi.

133 *"We have a very nice family life"*: Mary Daniels, "Preteen Readers Find Their Boswell in Blume," *Chicago Tribune*, June 23, 1978, p. D3.

134 *by November 1979, there were a reported three million copies*: Eric Pace, "Fictional Heroines with a Will," *New York Times*, November 22, 1979.

134 *"I think divorce is a tragedy, traumatic and horribly painful for everybody"*: Peter Gorner, "Tempo: The Giddy/Sad, Flighty/Solid Life of Judy Blume," *Chicago Tribune*, March 15, 1985, p. D1.

135 *"My breasts were growing or else they were just fat"*: Judy Blume, *Just as Long as We're Together* (New York: Orchard Books, 1987), p. 190.

135 *"I hate not knowing what's going to happen!"*: Ibid., p. 263.

136 *Most of the kids who contacted Judy received a mailer in return*: Mailer viewed at the Elizabeth Public Library's main branch, June 28, 2022.

137 *"Could you sort of be a second mother to me and tell me the facts of life?"*: Judy Blume, *Letters to Judy*, p. 179.

137 *Besides family and doctors you are the only person I've ever told this to*: Ibid., p. 259.

137 *"With her own children, Judy Blume concedes"*: Joyce Maynard, "Coming of Age with Judy Blume," *New York Times*, December 3, 1978.

137 *"During a particularly rough time for our family my daughter, Randy"*: Judy Blume, *Letters to Judy*, p. 10.

## Chapter Seventeen
### Fame

138 *"One day, there's going to be Judy Blume tampons"*: Barbara Karlin, "Blume Speaks Out on Speaking Out," *Los Angeles Times*, October 18, 1981, p. E6.

138 *"The book struck me as incredibly candid"*: Telephone interview with Dean Butler, April 5, 2023.

139 *"Oh come on," Michael says in an early sequence*: John Korty, director, *Forever*, 1978.

140 *"She was resolute about that," he remembered*: DB to RB, April 5, 2023.

140 *"I see a bright young girl with a full life ahead of her"*: John Korty, director, *Forever*, 1978.

141 *Judy loved the adaptation*: Box 34 of the Judy Blume Papers at Yale University's Beinecke Rare Book and Manuscript Library. Accessed April 28, 2022.

141 *"I remember my father looking at me afterwards"*: DB to RB, April 5, 2023.

142 *which she'd been calling "After the Sunset"*: Box 115 of the Judy Blume Papers at Yale University's Beinecke Rare Book and Manuscript Library. Accessed April 28, 2022.

143 *"I love to make kids laugh, and I laugh a lot myself"*: Jennifer Hooker, Eileen

Duffy, Kristen Pfeffer, and Jamie Liguiori, "Talking with Judy Blume," *Newsday*, November 10, 1980, p. B16.

143  *Blume received a reported $500,000 advance for* Superfudge: N. R. Kleinfeld, "Young Readers: A Good Market," *New York Times*, March 27, 1981, p. D1.

143  *A rep for Jordache jeans got in touch*: Box 10 of the Judy Blume Papers at Yale University's Beinecke Rare Book and Manuscript Library. Accessed April 28, 2022.

144  *In December of 1980, six of her books topped the bestsellers list at B. Dalton*: Box 25 of the Judy Blume Papers at Yale University's Beinecke Rare Book and Manuscript Library. Accessed May 11, 2022.

## Chapter Eighteen
## Gatekeepers

145  *"Perhaps the best thing to do with Ms. Blume would be to ignore her altogether"*: David Rees, "Not Even For a One-Night Stand: Judy Blume," *The Marble in the Water* (Boston: The Horn Book, 1980), pp. 173–84.

145  *"a scatological and soft-porn* cinema verité *of childhood, of puberty, of growing up"*: Sandy Rovner, "Talking It Out with Judy Blume," *Washington Post*, November 3, 1981, p. B1.

146  asserting that she *"may never win any prizes for literary quality"*: Patricia O'Brien, "Judy Blume—Banned Again," *Hartford Courant*, March 12, 1980, p. 15.

146  *"He really hated stuffy children's books"*: PS to RB, May 27, 2022.

146  *"shopping list . . . entirely forgettable, drab, flat"*: David Rees, "Not Even For a One-Night Stand: Judy Blume," *The Marble in the Water* (Boston: The Horn Book, 1980), pp. 173–84.

147  *"The reader's reaction is laughter—anything from an embarrassed snigger"*: Ibid.

148  *"In children's books, since they became a thing at the beginning of the twentieth century"*: RS to RB, June 10, 2022.

149  *"Dick, he once said to me, 'We're writing sugar-coated bitter pills'"*: PS to RB, May 27, 2022.

149  *"anti-American, anti-Christian, anti-Semitic and just plain filthy"*: Edward Labaton, "The Board and the Books," *New York Times*, August 29, 1982, sec. 11, p. 22.

149  *"Two of the authors banned in Island Trees were among the most important"*: Email with Steven Pico, April 19, 2022.

150  *"They [the members] did not read the books in their entirety"*: Nicole Chavez, "He Took His School to the Supreme Court in the 1980s," CNN.com, June 25, 2022. https://www.cnn.com/2022/06/25/us/book-bans-island-trees-union-free-school-district-v-pico/index.html.

150  *He did, in fact, get accepted to Haverford College*: Lini S. Kadaba, "Standing Up for Freedom," Haverford.edu, September 20, 2022. https://www.haverford.edu/college-communications/news/standing-freedom.

151 *"Until the day I die, I refuse to budge on my position"*: Michael Winerip, "L.I. School Board Ends Its Fight to Ban Books," *New York Times*, January 31, 1983, sec. B, p. 7.

152 *"He was a real nonconformist and he was someone who believed"*: Zoom interview with Karen Fleshman, April 3, 2023.

152 *"By the time I'm growing up, it's a big hotbed of the John Birch Society"*: Ibid., April 3, 2023.

152 *"For Karen, a brave young woman and a real friend"*: Ibid., April 3, 2023.

153 *"It really gave me confidence the rest of my life"*: Ibid., April 3, 2023.

## Chapter Nineteen
## Allies

154 "Democracy *is exhausting*": Betty Miles, *Maudie and Me and the Dirty Book* (New York: Avon Books, 1980), p. 140.

155 *"Just then, Blackie gave a little moan, and her stomach began to ripple"*: Ibid., p. 47.

155 *"How did the puppy get in there . . . inside his mommy"*: Ibid., p. 48.

155 *"Kids this age can be embarrassingly frank!"*: Ibid., pp. 50–51.

155 *"it was a crime to spend public funds on smut like that!"*: Ibid., p. 89.

156 *"You've probably heard," the ringleader tells Kate's mother*: Ibid., p. 115.

156 *"I'm Kate Harris," she announces in front of the board*: Ibid., p. 135.

156 *"Norma Klein was my first writer friend," Blume told Terry Gross*: "Judy Blume Was Banned from the Beginning but Says 'It Never Stopped Me from Writing,'" *Fresh Air*, April 24, 2023. https://www.npr.org/2023/04/24/1171112806 /judy-blume-are-you-there-god-its-me-margaret-forever.

157 *"Well, that's just plain silly!" her father says*: Norma Klein, *Girls Can Be Anything* (New York: Dutton, 1973), no page numbers.

158 *"She was a very strong feminist," said Fleissner*: Telephone interview with Jennifer Fleissner, April 3, 2022.

158 *"Here is Mother with her Planned Parenthood meetings"*: Norma Klein, *Hiding* (New York: Pocket Books, 1976), p. 15.

158 She describes herself as *"the silent, clinging, frightened one"*: Ibid., p. 16.

159 *"I was afraid of the potential for failure and humiliation"*: Ibid., p. 35.

159 *"Where are you when we make love?"*: Ibid., p. 52.

159 *"People say: Take off your mask," Krii explains*: Ibid., p. 80.

159 *"I think she wanted to take the pleasure of girls seriously"*: JF to RB, April 3, 2022.

160 *"sometimes fear[s] that my husband and I will be hauled off"*: Norma Klein, "Growing Up Human: The Case for Sexuality in Children's Books," *Children's Literature in Education*, 1977, pp. 77–84.

161 *In 1979, when Judy was still living in Santa Fe, Klein wrote her a long letter*: Box 25 of the Judy Blume Papers at Yale University's Beinecke Rare Book and Manuscript Library. Accessed May 11, 2022.

161 *"It's funny, she could be very shy with people that she didn't know"*: JF to RB, April 3, 2022.

161 *"In New York girls like me are a dime a dozen"*: Norma Klein, *It's OK if You Don't Love Me* (New York: Fawcett Juniper, 1977), p. 16.

162 *"That's okay. I'm not sure I'm in love with you," Jody says*: Ibid., p. 98.

162 *"First, most of the boys couldn't believe that there was a boy"*: Ibid., p. 107.

163 *"There was just this very peaceful, contented feeling"*: Ibid., p. 134.

163 *"To take Lyle along and have him meet Daddy would, for me, be an act"*: Ibid., pp. 152–53.

163 *"I wish I could be looking back ten years from now"*: Ibid., pp. 254–55.

## Chapter Twenty
## Censorship

165 *"I willed myself not to give in to the tears of frustration and disappointment I felt coming"*: Judy Blume, "Places I Never Meant to Be: A Personal View," *American Libraries*, June/July 1999, pp. 62–67.

166 *"When we elected Ronald Reagan and the conservatives decided"*: Alison Flood, "Judy Blume: 'I Thought, This Is America: We Don't Ban Books. But Then We Did,'" *The Guardian*, July 11, 2014. Accessed online: https://www.theguardian.com/books/2014/jul/11/judy-blume-interview-forever-writer-children-young-adults.

166 *The tide against her turned practically "overnight"*: Judy Blume at the Arlington Public Library event on October 22, 2015. Accessed on YouTube: https://www.youtube.com/watch?v=PUDBcovfFjM.

166 *the* New York Times *reported that challenges against books had "shot up" since the late 1970s*: Colin Campbell, "Book Banning in America," *New York Times*, December 1, 1981, sec. 7, p. 1.

167 *"a best-selling author of sexually explicit books for children and young adults"*: Ibid.

167 *"We began to get letters from these people"*: PS to RB, May 27, 2022.

168 *"Thanks to Jerry Falwell and his Moral Majority I went from being called a 'Communist'"*: Judy Blume, "Is Puberty a Dirty Word," *New York Law School Review* 38, nos. 1–4 (1993): 37–43.

168 *"We didn't create the law that we would have liked"*: "Inside the SCOTUS Case on School Library Censorship," WNYC, February 24, 2022. https://www.wnycstudios.org/podcasts/otm/segments/first-supreme-court-case-banned-school-books-on-the-media.

168 *"In Florida, pornographic and inappropriate materials"*: "Governor Ron DeSantis Debunks Book Ban Hoax," FLGov.com, March 8, 2023. https://www.flgov.com/2023/03/08/governor-ron-desantis-debunks-book-ban-hoax/.

169 *Covering it for the* New York Times, *reviewer Linda Wolfe described paging through* Show Me!: Linda Wolfe, "The Birds and the Bees Were Never like This," *New York Times*, July 13, 1975, p. 203.

170 *"This book poses a problem for enlightened parents and sex educators"*: E. James Lieberman, *SIECUS Report* 5, no. 1 (September 1975): 6.

170 *"Until the Supreme Court decision of July"*: Edwin McDowell, "Picture Book on Sex Is Withdrawn," *New York Times*, September 19, 1982, Sec. 1 p. 61.

171 *"I distinguish pornography in terms of intent"*: CS to RB, October 26, 2022.

171 *As part of their decision, the judges created the "Miller Test"*: Miller v. California, 413 U.S. 15 (1973). https://supreme.justia.com/cases/federal/us/413/15/.

172 *In the draft, Davey wakes up and starts touching herself*: Box 115 of the Judy Blume Papers at Yale University's Beinecke Rare Book and Manuscript Library. Accessed April 28, 2022.

172 *"I get Jane undressed down to her shirt and her underpants"*: Judy Blume, *Tiger Eyes* (New York: Bradbury Press, 1981), p. 134.

172 *"We want this book to reach as many readers as possible, don't we?"*: Judy Blume, "Places I Never Meant to Be: A Personal View," *American Libraries*, June/July 1999, pp. 62–67.

173 *"Why deprive kids in some parts of the country of what is, essentially"*: Pat Scales, "Natural Born Editor," *School Library Journal*, May 2001, pp. 50–53.

173 *"Without a doubt, the upheavals of the 1960s"*: Marie Winn, "What Became of Childhood Innocence," *New York Times*, January 25, 1981, sec. 6, p. 15.

174 *"Ultimately, I was not strong enough or brave enough"*: Judy Blume, "Places I Never Meant to Be: A Personal View," *American Libraries*, June/July 1999, pp. 62–67.

## Chapter Twenty-One
## Morals

175 *"They call her a Pied Piper leading kids down the wrong path"*: Gay Andrews Dillin, "Judy Blume: Children's Author in a Grown-Up Controversy," *Christian Science Monitor*, December 10, 1981, p. B4.

175 *"How to Rid Your Schools and Libraries of Judy Blume Books"*: Judy Blume, "Places I Never Meant to Be: A Personal View," *American Libraries*, June/July 1999, pp. 62–67.

175 *created a flyer with the frightening title "X-Rated Children's Books"*: Found in Box 32 of the Judy Blume Papers at Yale University's Beinecke Rare Book and Manuscript Library. Accessed May 11, 2022.

176 *"Blubber is a good name for her"*: Judy Blume, *Blubber* (New York: Dell, 1986), p. 5.

177 *"If we're going to do this we're going to do it right"*: Ibid., p. 130.

177 *As Fogel told the* Washington Post: Lawrence Feinberg, "School's Use of Candid Novels Draws Parents' Fire," *Washington Post*, February 25, 1980, p. A1.

178 *"It's not a great piece of literature"*: Ibid.

178 *"The fact that it is not resolved is the most important part of the book"*: Ibid.

178 *"Blubber, she told her mother, is 'the best book I ever read'"*: Ibid.

179 *"Blume's books are sympathetic stories of ordinary children"*: Kathleen

Hinton-Braaten, "Writing for Kids Without Kidding Around," *Christian Science Monitor*, May 14, 1979, p. B10.

179  *"A growing number of iconoclasts are out to take the bloom"*: Gay Andrews Dillin, "Judy Blume: Children's Author in a Grown-Up Controversy," *Christian Science Monitor*, December 10, 1981, p. B4.

179  *"They're trying to use us to sell more of their books"*: Ibid.

180  *"It's the writers and advertisers who are the ones putting"*: Ibid.

180  *"Judy Blume writes what she calls 'honest' books for children"*: Cal Thomas, "In Kids' Books, Guess What 'Honest' Means," *Philadelphia Daily News*, November 23, 1984.

180  *"Arguing that Blume is just giving kids what they want is no argument at all"*: Ibid.

182  *"Congress soon passed the so-called squeal rule," he wrote*: Jeffrey P. Moran, *Teaching Sex: The Shaping of Adolescence in the 20th Century* (Boston: Harvard University Press, 2000), p. 205.

## Chapter Twenty-Two
## Notoriety

183  *"Isolated and alone"*: Judy Blume in conversation with Samantha Bee at an event at the 92nd Street Y on June 2, 2015. Accessed on YouTube: https://www.youtube.com/watch?v=l7svP4zqCc0.

185  *"I had letters from angry parents accusing me of ruining Christmas forever"*: Judy Blume, "Places I Never Meant to Be: A Personal View," *American Libraries*, June/July 1999, pp. 62–67.

185  *"there's a whole chapter that blows up Santa Claus"*: LH to RB, October 25, 2022.

185  *"Some sent lists showing me how easily I could have"*: Judy Blume, "Places I Never Meant to Be: A Personal View," *American Libraries*, June/July 1999, pp. 62–67.

185  *"Judy Blume and I were the only women writers on the list"*: Norma Klein, "On Being a Banned Writer," *The Lion and the Unicorn* 10 (1986): 18–20.

185  *Klein was "happy to be a quiet pioneer"*: JF to RB, April 3, 2022.

186  *Donelson tallied up protests against books as reported by the Office for Intellectual Freedom*: Ken Donelson, "'You Can't Have That Book in My Kid's School Library': Books Under Attack in the *Newsletter on Intellectual Freedom*, 1952–1989," *High School Journal* 74, no. 1 (October/November 1990): 1–7.

186  *because there were no Black people in Old Town, "prejudice was no problem"*: Ibid.

186  *"There's an obvious drop-off after Steinbeck," Donelson wrote*: Ibid.

187  *"a deadly and frightening thing to observe"*: Norma Klein, "On Being a Banned Writer," *The Lion and the Unicorn* 10 (1986): 18–20.

188  *In the* Times, *Richard Jackson called the decision "lunatic"*: "Peoria, Ill. Bans 3 Books from School Libraries," *New York Times* via AP, November 11, 1984, sec. 1, p. 34.

188 *"99 percent" of callers outside of Peoria agreed with the decision*: "Peoria School Board Restores 3 Judy Blume Books," *New York Times* via AP, December 5, 1984, sec. A, p. 16.

188 *"the wrong lesson, one of intolerance, distrust and contempt"*: "8 Who Write Children's Books Protest Ban on Blume Works," *New York Times*, November 20, 1984, sec. A, p. 17.

189 *"This is what I first suggested as a compromise," she said*: "Peoria School Board Restores 3 Judy Blume Books," *New York Times* via AP, December 5, 1984, sec. A, p. 16.

189 *"The first page I opened to talked about masturbation," she explained to a reporter*: Michael Hirsley, "ACLU Senses an Upturn in School-Book Censorship in South," *Chicago Tribune*, December 29, 1985.

190 *"No one is obligated to read this book"*: Ibid.

191 *she demanded that the school system remove the Harry Potter books from libraries*: "Hearing to Determine Fate of 'Harry Potter' Book in GCPS," *Gwinnett (GA) Daily Post*, April 10, 2006.

191 *"That's what happens when they start banning books"*: "Deenie Sales Soar," *Galveston Daily News*, September 10, 1985, p. 9A.

191 *In June 1984, she received a letter from a board member*: Box 32 of the Judy Blume Papers at Yale University's Beinecke Rare Book and Manuscript Library. Accessed May 11, 2022.

192 *"My life changed when I learned about the National Coalition Against Censorship"*: Judy Blume, "Places I Never Meant to Be: A Personal View," *American Libraries*, June/July 1999, pp. 62–67.

192 *"The intense battles around the control of sexuality"*: Leanne Katz, "Introduction: Women, Censorship and Pornography," *New York Law School Review* 38 (January 1993): 9–23.

192 *"I used to feel so alone when I heard my books were being challenged"*: Judy Blume, "Is Puberty a Dirty Word," *New York Law School Review* 38, nos. 1–4 (1993): 37–43.

## Chapter Twenty-Three
### Daughters

194 *"I gave you a lot of shit this year, didn't I, Mother?"*: Judy Blume, *Smart Women* (New York: Berkley Books, 1983). I worked from the 2004 reprint by Berkley Books, p. 350.

195 *The next night they got tickets to see* Apocalypse Now: Carlin Flora, "Judy Blume: Mating IQ," *Psychology Today*, January 1, 2007. Accessed via the New York Public Library.

195 *"Falling in love at forty (or any age) is s'wonderful"*: Judy Blume, *Smart Women*, Introduction, p. IX.

195 *"She did not understand how or why Michelle had turned into this impossible creature"*: Ibid., p. 16.

195 *"believes that Michelle is based on her (when she was that age)"*: Ibid., Introduction, p. x.

196 *"look[s] like the girl on the Sun-Maid raisin box"*: Ibid., p. 6.

196 *"No more affairs going nowhere"*: Ibid., p. 93.

196 *"She tried to think reasonably, but she couldn't"*: Ibid., p. 135.

197 *"Did you know when we first moved to town my mother joined Man-of-the-Month club?"*: Ibid., p. 140.

197 *"I'm the one who has to suffer through it every time one of her love affairs fizzles"*: Ibid., p. 144.

197 *"One day, Margo would be sorry"*: Ibid., p. 146.

198 *"You've become so self-absorbed that you probably never even considered"*: Randy Blume, *Crazy in the Cockpit* (New York: DK Publishing, 1999), pp. 5–6.

198 *"It turned out my mother wouldn't have noticed if I'd flown an airplane through the living room"*: Ibid., p. 19.

198 *"My mother and Norman got up early every morning to bike, snorkel, or sail"*: Ibid., p. 24.

199 *"How could she have let me come to this intellectual and cultural wasteland"*: Ibid., p. 213.

199 *"She felt a pouring out of motherly love"*: Judy Blume, *Smart Women*, p. 351.

## Chapter Twenty-Four
## Libraries

201 *"It's really scary being a librarian right now"*: AL to RB, October 12, 2022.

201 *the breadwinner/homemaker model of marriage is still "super baked in"*: SK to RB, October 14, 2022.

202 *"Of course, [he] opened it initially to the perfect page"*: Skype call with Michael Dishnow, May 2, 2023.

202 *"at one point I made a statement to the effect, I used a curse word"*: Ibid., May 2, 2023.

202 *"the realities I knew having been in the Marine Corps overseas"*: Ibid., May 2, 2023.

202 *"They fired me . . . for being insubordinate"*: Ibid., May 2, 2023.

203 *"But I wasn't in it for the money to begin with,"* *Dishnow said*: Ibid., May 2, 2023.

203 *"Guidance counselor Mike Dishnow was fired for writing critically"*: Judy Blume, "Places I Never Meant to Be: A Personal View," *American Libraries*, June/July 1999, pp. 62–67.

204 *"From my mom's point of view and the other seventies-era writers, it was such a step backwards"*: JF to RB, April 3, 2022.

204 *"so much worse than it was in the '80s"*: Steven McIntosh, "Judy Blume Worried About Intolerance and Book Banning in the US," BBC.com, April 1, 2023. https://www.bbc.com/news/entertainment-arts-65142127.

204 *"Critical Race Theory is not taught in K–12 education"*: AL to RB, October 12, 2022.

205 *"they looked over a kid's shoulder and, excuse my language, they saw the word 'fuck'"*: Ibid., October 12, 2022.

206 *"I loved that book, the kids loved it"*: LH to RB, October 25, 2022.

206 *"Well, it ended up being so controversial and difficult"*: Telephone interview with Carol Waxman, October 27, 2022.

207 *"I wholly support the trans community"*: Judy Blume (@judyblume) on X (Twitter), April 16, 2023: https://x.com/judyblume/status/16477133238306 44736?s=20.

207 *"Augustus Gloop is no longer fat, Mrs. Twit is no longer fearfully ugly"*: Anita Singh, "Augustus Gloop Is No Longer Fat as Roald Dahl Goes PC," *The Telegraph*, February 17, 2023. https://www.telegraph.co.uk/news/2023/02/17 /roald-dahl-woke-overhaul-offensive-words-removed/.

207 *oft-censored author Salman Rushdie tweeted that Puffin Books*: Salmon Rushdie (@salmonrushdie) on X (Twitter), February 18, 2023. https://x.com/Sal manRushdie/status/1627075835525210113?s=20.

207 *"The mother is always home, never works, always wearing a dress"*: CW to RB, October 27, 2022.

208 *"Parents don't want to admit that their children are growing up"*: AL to RB, October 12, 2022.

209 *"They said, 'Well, they couldn't read or write because maybe many of them'"*: JL to RB, November 8, 2023.

209 *"I always say, the reason [to have] inclusivity and diversity in our collections"*: Ibid., November 9, 2023.

## Chapter Twenty-Five
## Legacy

210 *"We didn't have the internet; we didn't have any places where we could find the answers"*: Telephone interview with Shannon Dressler, October 31, 2023.

210 *"in every age . . . there are books that answer the needs of the moment"*: Gay Andrews Dillin, "Judy Blume: Children's Author in a Grown-Up Controversy," *Christian Science Monitor*, December 10, 1981, p. B4.

211 *"The way that sex education is usually done is to put up one picture"*: CS to RB, October 26, 2022.

212 *"It's really helping [students] learn how to have healthy relationships"*: SD to RB, October 31, 2023.

212 *"These kids have access to so much"*: Ibid., October 31, 2023.

213 *"I get why parents don't want to talk about where babies come from"*: CS to RB, October 26, 2022.

214 *authors gathered at the Atlanta-Fulton central library to read aloud*: Cynthia Durcanin, "Atlanta Writers Read from Rushdie amid Moslem Protests," *Atlanta Constitution*, February 26, 1989.

214  *the then-forty-nine-year-old Judy was dubbed a Library Lion by the New York Public Library*: Patricia Leigh Brown, "A Literate Night of Dining and Lionizing," *New York Times*, November 13, 1987, sec. A, p. 22.

214  *On June 6, 1987, just a week after his fiftieth birthday*: Box 34 of the Judy Blume Papers at Yale University's Beinecke Rare Book and Manuscript Library. Accessed April 28, 2022.

215  *"She always said, 'I should only live to see this wedding'"*: Weidt, *Presenting Judy Blume*, p. 15.

215  *"I used to think that when my kids grew up"*: Judy Blume at the Arlington Public Library event on October 22, 2015. Accessed on YouTube: https://www.youtube.com/watch?v=PUDBcovfFjM.

# Index

# About the Author

R achelle Bergstein is a lifestyle writer, author, and editor, focused on style, pop culture, and families. Her work has appeared in the *New York Post*, the *New York Times*, NPR, and more. She is the author of three books: *Women from the Ankle Down, Brilliance and Fire*, and *The Genius of Judy*. She lives with her husband and son in Brooklyn. Find out more at RachelleBergstein.com.